D1544201

The Economics
of Inflation

GLASGOW SOCIAL AND ECONOMIC RESEARCH STUDIES

AN INTRODUCTION TO THE ITALIAN ECONOMY

Kevin Allen and Andrew Stevenson

THE INDUSTRIAL RELATIONS ACT

A. W. J. Thomson and S. R. Engleman

The Economics of Inflation

James Anthony Trevithick & Charles Mulvey

GLASGOW SOCIAL & ECONOMIC RESEARCH STUDIES 3

MARTIN ROBERTSON

First published in 1975 by Martin Robertson & Co. Ltd., 17 Quick Street, London N1 8HL

ISBN 0 85520 086 3

Printed in Britain at The Pitman Press, Bath

Preface

In recent years the economics of inflation has come to occupy a central role in discussion of economic matters both among laymen and professional economists. This is principally because inflation is now regarded as the most intractable economic problem which faces the western world, but it is also of special interest to the economist in that it is a topic which cuts across almost every field of economics in one form or another. In consequence the literature on the subject is as diverse as it is vast and has evolved in a wide variety of academic journals. There is therefore a great deal of difficulty in sorting out the rival claims of competing schools of thought. What appears to one group to be simply the result of monetary mismanagement appears to another group as the outcome of the class struggle in which the crumbling edifice of capitalism will finally collapse. The reticence of economists in surveying this highly contentious area of debate is quite understandable. Nevertheless a beginning must be made in disentangling the various approaches to the inflationary process which have emerged over the last few years.

With this object in mind we have attempted in this book to survey the literature on the diverse and frequently contradictory views of the inflationary process which are current in contemporary discussion of the problem. In some chapters, more especially those concerned with the macroeconomic approaches to inflation, only the broad lines of the debate are sketched out, the interested reader being left to fill in the details for himself. In other chapters, most notably chapters 4, 5 and 6, the survey of the theoretical and empirical literature is more thorough and complete.

This book is primarily intended to be a text on the economics of inflation for students in the later years of an undergraduate course or in the preliminary year of a postgraduate course. In general it is assumed that the reader is acquainted with the elementary principles of macroeconomics and is able to follow the manipulation of the Hicksian *IS-LM* apparatus without difficulty. Nevertheless certain aspects of the theory of inflation are not easily accessible to those who lack a solid grounding in economic theory or who are not at home with a mathematical form of presentation. As far as possible these aspects have been relegated to appendices.

In attempting to evaluate the state of play in the debate between rival camps and to draw certain tentative conclusions, we run the risk of being accused of partiality or prejudice by various commentators who disagree with the emphasis accorded to certain aspects of the inflationary process at the expense of others which they regard as more important. This kind of accusation is inevitable in an area of economics in which not only every economist has his own opinions concerning the sources of inflationary pressure but every 'man in the street' has also formed an embryonic theoretical framework. We have endeavoured to present the arguments as fairly and as carefully as possible and to assemble as broad a cross-section of professional opinion as a book of this length will permit.

We have many people to thank for assisting us in the preparation of this book. In particular, John Foster has spent much time in reading drafts and making comments and suggestions and generally saving us from ourselves. We owe much to Professor Ken Alexander for encouraging us to write the book in the first place. Professors John Williamson and Frank Brechling and Miss Diane Dawson have read certain chapters in draft and have made helpful comments. Patrick Kinsella and Andrew Sommerville, two of our former students in Trinity College, Dublin, were particularly severe critics of earlier drafts. We are also deeply indebted to the ladies who ungrudgingly typed the manuscript in its various stages of preparation — Elizabeth Cousin, Frances Stevenson, Christine Kerr, Enda Hennigan and Mary Ruane.

University of Glasgow

James A. Trevithick
Charles Mulvey

Contents

Contents

CHAPTER 1

Introduction

Inflation surely helped to make Mr Edward Heath Prime Minister in 1970 and, even more surely, ex-Prime Minister in 1974. The popularity of Japan's Prime Minister, Mr K. Tanaka, is at an alltime low because of inflation. President Allende of Chile lost his life at least partly because of inflation. Throughout the world, inflation is a major source of political unrest. (Friedman, 1974)

1.1 The modern experience of inflation

Inflation is probably best defined as a persistent tendency for the general level of prices to rise. This definition is sufficiently elastic to embrace phenomena such as 'hyper-inflation', 'stagflation' and 'creeping inflation' while still remaining simple and precise. Inflation is not exclusively a modern phenomenon. It is well known that inflation was experienced in ancient times. However, we propose to concentrate for the moment on the modern experience of inflation in order to describe the phases of inflation which preceded the wage and price explosion which is presently raging throughout the non-communist world.

1.1.i Before the Second World War

Prior to the Second World War inflations tended to occur during and immediately after wars, when governments financed the war by resort to the printing press, or during periods when gold discoveries of a significant kind have been made. In other instances, such as the German hyper-inflation of 1923, weak governments have attempted to buy their way out of economic crises by printing vast sums of money. These inflations generally had two important characteristics:

(a) they occurred in response to some particular event, such as a war, gold discovery or unmanageable economic crisis;
(b) they lasted only as long as the event with which they were associated and that was normally not very long.

1

Thus prior to the Second World War inflations tended to flare up from time to time and then die down as the exceptional circumstances which caused them ended.

1.1.ii   The Second World War and its aftermath

The Second World War was accompanied, as were all wars, by a rapid world inflation. As had happened often before, the wartime inflation continued into the postwar period and ' . . . seemed part and parcel of the process of postwar reconstruction' (OEEC, 1961). Before this postwar inflation had had time to unwind itself as historical precedent would lead us to expect, the Korean War broke out and another war inflation was precipitated. By 1953 war and postwar hangovers were behind us and ' . . . a new period of economic expansion began in which persistent inflation was not generally anticipated or feared' (OEEC, 1961).

1.1.iii   1953–9

Governments in the industrialised countries were now committed to policies of rapid growth and full employment. These policies were, on the whole, highly successful. Most European countries steadily approached full employment during the 1950s, and many had achieved this objective by the mid-1950s. At the same time growth rates were running at satisfactorily high levels in most countries although the UK and the USA grew at markedly slower rates than the main European industrial countries. There were however disturbing signs that inflation was not going to disappear. Between 1953 and 1959 retail prices in the main industrial countries rose at an annual average rate of about 2–4% per annum. In addition to the persistence of inflation, balance of payments problems became an increasing cause for concern in some countries and were generally dealt with by sharp bouts of deflation.

1.1.iv   1960–74

In the first half of the 1960s the rate of inflation in many of the industrialised countries quickened. In most European countries prices rose between 1960 and 1966 at a rate of about 3–5% per annum. In the USA and Canada inflation proceeded more slowly than in Europe and there is no evidence of any quickening during the early 1960s in those countries. From 1967 onwards however the rate of inflation in all the main industrial countries began to accelerate. By 1970 it was clear that a worldwide price and wage explosion was occurring and by mid-1974 inflation had accelerated to levels ranging from 24% in Japan to 7% in Germany. In fig. 1.1 the inflationary experience of the UK,

Fig. 1.1   *Rates of Inflation in Five Industrial Countries 1960—74*

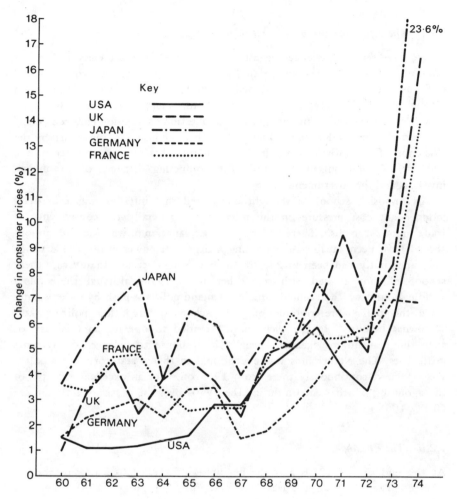

USA, Japan, France and Germany since 1960 is charted. (The data are set out in Appendix 1 of this chapter.)

Postwar experience of inflation in the main industrial countries may be briefly summarised as follows: inflation ran at high rates from 1945 to 1953 and this was understood to be the result of postwar reconstruction followed by the effects of the Korean War; from 1953 to 1959 inflation persisted at relatively low rates, with much cyclical variation, and appeared to be tailing off in 1959; from 1960 to 1966 the inflation rate quickened in most countries; after 1967 inflation began to accelerate and by the early 1970s had developed into a worldwide price and wage explosion.

1.2   Economic policy and inflation

1.2.i   *The inflationary gap and cost-push theories*

As we have seen, experience suggested to the observer in the early 1950s that inflation was a phenomenon associated with particular events and would unwind itself as the event which occasioned it ended. The persistence of inflation through the 1950s therefore perplexed economists and governments alike. In a general way two schools of thought on the question of inflation emerged during this period. The neo-Keynesian school held that the inflation was caused by the existence of an 'inflationary gap' which in turn was the consequence of the inability of total output to satisfy the competing demands of consumers, investors and the government.

An opposing school of thought contended that inflation was caused by independent cost pressure on the price level – generally the consequence of trade union wage-push. There was no clear explanation of why the trade unions should have been capable of exercising a degree of power in the 1950s which they apparently had been unable to do in previous periods. In any case these schools of thought vied with each other in the 1950s, although there was a middle ground which accepted a mixed demand-pull/cost-push hypothesis, and, since the policy prescriptions of each school differed, left policy-makers somewhat bemused. In the event policy tended to operate on the basis of short-run demand management, usually in response to balance of payments difficulties. The Netherlands was exceptional in that a statutory wages policy was operated continuously there from 1945 on. (For an excellent example of the agonising which went on during the 1950s over the causes of inflation see OEEC, 1961.)

1.2.ii   *The Phillips Curve*

At the end of the 1950s and the beginning of the 1960s a new orthodoxy emerged. The 'Phillips Curve' was discovered in 1958 (Phillips, 1958) and given a theoretical rigour in 1960 by Lipsey (1960). Broadly the Phillips/Lipsey hypothesis held that in the long run, the rate of change of money wages would be determined by the level of excess demand in the labour market (measured by the unemployment rate), while in the short run fluctuations in import prices and productivity growth would combine with excess demand in determining the rate of inflation. Thus there would according to this hypothesis be a long-run trade-off between wage inflation and unemployment since the growth of import prices would tend to be equal to that of domestic prices and productivity would tend to grow at a steady rate. The Phillips curve was quickly absorbed into the theory of inflation in its own right. The effect was to lend weight to the demand-pull explanation of inflation, although some writers have argued that the Phillips curve is 'neutral' as between cost-push and demand-pull theories. The main proponents of the cost-push hypothesis however did not normally deny the demand-pull implication of the Phillips curve but still asserted the view that trade unions could and did push up the wage level independently of the level of excess demand. The most determined proponent of this view was Hines who showed that changes in the percentage of the workforce unionised 'were highly correlated with the rate of change of money wages (Hines, 1964). The demand-pull orthodoxy however remained virtually intact.

The Phillips curve was found to exist for most industrialised countries in varying shapes and forms. Its policy implications posed certain political dilemmas for governments. The rate of unemployment associated with a rate of change of money wages equal to the trend rate of growth of productivity (and therefore compatible with price stability) was, politically, too high to contemplate. For the UK this unemployment rate was about 2½%; for the USA somewhere between 6% and 8%; and for Canada between 5% and 6½%. The trade-off between inflation and unemployment was sufficiently alarming to governments (committed as they were to 'full employment') for incomes policies to be seized on as an alternative to demand restraint. In the UK a succession of 'incomes policies' beginning with the abortive National Incomes Commission in 1962 followed by Labour's National Board for Prices and Incomes from 1965 to 1971, the Tories' Pay Board and Prices Commission between 1972 and 1974 and the 'Social Contract' of 1974 have been the principal weapons of anti-inflationary policy. Similarly in the USA the Wage/Price Guideposts, in Holland the National Wages Policy, in Germany wage freezes and similar measures elsewhere have reflected governmental preferences to bypass or at least shift the Phillips curve in tackling inflation. It should be recognised however that, if inflation was indeed a response to the pressure of demand, the incomes policy approach was not a real alternative to a policy which eliminated excess demand. At best incomes policies could temporarily hold back wages only by rationing labour and thereby distorting the allocation of resources. Minor merits of incomes policies arise where an active manpower policy is also employed to shift the Phillips curve and where conventional 'wage contours', which have no economic justification, are loosened up.

1.3 Proposals for economic policy

It may be useful at this stage if we were to declare our hand and outline what we consider to be the appropriate policy measures which the government should undertake to tackle inflation. Needless to say not everyone will agree with the stance we adopt but we regard inflation as such a pressing problem that to write a book on the subject without coming out with at least tentative proposals for its cure would be irresponsible.

In brief we regard the 'expectations-augmented' Phillips curve as eminently more plausible than the original version. Moreover not only does it perform *reasonably* well within a closed economy, but it also works well within a system of fixed exchange rates in explaining international inflationary experience. As the motive force behind this worldwide relationship, we consider the massive increase in world liquidity which has been occurring since the 1960s as being the principal culprit.

In our opinion the monetarist explanation of inflation is superior to the 'institutionalist' or cost-push explanations of inflation for it explains in very simple terms the following two phenomena:

(i) it explains why the inflation rate has accelerated in the UK, the United States, Japan and many other advanced economies since around 1967 — there is no evidence of substantial changes in the structure of these economies around this time;

(ii) it explains why, despite ripples of relatively minor magnitude, inflation is, under a system of fixed exchange rates, essentially a worldwide phenomenon.

Although we accept the hypothesis that the existence of trade unions imparts an inflationary bias to the system, we see no reason to believe and no evidence to indicate that the extent of this bias has markedly increased both within and between nations after 1967.

Our policy conclusions are therefore:

(a) There should be a *gradual* reduction in the rate of domestic credit expansion. A sudden reorientation of monetary policy could have very serious repercussions which a gradualist posture would seek to avoid.

(b) There should be complete indexation of all nominal contracts to erode more rapidly the firmly held expectations of inflation.

(c) In the absence of any form of international co-operation to reduce the world rate of monetary expansion, individual economies should float their exchange rates 'cleanly', thereby effectively isolating themselves from inflationary pressure occurring elsewhere in the world.

(d) Contrary to the monetarist proposals outlined above, we do see a short-run role for prices and incomes policy in lowering inflationary expectations, provided that proposals (a)–(c) are implemented simultaneously. Although we accept that such a policy may produce certain resource misallocations, there is a sufficient volume of evidence to indicate that a large number of prices (and especially wage rates) are administered by convention and rule of thumb, rendering, for example, the structure of wage differentials highly rigid. In such circumstances a 'freezing' of the vector of relative prices for a short period may not be too disastrous and will probably be a useful adjunct to indexation in accelerating the speed of adjustment of the 'real' economy to a lower rate of monetary expansion.

1.4 The layout of this book

In this introductory chapter so far, we have attempted to sketch in the broad facts about modern inflation, the theories which have purported to explain it and the policies which governments have employed to try to suppress it. Because we have been concerned here to present the facts of inflationary experience, theories of inflation and economic policy in the way in which they actually evolved we have not compared theories or evaluated policies in any coherent way. Further, we have discussed concepts which may be unfamiliar to many readers and which may therefore have mystified rather than enlightened. It is nevertheless useful to approach a subject as complex as the economics of inflation with a broad scheme in mind, even though much of it is mysterious, and the scheme of the remainder of this book is designed systematically to develop and relate the principal themes touched on above.

Chapter 2 is devoted to presenting a set of macroeconomic models of the inflationary process. The simple quantity theory of money is considered first. The Keynesian model is then considered and a novel interpretation of Keynes's views on the inflationary process, as contained in *How to Pay for the War*, is advanced. Money is then introduced into the Keynesian model and it is demonstrated that it is only under two restrictive and unlikely assumptions that an increase in the supply of money will not affect the price level. Lastly, the remarkably complete dynamic model of inflation of Hansen, which has been much neglected, is outlined. In chapter 3 a simple macroeconomic model of cost inflation is set out. The model is highly generalised and the inflationary impact of trade unions is not discussed in detail until chapter 6. In addition to the general model of cost inflation two specific and controversial theories which have been advanced to explain the recent inflation are critically examined.

In chapter 4 the elementary theory of the Phillips curve is outlined and the detailed problems of the dispersion of unemployment, the 'loops', and the empirical evidence are considered. Chapter 5 takes up a number of issues which were central to the post-Phillips curve debate and introduces price inflation into the analysis. Chapter 6 deals with the impact of trade unions on inflation and, after reviewing the empirical evidence, concludes that trade unions do affect the rate of inflation in certain circumstances. Chapter 7 outlines the expectations hypothesis and reviews the empirical evidence in relation to it. The conclusion is that the expectations hypothesis is supported by the evidence although there may be some threshold effect involved. Taken together these four chapters contain the most detailed account of the relation between excess demand and inflation that we are aware of.

Chapter 8 discusses the monetarist theory of inflation in detail and highlights aspects of it which are often neglected. The persuasive logic of the model is examined against the facts of the recent inflation and its explanatory capacity is shown to be considerable. Chapter 9 discusses the effects of inflation, both anticipated and unanticipated. In chapter 10 we present our conclusions and draw implications for economic policy.

Appendix 1

Table 1.1   Rates of Inflation in Five Industrial Countries 1960—74

% per annum

Year	USA	UK	Japan	Germany	France
1960	1.5	1.0	3.6	1.5	3.6
1961	1.1	3.4	5.4	2.3	3.4
1962	1.1	4.5	6.7	4.5	4.7
1963	1.2	2.5	7.7	3.0	4.8
1964	1.4	3.9	3.9	2.3	3.4
1965	1.6	4.6	6.5	3.4	2.6
1966	2.8	3.7	6.0	3.5	2.7
1967	2.8	2.4	4.0	1.5	2.7
1968	4.2	4.8	5.5	1.8	4.5
1969	5.0	5.2	5.1	2.6	6.4
1970	5.9	6.5	7.6	3.7	5.5
1971	4.3	9.5	6.3	5.3	5.5
1972	3.4	6.8	4.9	5.4	5.9
1973	6.2	8.4	12.0	7.0	7.5
1974*	11.1	16.5	23.6	6.9	13.9

Source: *National Institute Economic Review.* Table 'Industrial Countries: consumer prices
and the labour market'. Data for 1974 from OECD *Main Economic Indicators.*
* Data refer to change in prices between June 1973 and June 1974.

CHAPTER 2

The Quantity Theory, the Keynesian Revolution and the Rate of Inflation

In order to understand the context within which the modern debate on the sources of inflationary pressure is taking place, it is necessary to devote some time to an examination of some of the controversies on inflation which were raging in the 1920s, the 1930s and the 1940s. With this object in mind we shall summarise briefly two of the main approaches to inflation, the quantity theory of money and the neo-Keynesian approach.

2.1 The traditional quantity theory of money

Consider Irving Fisher's famous equation of exchange:

$$Mv = pT \qquad (2.1)$$

where M is the nominal stock of money, p is the transactions price level, v is the transaction velocity of circulation of money and T is the number of transactions undertaken over a period of time.

What preoccupied the attention of quantity theorists were the repercussions upon the economic system of an increase in the stock of money due, for example, to a new discovery of gold or to an expansive monetary policy. As it stands, equation (2.1) is incapable of assisting in this line of inquiry. It is merely an identity, possessing exactly the same characteristics as the proposition 'The amount sold will equal the amount bought'. In order to furnish some information on how the economy works, equation (2.1) will have to be subjected to various modifications which will constrain the behaviour of certain variables. In cruder versions of the quantity theory, severe restrictions were placed upon the variation in v and in T. The transactions velocity of circulation and the total number of transactions were taken to be constant *even in the short run*. According to Fisher, v was fixed by 'objective' economic factors; T was determined at its full employment equilibrium level by the free interaction of the forces of supply and demand, i.e. by 'real' forces. These rigid characteristics made the model fair game for its neo-Keynesian detractors and called for drastic revision if a fundamentally monetarist model were to be taken at all seriously. That modern monetarists have taken up the gauntlet will be seen in chapter 8.

We have seen that one of the great weaknesses of Fisher's version of the quantity theory lay in his mechanistic approach to the determination of the transactions velocity, v. The velocity of circulation of money was determined by institutional factors such as the average length of the payments period and was not considered to be the outcome of utility maximising decision-making on the part of individuals.

This deficiency was partially remedied in the Cambridge equation of the demand for money:

$$M_d = kPX \tag{2.2}$$

where M_d is the level of demand for nominal cash balances, X is the level of output, P is the price level (different from p in equation (2.1)) and k is the desired ratio of cash balances to money income. In this formulation the demand for money is the outcome of choices by individuals on what proportion of their money income they are to hold in the form of cash balances. The Cambridge version of the quantity theory laid much greater emphasis on *income* transactions as opposed to *gross* transactions so that nominal income, *PX*, i.e. payments for *final* goods and services, appears on the right hand side of equation (2.2) instead of the nominal value of all transactions, pT. It follows that a different concept of velocity is associated with the Cambridge equation as compared to the Fisherine equation of exchange. In particular we may define the *income* velocity of circulation as 'the number of times per unit time that the money stock is used in making *income* transactions' (Friedman, 1970). This definition may be expressed symbolically by the formula

$$V = \frac{PX}{M_d} = \frac{1}{k}$$

where V is the income velocity of circulation of money. In subsequent discussion of the traditional quantity theory we shall concentrate on the Cambridge formulation so that when the velocity of circulation of money is referred to, it is to be understood as the income velocity of circulation, V. On the other hand, in analysing the properties of the Cambridge equation, we shall retain the Fisherine (and Pigovian) assumption that V, and hence k, are constant. This is the first step in transforming equation (2.1) into a useful operational relation.

There is still a great deal of controversy over what neoclassical monetary theory actually was. Although it would be inappropriate in a book of this nature to delve too deeply into the history of economic thought, it may be useful at this stage to introduce a highly simplified model of the neoclassical macroeconomic system with a view to examining how monetary disturbances affect individual variables.

Consider a labour market in which the supply of labour, N_s, is an increasing function of the real wage rate (W/P), where W is the money wage rate and P is the price level; that is $N_s = N_s(W/P)$. Similarly assume that the demand for labour, N_d, is also a function of the real wage rate, but this time a diminishing function reflecting the hypothesis that the marginal productivity of labour decreases with the level of employment; that is $N_d = N_d(W/P)$. With flexible wages and prices, an equilibrium level of employment, N_F, and an equilibrium real wage rate $(W/P)_F$, will be established simultaneously. Clearly in this system no valid distinction may be drawn between the equilibrium level of employment and the 'full employment' level of employment since both concepts are defined identically.[1] These properties of labour market equilibrium are depicted in fig. 2.1(a).

In order to determine the level of national income corresponding to the equilibrium level of employment, N_F, we need to introduce the notion of a short-run production function, $X = X(N)$: for a given state of technology and a fixed capital stock, the level of output, X, is positively related to the level of employment. The production function is concave to the N-axis, reflecting the presence of diminishing marginal productivity of labour.[2] This short-run production function is depicted in fig. 2.1(b).

Fig. 2.1

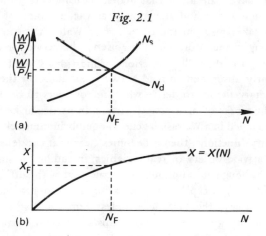

(a)

(b)

The above diagram represents a completely self-contained subsystem of the neoclassical macroeconomic model. The characteristics of equilibrium in this subsystem depend solely upon (a) the state of technology which provides information concerning not only the shape and position of the production function but also the properties of the labour demand function; and (b) the utility functions of individual suppliers of labour (unspecified in the above model) which, in this highly simplified system, will provide information on the number of man-hours which workers are willing to work in return for a pre-specified real wage rate. The only price which enters the picture is a *relative* price, viz. the real wage rate, (W/P). The level of *absolute* prices (e.g. the levels of

W and P measured separately) cannot be ascertained with reference to this subsystem alone.

This analytical breach is filled by introducing the quantity theory of money into the picture. Since the level of output has been determined independently in a completely separate part of the system, the final restriction necessary to turn an identity into a useful behavioural equation has been imposed. That is, not only has k been fixed by exogenous institutional factors, but X has also been determined exogenously by the equations of a distinct subsystem of the neoclassical model. We are left with one equation in only one unknown, viz. the price level, P. This leads to the inevitable conclusion that in naive versions of the quantity theory of money the price level is uniquely determined by the supply of money. The corollary of this proposition is that the rate of price inflation is uniquely determined by the rate of increase of the supply of money. This relationship between the rate of inflation and the rate of monetary expansion is central to a monetarist interpretation of the origins of inflationary pressure.

The naive version of the quantity theory of money has been under attack for many decades for being rigidly mechanistic. In the model which has just been described, no reason is given as to why k (or V) should take on any particular value, constant or otherwise. Many writers (e.g. Hicks, 1935, but especially Samuelson, 1968) have maintained that neoclassical monetary theory implicitly concentrated upon the demand for money as the outcome of an optimising procedure which takes place in the context of a Walrasian general equilibrium system[3] containing money (or, more precisely, the services rendered by the possession of money) in the utility functions of individuals. Professor Samuelson (1968) has recently attempted to read between the lines (or the equations) of neoclassical monetary theory to derive what he considers to be the correct way of interpreting the works of neoclassical writers. In particular he points out that when money is included in a Walrasian general equilibrium model as an argument in individual utility functions, then it becomes clear that the demand for money is a function of a wide variety of real variables, including the interest rate. On the other hand, although it is undoubtedly true that with sufficient manipulation neoclassical theory is capable of generating quite sophisticated theories of the demand for money, the fact nevertheless remains that it was the naive version of the quantity theory which economists and policy-makers adhered to until well into the 1930s. But such doctrinal disputes are out of place in a book of this nature so that we shall henceforward confine our attention to what is *popularly considered* to be the traditional version of the quantity theory of money.

The precise nature of the demand for money function implied in naive versions of the quantity theory may be illustrated in fig. 2.2. According to Samuelson neoclassical theorists had no doubt in their minds when they referred to the demand for money curve. If the value of money, $1/P$, measured by the reciprocal of *any* absolute money price or any average price level is measured on the vertical axis, and the demand for money is measured on the horizontal axis,

Fig. 2.2

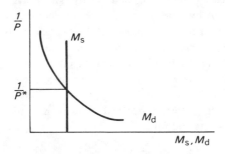

then the resultant demand curve for money '. . . would be a rectangular hyperbola with a geometrical Marshallian elasticity of exactly minus one'. The supply of money in nominal terms is exogenously determined by the monetary authorities and is represented by the vertical line M_s in fig. 2.2. The intersection of the demand for money function M_d, with the vertical supply function determines the value of P at P^*. In other words, the only way in which desired real cash balances, (M_d/P), can be brought into line with *actual* real cash balances, (M_s/P), is by variations in the price level.[7] More specifically, if $(M_s/P) < (M_d/P)$, the price level will have to fall; and if $(M_s/P) > (M_d/P)$, the price level will have to rise.

The problem now arises as to how disequilibrium in the money market $[(M_d/P) \neq (M_s/P)]$ *generates* price changes. When individuals as a group find that the supply of a particular good exceeds their demand for that good, they arrive at their equilibrium consumption of that good by restricting their purchases of it. And the same is true on the individual level for the holding of real cash balances. Individuals acting independently can reduce their real cash balances by spending the excess and can increase them by curtailing expenditure. The same principle does *not* apply to individuals considered collectively. Once more money is made available by a rightward shift in the M_s function, individuals taken as a whole have no option but to hold that higher volume of nominal money. If initially $(M_s/P) = (M_d/P)$, such an increase in the supply of money will set in motion forces which will drive up the price level. These forces were never elucidated in any detail by neoclassical writers, but it is clear that the initial reaction of the economy to an excess of actual over desired real balances is to attempt to spend the difference on goods and services. But the real output levels of goods and services have already been determined in the real sector of the economy and only real changes such as shifts in production functions or utility functions can alter such variables. Attempts to deplete the level of real cash balances in these circumstances will simply raise the price level. This process will continue until the price level has been driven upwards by an amount sufficient to bring (M_s/P) into equality with (M_d/P).

An alternative transmission mechanism, one which is more suited to advanced monetary systems where changes in the money supply are brought about by government open market operations and not by random variations in the supply of gold, is provided by the *interest rate mechanism* of Alfred Marshall. According to Marshall, the initial impact of an increase in the nominal supply of money is to reduce the rate of interest. On traditional neoclassical grounds, it was thought that such a decline in the rate of interest would stimulate desired investment and perhaps even consumption. But since the economy was assumed to be working at its full-employment level of output (as is an implication of a stable Walrasian system), greater planned investment and consumption would only issue in higher wages and prices.

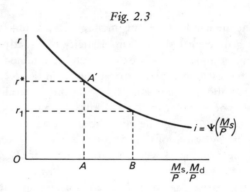

Fig. 2.3

The interest rate mechanism is illustrated in fig. 2.3. The nominal (and real) rate of interest, r, is measured on the vertical axis and the demand for and supply of real cash balances is measured on the horizontal axis. For a given level of real income, the demand for real cash balances is fixed and may be represented by the vertical line AA'. The rate of interest is a function ψ of the supply of real cash balances. When $(M_d/P) = (M_s/P)$, the rate of interest is at its natural level r^*, to borrow Wicksell's terminology. If the government increases the nominal supply of money, the *market* rate of interest will fall, say, to r_1 as a result of the rise in the supply of real cash balances from OA to OB. The consequent rise in the level of planned investment will create a sort of inflationary gap which will continually depress the real value of the greater nominal supply of money. Inflationary pressures persist until M_s/P is once again brought into equality with M_d/P and the gap between the market and natural interest rates is bridged. Once monetary disequilibrium has been eliminated by inflation, the economy will revert to a situation of long-run equilibrium in which the rate of interest will be at a level determined (a) by the supply of savings (governed by the rate of time preference) and (b) by the demand for savings (determined by the marginal productivity of investment). Monetary factors only exert a short-run influence on the rate of interest.

2.2 The income—expenditure approach to inflation

No student of economics can be unaware of the devastating theoretical impact which Keynes' *General Theory of Employment, Interest and Money* (1936) had in undermining the foundations of the neoclassical world in which lapses from full employment were regarded as transitory deviations from an otherwise stable equilibrium. The powerful principle of *effective demand* attempted to demonstrate that the equilibrium[9] level of output and employment, X_E and N_E respectively, would in general not coincide with their full-employment values. By focusing upon the relationship between variations in *ex ante* expenditure and variations in real income and employment, Keynes established the *income-expenditure* approach to the determination of the level of economic activity. In this section we shall be concerned with the application of the extremely versatile principle of effective demand to the problem of inflation in the context of a fully employed economy. Section 2.2.i will deal with the model of inflation contained in *How to Pay for the War* and with other inflationary gap models current at this period (the early 1940s). In general these models excluded any specific mention of the monetary forces which may be operative either in bringing inflationary pressure under control or in exacerbating the upward spiral of wages and prices. This omission is remedied to some extent in Section 2.2.ii in which money is explicitly incorporated into the Hicksian *IS—LM* interpretation of the complete Keynesian model. Finally in Section 2.2.iii we shall examine another non-monetary theory of the inflationary process, Hansen's two-gap model, which is in direct line of descent from the earlier inflationary gap models but which expressly distinguishes between inflationary pressure emanating from the goods market on the one hand and from the factor market on the other.

2.2.i Inflationary gap models

Following upon the success of Keynes' *General Theory* in explaining the phenomenon of under-employment equilibrium, the onset of the Second World War appeared to undermine the claim to generality of the *General Theory*. The neoclassical world of full employment appeared to have made a startling comeback; capacity was being fully utilised and unemployment had been reduced to a minimum. From the economic point of view however there seemed to be one untidy blemish in an otherwise quite rosy picture: inflation was taking place at a rather alarming rate. The explanation of this phenomenon was to pose an important challenge to Keynes and his followers who had to answer the claim that the *General Theory* was nothing more than a description of the forces at work in a chronically depressed economy. In fact the principle of effective demand was to exhibit remarkable robustness in the decade which followed. The notion of deficient aggregate demand had been advanced to explain the unemployment problem of the 1920s and 1930s; the notion of *excessive* aggregate demand was subsequently advanced to explain the phenomenon of inflation in the 1940s.

This is the essence of the inflationary gap approach to inflation. The problem of inflation could be explained in terms of an excess of aggregate *ex ante* real expenditure over producible real output. The real expenditure plans of consumers, investors and the government could not be met simultaneously since the equilibrium level of national income was unattainable. In terms of the familiar 'Keynesian cross' diagram of a closed economy, the problem was stated as follows. Let aggregate real expenditure be measured on the vertical axis and real income on the horizontal axis. According to traditional Keynesian taxonomy, real expenditure may be subdivided into consumption expenditure, C, investment expenditure, I, and government expenditure, G. The aggregate expenditure function, $C + I + G$, relates the level of desired real expenditure to the level of real income (see fig. 2.4).

The intersection of the total expenditure function with the 45° line determines the equilibrium level of real national income, X_E. When national income is at X_E, the total amount of goods and services produced within the economy is equal to aggregate planned expenditure in real terms. But suppose now that X_E represents an unfeasible level of income; suppose, for example, that X_F represents the absolute maximum level of output obtainable from the resources of capital and labour; it will represent an effective ceiling beyond which output cannot rise. The fact that X_E exceeds X_F will imply that *ex post* real expenditure will fall short of its *ex ante* value. There will consequently be upward pressure on prices and an inflationary gap of magnitude AB will be said to exist.

Keynesians are in general agreement as to the origins of the inflationary process, viz. the emergence of an inflationary gap. This concord becomes somewhat diluted when it comes to sorting out what happens afterwards. Discussion tended to be concentrated upon whether the price level (or the level of money national income) would converge automatically to some new higher

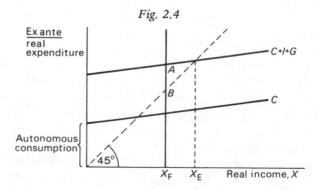

Fig. 2.4

level or whether the process of inflation would continue indefinitely, and perhaps even degenerate into hyper-inflation. These are some of the questions which Keynes and his followers attempted to answer.

How to Pay for the War. In his classic pamphlet *How to Pay for the War* (1940), Keynes addressed himself to one central problem: how to finance the government expenditure and private investment necessary for the successful completion of the war effort while at the same time avoiding the evils of inflation. In the course of writing and advising on this problem, Keynes advanced a theory of inflation which served as the basis for subsequent inflationary gap models of inflation. An examination of the original model contained in *How to Pay for the War* would therefore appear to be a natural starting point for a more general discussion of subsequent inflationary gap models.

His argument runs along the following lines: suppose that the value of output (valued, as are all the subsequent variables, at prewar prices) is Q and that the value of government expenditure and private investment necessary for the effective waging of war is G. The value of output which remains for individuals to consume if they so wish is $Q - G$; this is the supply of consumer goods. The demand for consumer goods is arrived at by considering how individuals divide their disposable income between consumption and saving. If X is the level of national income and T is the amount paid in taxation, then disposable income will be $X - T$. The aggregate amount which individuals decide to save is denoted by S so that desired consumption expenditure will be $X - (T + S)$. If $Q - G < X - (T + S)$, then the supply of consumer goods will fall short of the demand for those goods and an inflationary gap is said to exist.

Assuming that the ratio of real government expenditure plus private investment to real final output is constant, Keynes argued that the initial response of the system would be to hoist up the money value of $Q - G$ so as to clear the goods market. This initial response will lead to windfall gains which will benefit 'profiteers' who may either consume or save these gains. If they consume them, the very high rates of personal and profits taxation will siphon off a sizeable amount — moreover the increased consumption of profiteers could be offset 'by a modest increase of taxation on the general public'; if they save them, the inflation will be halted since the fall in aggregate consumer demand will bring about equilibrium between income and expenditure; if a mixture of the two effects occurs, it is clear that the inflationary process will cease and the price level will rise to a new higher level.

These conclusions have been arrived at on the assumption that workers are willing to stand idly by and see the erosion of the real wage rate consequent upon an inflation in the price of final output. This is an extreme assumption even in times of war. In a situation of excess demand for labour resulting from the existence of an inflationary gap, profiteers may see no disadvantage in diverting some of their windfall gains to finance an increase in money wages rather than allow most of these gains to be taxed away. If wages are continually chasing prices, there would appear to be no escape from this wage-price spiral.

The distribution of national income plays an important role in Keynes' theory of inflation. An inflationary gap may be eliminated by a redistribution of national income away from those classes of society which save little and are taxed at low rates in favour of those classes which save a great deal and who are taxed quite heavily on the income they do not save. Wage-earners constitute the majority of the high-consumption—low-taxation group whereas profiteers constitute the majority of the low-consumption—high-taxation group. We may write the marginal propensities to consume of profiteers and wage-earners as c_p and c_w respectively, where $c_p < c_w$. Assuming that non-consumption expenditure, G, is a constant proportion, g, of national income, the equation for income-expenditure equilibrium becomes:

$$X_t = c_w a_t X_t + c_p(1 - a_t)X_t + gX_t \qquad (2.3)$$

where a_t is defined as the equilibrium share of wages in national income. Since national income is assumed to be at its full-employment level, equation (2.3) defines a unique distribution of national income between workers and profiteers such that:

$$a_t = \frac{1 - g - c_p}{c_w - c_p}. \qquad (2.4)$$

Clearly the greater is the ratio of war expenditure to national income, the lower will have to be the share of wages if equilibrium is to be maintained.

But suppose that

$$a_t > \frac{1 - g - c_p}{c_w - c_p};$$

in this case an inflationary gap exists. The way in which the share of wages falls in response to inflationary pressure to an equilibrium level defined by equation (2.4) is the subject of chapter 9 of *How to Pay for the War*. In his numerical example,[6] Keynes illustrated a situation in which prices would have to remain 15% ahead of wages in order to effect the necessary depression of the real wage rate. The equilibrium relationship between wages and prices compared to the prewar situation would have to be:

$$P_t = (1 + 0.15)W_t; \quad t > 0 \qquad (2.5)$$

where W_0 and P_0, the initial prewar levels of wages and prices, are set at their base values of unity. The precise mechanism whereby the equilibrium condition embodied in equation (2.5) is satisfied rests almost exclusively upon the presence of certain lags in adjustment. Keynes assumed (a) that prices reacted instantaneously to wage increases and (b) that wages reacted with a one-year lag to price increases (see Trevithick, 1975). These two assumptions are formalised in equations (2.6) and (2.7):

$$P_t = (1 + 0.15)W_t \tag{2.6}$$

and

$$W_t = P_{t-1}. \tag{2.7}$$

Equation (2.6) states that profiteers will always attempt to keep prices 15% ahead of wages in order to clear the goods market while equation (2.7) implies that wages will respond fully to a given change in prices but with a lag of one year. By combining equations (2.6) and (2.7), equation (2.8) is obtained which contains current and lagged values of the price level alone:

$$P_t = (1 + 0.15)P_{t-1}. \tag{2.8}$$

If we follow convention and define the proportional rate of change of prices, $\dot{P}_t$, as

$$\dot{P}_t = \frac{P_t - P_{t-1}}{P_{t-1}}$$

then it is evident that one of the predictions of the above model is that wages and prices will continue to rise at the same proportional rate (15% in Keynes' example) in all periods except for the initial period. It is in this period that the redistribution of national income occurs; in all subsequent periods, the process of inflation serves to perpetuate this new distribution by means of the lagged response of wages to prices. Inflation will not get out of hand for it will proceed at a constant proportional rate.

This conclusion must be modified if the assumption of money illusion[7] is inserted into equation (2.7). For example, if we define a parameter ϕ as the percentage change in money wages caused by a one per cent change in prices,[8] and if we assume that this parameter is a positive fraction, then the inflationary process will peter out and the price level will stabilise at a new higher level P_∞ where

$$P_\infty = P_0 + \pi = 1 + \pi.$$

The value of π, the *once and for all* increase in prices needed to redistribute income and restore equilibrium, will be determined by the following equation:

$$\pi = \frac{a_0 - a_t}{a_t - \phi a_0} \tag{2.9}$$

where a_0 is the initial wage share and a_t is the wage share after the new equilibrium has been established.[9] (For a detailed derivation of this formula, see Maital, 1972.)

Nevertheless, whether or not money illusion is assumed, equilibrium will be restored by a reduction of *ex ante* real consumption expenditure (a rise in 'voluntary' savings). In the money illusion case, the wage-lag effect upon which Keynes laid such great emphasis is relegated to a rather subordinate role. Money illusion however was far from central to Keynes' argument. The more crucial wage-lag effect, while still restoring equilibrium between income and expenditure, produces a rather paradoxical result: persistent inflation becomes the means by which the inflationary gap is eliminated — it is the process of inflation which prevents the reappearance of the original excess of real expenditure over real national income.

The vital role of lags in Keynes' model cannot be overemphasised. The lag in adjustment of wages to prices will ensure that the real wage is depressed and that the pre-tax share of profiteers in national income will rise causing an overall fall in consumption and a rise in savings; if the fall in consumption is insufficient because of higher consumption expenditure by profiteers out of their windfall gains, this can be offset by increased taxation. Keynes concluded:

> *Thus the system of voluntary savings will have worked successfully.*
> *That is to say, the money will have been raised 'voluntarily' without*
> *an unlimited increase of prices. The only condition for its success is*
> *that prices should rise relatively to wages to the extent necessary to*
> *divert the right amount of working class and other incomes into the*
> *hands of the profiteers and thence into the hands of the Treasury,*
> *largely in the form of taxes and partly in the form of extra voluntary*
> *savings by profiteers.*

Several features of this model merit repetition. Firstly the financing of a higher level of real savings may have to be assisted by an active fiscal policy by the government whereby it may be obliged to increase the general level of taxes. Secondly the initial inflationary impulse takes place in the product market first of all and is *transmitted* into the factor market after a lag; it is not assumed that organised labour take advantage of their enhanced bargaining strength in order to jack up the level of real wages, merely that they take the steps appropriate to preventing the erosion of the real wage brought about by price inflation in the product market. Thirdly, in the absence of money illusion, the shorter the lag between wage increases and the prior increase in prices, the higher will be the rate of inflation (see Trevithick, 1975).

Neo-Keynesian developments. Keynes was not alone in inquiring into the repercussions of an exogenous increase in aggregate expenditure at full employment. The resource strains experienced by an economy at war had already become apparent in the United States in the early 1940s and the great fear at this time was, quite naturally, that inflation would erupt and wreak unacceptable havoc. Many American economists turned their attention to the development of formal models of the inflationary process which took as their foundation the income-expenditure approach, suitably modified to cater for situations of excess demand.

A typical example of how basic Keynesian principles were applied to the question of inflation is to be found in a celebrated article by A. Smithies (1942). Once again, Smithies was concerned with the situation depicted in fig. 2.1 in which *ex ante* expenditure exceeds the productive capacity of the economy. There is one important difference, however, between Smithies' model and the scheme outlined in *How to Pay for the War*: instead of deflating by an appropriate price index, Smithies defined all of his expenditure functions in *money* terms. That is, the total expenditure function may be written in the following manner

$$E' = \sigma + \epsilon Y + G' \qquad (2.10)$$

where Y is *money* national income (= $P \cdot X$) and the 'prime' superscripts indicate the money values of aggregate expenditure (i.e. $E' = P \cdot E$) and government expenditure plus private investment (i.e. $G' = G \cdot P$); ϵ is the marginal propensity to consume and σ is the level of autonomous consumption. The fact that σ is fixed in *money* terms is of cardinal importance to the model for it implies that inflation will gradually erode the real value of autonomous consumption until the point has been reached at which full-employment equilibrium has been established. Thus by couching the aggregate expenditure function in money terms, Smithies has indicated one possible escape route from a situation of chronic excess demand: the value of the intercept of the consumption function will decline in real terms in the presence of inflation (see fig. 2.3).

Unfortunately there is no economic reason to assume that real autonomous expenditure will in fact decline in an inflationary situation. By framing all of his expenditure functions in nominal terms, Smithies has inserted an arbitrary assumption concerning the behaviour of aggregate expenditure.

Fortunately one alternative escape route remains in Smithies' model. This is the conventional neo-Keynesian assumption that the presence of money illusion in the labour market will serve to redistribute income away from high-consumption groups (workers) and in favour of low-consumption groups (non-wage-earners).[10] This hypothesis introduces an asymmetry into the expenditure plans of different groups: capitalists and rentiers are not subject to money illusion but workers are. Inflation will therefore tilt the distribution of income in favour of the former group which, on average, saves a greater proportion of its real income than the latter group. The consequent flattening of the consumption function will bridge the inflationary gap and save the day.[11]

Many of the features of the Smithies model were incorporated into subsequent theoretical studies on inflation. For example the assumptions of money illusion in the labour market and of differential consumption patterns between wage-earners and non-wage-earners were common elements in later models. For instance passive economic groups who live on incomes fixed in nominal terms and whose expenditure figures significantly in total spending will find their real purchasing power eroded by inflation. Once again *ex ante* expenditure will gradually be brought into line with full-employment income. A similar result can be produced by assuming that some sort of Pigou effect is operative. If consumption varies directly with the real value of liquid assets, inflation may reduce consumption by diminishing the value of such assets. The scope for elaboration on the same theme is without limit.

Most of the models which followed *How to Pay for the War* are formally very similar to each other. As in the Smithies model, they in general reduce to a first or second order difference equation in either the price level or equivalently (since output was assumed constant) in money national income. Conclusions concerning the existence and stability of the equilibrium levels of these variables are drawn through an examination of the magnitudes and signs of the original structural parameters. On the whole the economic justification for restricting the parameters to taking certain values or ranges of values does not receive extensive treatment, with the result that such models are vulnerable to the criticism of being somewhat arbitrary; greater emphasis tended to be laid, for example, on how different lag structures affected the mathematical properties of the solution.

In general neo-Keynesian theories predict either that the rate of price inflation will eventually fall towards zero or (less commonly) that it will accelerate progressively; very rarely do they predict that the rate of inflation will remain constant over time as in Keynes' own model. Moreover nearly all such theories (Keynes' being no exception) predict that provided certain key parameters have the right sign and magnitude and that the system is characterised by the existence of lags of sufficient length, then equilibrium will be restored *automatically*: the inflationary gap would be closed even in the absence of discretionary government intervention although a contractionary fiscal policy would considerably accelerate the process and was therefore desirable.

2.2.ii *Money in a simple Keynesian model*

One of the most damaging criticisms of the quantity theory approach is contained in chapters 20 and 21 of the *General Theory* where Keynes examines the manner in which the price level may be affected by an increase in the money supply. An increase in the supply of money will raise the level of absolute prices if the following two elasticities are positive: (a) the elasticity of aggregate demand with respect to changes in the quantity of money, labelled e_d in the *General Theory*; and (b) the elasticity of absolute prices with respect to aggregate demand, e_p. The former elasticity will depend upon a complex set of factors such as the elasticities of the liquidity preference function and the investment function. The latter elasticity, e_p, will depend primarily upon the degree of capacity utilisation. The Marshallian k will be constant only if *both* e_d and e_p are equal to unity. In fact, e_d will typically be less than unity whereas there is no way of predicting the value of e_p on *a priori* grounds: e_p may indeed exceed unity when, for example, there is a 'flight from currency' as occurred in several post-First World War European economies.

The upshot of this line of reasoning is the Keynesian contention that not only is the velocity of circulation of money a variable (as many modern quantity theorists are prepared to admit), but also that its variation is largely unpredictable *a priori*. The behaviour of the velocity of circulation will depend upon the complex interrelationship of a whole string of elasticities some of which vary with the degree of capacity utilisation.

On the other hand, Keynes should not be interpreted as denying a stable velocity of circulation in the long period: ' . . . there may well be some sort of rough relationship between the national income and the quantity of money required to satisfy liquidity preferences, taken as a mean over periods of optimism and pessimism together.' (Keynes, 1936, p. 306). What Keynes was calling into question was the practical relevance of such historical proportionality from the point of view of economic policy.

In the passage of the *General Theory* which has just been cited, Keynes was focusing his attention on the complicated series of interactions which must be generated before an increase in the supply of money can have any effect on the price level. We have seen that one of the relevant elasticities, e_p, will depend upon the degree of capacity utilisation which, in the *General Theory*, was assumed to be incomplete. The question which must now be asked is this: in the context of a *fully employed* economy, under what circumstances will an increase in the supply of money *not* produce a rise in the price level?

To answer this question, we must first of all introduce the familiar Hicksian *IS–LM* framework of analysis. Let the real interest rate, r, be measured on the vertical axis and the level of real income, X, be measured on the horizontal axis. Once again we shall denote the full-employment level of output by the symbol X_F. Moreover we shall assume that the economy is in the liquidity trap so that the *LM* curve is horizontal over the relevant range. An initial position of full-employment equilibrium may be depicted by allowing the *IS* curve to intersect with the *LM* curve at a level of income X_F (see fig. 2.5). An increase in the supply of money will shift the *LM* curve from LM_1 to LM_2 but aggregate demand will remain unchanged at X_F. No wedge has been driven between the equilibrium and full-employment levels of output and an inflationary gap has failed to emerge. In consequence prices will remain steady.

There is one other situation in which an increase in the supply of money will fail to produce an inflationary gap. This is the case in which the *IS* function is

Fig. 2.5

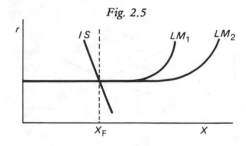

vertical at the full-employment level of output. Even if the *LM* function is
positively sloped, an increase in the supply of money will simply depress the rate
of interest and will not raise the level of demand. Such an outcome is illustrated
in fig. 2.6. Once again an inflationary gap fails to materialise.

Fig. 2.6

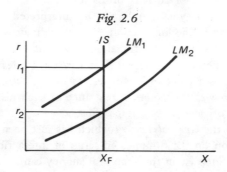

The intermediate case is illustrated in fig. 2.7. Owing to the Keynesian
assumption of downwardly inflexible wages and prices, at all levels of output
below full utilisation of capacity there will be a unique *LM* curve corresponding
to a given supply of money.[12] Once full capacity has been reached, however,
prices start to respond in an upward direction to increases in the pressure of
demand. At or above X_F, a unique *LM* curve corresponds to a given level of *real*
balances, M/P.[13] Thus the curve $LM(M_0/P_0)$ corresponds to a level of real
balances M_0/P_0 (see Laidler, 1969).

The initial impact of increase in the supply of money from M_0 to M_1 is to
displace the *LM* function from $LM(M_0/P_0)$ to $LM(M_1/P_0)$. The intersection of
this latter curve with the *IS* curve produces an equilibrium level of real income in
excess of X_F. In other words an inflationary gap will exist. Prices will continue
to rise for as long as X_E exceeds X_F. Prices will stabilise only when the new
supply of money, M_1, has been deflated in real terms by a sufficiently large
price increase. Full-employment equilibrium will be restored when
$(M_1/P_1) = (M_0/P_0)$; that is, when the *LM* curve has drifted back to its initial
position.

Fig. 2.7

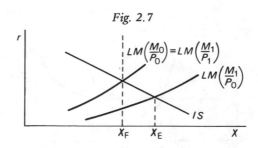

But the above prediction is perfectly consistent with the quantity theory approach for in equilibrium the level of real balances remains a constant proportion of real income. Indeed as it stands it is simply a more elaborate way of presenting the Marshallian transmission mechanism outlined in section 2.1. It must therefore be concluded that 'money does not matter' in an income-expenditure model (a) if the liquidity preference function is infinitely elastic with respect to the rate of interest and/or (b) if the investment function is completely interest inelastic. Only when one or both of these two conditions is fulfilled will an increase in the supply of money have no effect on the price level.[14]

2.2.iii *The Hansen two-gap model*

The income-expenditure approach to inflation bore copious fruit in the shape of the numerous theoretical studies in the inflationary gap tradition which appeared during and after the war. This apparent success however did not go unchecked. Towards the end of the 1940s, certain writers began to express their dissatisfaction with the high degree of aggregation associated with the simplest Keynesian models. In particular they were uneasy about the seemingly subordinate role which was accorded to the labour market during times of inflation. In early neo-Keynesian theories, the labour market reacted in a highly defensive manner to increases in the price of goods and services. Increases in money wages were simply attempts to restore the initial level of real wages in the face of rising prices. The role of the labour market in *initiating* price increases was seldom investigated. An important contribution to our understanding of how demand conditions in both the product market and the labour market affect the rate of inflation is contained in the writings of the Swedish economist, Bent Hansen (Hansen, 1951).

The essence of Hansen's model is illustrated in fig. 2.8. The real wage is measured on the vertical axis and the level of real national income is measured on the horizontal axis. The η (W/P) function relates the *demand* for real output to the real wage rate. The higher the real wage rate, the higher is the level of real *ex ante* demand (i.e. $\eta' > 0$). This proposition is justified on the basis of two assumptions: firstly that as the wage rate rises, the real wage bill will rise; and secondly that as the real wage bill rises relative to other incomes, real demand will rise due to the higher marginal propensity to consume of wage-earners. The $\rho(W/P)$ function on the other hand indicates how the output decision of entrepreneurs is affected by rising real wages. Its negative slope reflects the phenomenon of diminishing marginal productivity of traditional neoclassical theory. The higher the real wage rate, the lower will be the demand for labour; if this lower demand translates itself into a lower level of employment, as is assumed in elementary comparative static analysis, the supply of real output will fall. The equilibrium level of output, X_E, occurs at the intersection of the η and ρ functions at point A.

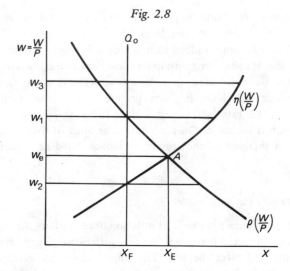

Fig. 2.8

But suppose that X_E represents an infeasible level of output. Assume instead that there is a ceiling to output given by the vertical line Q_0.[15] The fact that the capacity curve Q_0 lies to the left of point A will give rise to either a goods gap or a factor gap or both, depending upon the level of the real wage rate. On the assumption that real wages are the most important component of factor incomes, an *index* of the factor gap may be obtained by measuring the horizontal distance between the Q_0 curve and the ρ function. The size of the goods gap is measured by the horizontal distance between the Q_0 curve and the η function. An inspection of fig. 2.8 reveals that at all wage rates between w_1 and w_2, there is both a positive factor gap $((\rho - Q_0) > 0)$ and a positive goods gap $((\eta - Q_0) > 0)$.

Two further behavioural assumptions are required to complete the model. The first is an equation linking the rate of change of prices to the size of the goods gap so that

$$\frac{dP}{dt} = f(\eta - Q_0) \text{ where } f'(\ ) > 0 \text{ and } f(0) = 0. \qquad (2.11)$$

The second is an equation linking the rate of change of money wages to the index of the size of the factor gap so that

$$\frac{dW}{dt} = g(\rho - Q_0) \text{ where } g'(\ ) > 0 \text{ and } g(0) = 0. \qquad (2.12)$$

The equation for the rate of change of *real* wages is therefore

$$\frac{d\left(\frac{W}{P}\right)}{dt} = \frac{g(\rho - Q_0) - \frac{W}{P} f(\eta - Q_0)}{P}. \qquad (2.13)$$

Quasi-equilibrium is said to prevail when $d(W/P)/dt = 0$. For this to occur, the following condition must be satisfied:

$$\frac{W}{P} = \frac{g(\rho - Q_0)}{f(\eta - Q_0)}. \tag{2.14}$$

The real wage rate which satisfied condition (2.14) is the quasi-equilibrium real wage rate, w_e. Its magnitude will depend upon the relative sluggishness of response of the money wage rate and the price level. The faster the speed of response of the money wage rate relative to that of the price level, the higher will be w_e. Moreover it can be easily verified that w_e will be located in the interval $w_1 > w_e > w_2$. Further inspection of the properties of the model will reveal that w_e is a stable quasi-equilibrium in the sense that, if any other real wage rate were to prevail initially, the process of money wage/price inflation will drive the real wage rate towards w_e. For example if the initial real wage rate is w_3, there will be a positive goods gap and a negative factor gap. The dynamic adjustment functions (equations (2.12) and (2.13)) will imply a continuous depression of the real wage rate to the point where equation (2.14) is satisfied, i.e. where the real wage rate is w_e. Once the real wage rate has been driven below w_1, the size of the goods gap will have been reduced but a positive factor gap will have emerged. It is for this reason that Hansen states that a necessary condition for full inflation is the existence of both a positive goods gap and a positive factor gap.

Hansen's separation of the goods and factor markets and his investigation of the role of excess demand for factors of production in pushing up money wages independently of prices provided a useful starting point for subsequent empirical studies of the determinants of the rate of change of money wages. Indeed much of the early theorising on the Phillips curve relation owed a great deal to his dynamic treatment of the factor market. Excess demand for labour services has always played a central part in determining the rate of change of aggregate money wages, even in the highly sophisticated theories which have appeared since the late 1960s. His separate treatment of the labour market was a distinct improvement on most neo-Keynesian models which tended to treat the behaviour of money wages in a fairly arbitrary manner (*vide* Smithies). Viewed in this light his model may be seen as bridging the gap between neo-Keynesian theory and the more empirically orientated models which were to follow.

Notes to chapter 2

1. The distinction between these two concepts which is made in neo-Keynesian economics arises from defining equilibrium in such a way as to be consistent with the persistence of an uncleared labour market. For a critical analysis of this position, the reader should consult Leijonhufvud (1968a).

2. Note that the demand curve for labour, $N_d(W/P)$, is simply the first derivative of the production function at different levels of employment.

3.   The reader who is unfamiliar with the properties of general equilibrium systems should consult Baumol (1972).

4.   Note that the choice of a price deflator, in our example the average price level P, is immaterial since all *relative* prices (e.g. the real wage rate) have been determined in the real sector of the economy and the choice of a *numéraire* to characterise the equilibrium vector of relative prices is arbitrary.

5.   Note that Keynes defined equilibrium in respect of the laws of motion of the economic system. An economy in which markets *persistently* fail to clear may be regarded as being in a state of rest and hence in equilibrium.

6.   *How to Pay for the War* p. 72. It should be noted that the wage and price columns are each wrongly headed.

7.   In much of what follows we shall be adhering to the analysis of S. Maital (1972) although we disagree with his emphasis on what appears to be a money illusion (or 'institutional' parameter). We would be inclined to pay greater attention to lags in adjustment. For a more detailed discussion of this matter the reader is referred to Trevithick (1975).

8.   Equation (2.7) would become $W_t = \phi P_{t-1}$.

9.   If, as is more probable in peacetime, the emergence of an inflationary gap is a result of an increase in consumer expenditure, a_0 may be interpreted as the share of wages in national income which workers are *attempting* to achieve.

10.   We have seen that, when writing on inflation at this period, Keynes made no such assumption. The term neo-Keynesian is a catch-all category designed to include economists who would tend on balance to subscribe to the income-expenditure method.

11.   Smithies introduced money illusion as a theoretical possibility in a more general model. His article is concerned more with investigating the mathematical conditions for the existence of a stable equilibrium at full employment and less with advancing tentative empirical estimates of the values of particular parameters.

12.   In fig. 2.6 it is clearly possible to have an infinite number of *LM* functions corresponding to equilibrium at full employment. This is due to the fact that increases in the supply of money do not provoke any increase in prices to restore the real value of the money stock to its initial value.

13.   It should be noted that this definition of an *LM* curve may easily be incorporated into a model in which monetary expansion and price inflation are occurring continually. All that is required is that the money supply and the price level grow at the same rate for the *LM* curve to remain in a given position.

14.   This conclusion must be slightly modified when dealing with a situation in which the supply of money and the price level are increasing continually. If one of the two elasticity conditions is satisfied, an increase in the rate of monetary expansion will have no effect upon the *rate of inflation*.

15.   The capacity constraint as we have drawn it is vertical. Alternative shapes for the constraint are clearly possible. For example Bronfenbrenner and Holzman (1963) assume that capacity will increase with the real wage rate up to a certain point, after which further increases in the real wage rate reduce the level of capacity.

CHAPTER 3

Theories of Cost Inflation

For many years now a controversy has been raging concerning the sources of inflationary pressure in which two distinct and rival camps have disputed with each other over the formulation and interpretation of empirical hypotheses. On the one hand there are those who believe that in any reasonable explanation of the inflationary process, some attention must be paid to excess demand forces and that a policy of demand restriction is of cardinal importance in any anti-inflation programme. Within this camp there is, of course, considerable scope for dissension regarding the sources of the excess demand both for goods and services and for factors of production. Nevertheless when it comes to formulating a policy for controlling inflation, all are unanimous in according pride of place to demand restraint.

On the other hand there are those who regard the inflationary process as a non-economic phenomenon, being essentially social and political in origin. The more generous in this camp are prepared to concede that, in certain circumstances, excess demand could play *some* role in raising or lowering the inflation rate but even they are not prepared to place anything but a minimal reliance upon a policy of demand management. Given that the inflation has socio-political origins, is sustained by a socio-political dynamic and is mainly independent of the pressure of demand, the problem can only be solved by devising an institutional framework which will restrain the worst excesses of individual avarice in the interest of the common good. A prices and incomes policy would therefore appear to be the logical extension of this diagnosis.

We may call this latter approach the *cost-push* interpretation of inflation and it is with this approach that we shall be principally concerned in this chapter. In section 3.1 a simple dynamic model will be constructed in which many of the elements of more formal and technically complex theories of cost inflation will be incorporated. In section 3.2 we shall consider three distinct but interrelated models of cost inflation: the models of (a) Ackley, (b) Wiles and (c) Jackson, Turner and Wilkinson. Section 3.3 will be devoted to a preliminary examination of the 'demand-pull versus cost-push' debate. This will provide an introduction to the detailed evidence concerning the role of trade unions in generating inflationary pressure which is contained in chapter 6.

3.1   A simple model of cost inflation

> *The current inflation consists of a social dispute about the
> distribution of the national income; persistent attempts by many
> social groups to increase their consumption faster than is consistent
> with the aims of other groups or with macroeconomic stability;
> persistent consequential bidding up of the price level in a wage-price
> or wage-wage spiral.* (Posner, 1973)

The logic of this position may be formalised by considering the following highly
simplified model in which W_B is the money wage bill, Z_B is the money profit bill,
the real value of national income is constant and money national income, Y, is
totally exhausted by the incomes of wage-earners and profit-earners; i.e.
$Y = Z_B + W_B$. Moreover let the subscript t denote the magnitude of any variable
at time t. A condition for zero inflation is that the following relationship should
hold *ex ante:*

$$Y_t = (\alpha_1 + \alpha_2)Y_t \qquad (3.1)$$

where α_1 and α_2 are the shares of wages and profits in national income. Clearly
$(\alpha_1 + \alpha_2) \equiv 1$ *ex post.* What is important is that each income-receiving group
should be satisfied with the realised division of national income. Should one
group be dissatisfied with its income share then the sum of the *desired* shares in
national income may exceed unity, i.e. $(\alpha_1 + \alpha_2) > 1$.

In order to determine the dynamic properties of this model we shall assume
that equation (3.1) is initially satisfied *ex ante* but that one group (in our
example, wage-earners) becomes dissatisfied with its share of national income.
More specifically we shall assume that, in period 1, the money wage bill rose in
an attempt to establish the following relationship between wages and money
income:

$$W_{B1} = \alpha_1' Y_0$$

where α' is the new *ex ante* wage share. It is now assumed that profit-earners, in
an effort to restore the *status quo ante*, raise prices by an amount just sufficient
to maintain the initial share of profits in national income. If profit-earners react
instantaneously in defence of their income shares, the following equation will
hold:

$$Z_{B1} = \alpha_2 Y_1.$$

If a similar reaction pattern persists for all succeeding periods, the resulting
equation for money national income will be:

$$Y_t = \alpha_1' Y_{t-1} + \alpha_2 Y_t = \left(\frac{\alpha_1'}{1 - \alpha_2}\right) Y_{t-1}. \qquad (3.2)$$

The first order difference equation (see Baumol, 1951) is of the simplest possible nature and produces a solution:

$$Y_t = Y_0 \left(\frac{\alpha_1'}{1 - \alpha_2} \right)^t. \tag{3.3}$$

Since we have been assuming throughout that real income is constant, equation (3.3) is also an equation in the price level, P_t. By the appropriate manipulation we may derive the following expression for the rate of inflation:

$$\dot{P} = \frac{\alpha_1'}{1 - \alpha_2} - 1 \tag{3.4}$$

The rate of inflation will be zero if and only if $\alpha_1' = 1 - \alpha_2$. That is, $\dot{P} = 0$ if the amount claimed by labour is equal to the amount conceded by capital. Should the two groups be engaged in some sort of class struggle for shares in national income then $\alpha_1' > (1 - \alpha_2)$ and the various claims on national income cannot be satisfied simultaneously. The more intense the struggle for income shares (i.e. the larger is the discrepancy between α_1' and $(1 - \alpha_2)$) the higher will be the rate of inflation.

The basic model can be elaborated and extended in a number of directions. For example the introduction of fixed income groups who are unable to defend themselves against the ravages of inflation could provide an important stabilising factor in reconciling the competing claims of other economic groups (see F. D. Holzman, 1950). Money illusion could also fill a similar role. Moreover a complex model could be devised in which competitive and non-competitive markets coexist side by side and in which inflationary impulses are transmitted from one group of markets to the other (see Duesenberry, 1950).

The cost-push hypothesis may also be expressed in what is possibly a more familiar guise by disaggregating the analysis to take account of rivalry, not between different broad categories of income recipient, but between different groups within the same broad income category. For example, a notable feature of recent British experience has been the growing friction between members of different unions, each union vying with others to establish or maintain a 'fair' pattern of wage differentials between comparable groups of workers. The evidence in support of this 'comparability' hypothesis will be surveyed in chapter 6. At this stage all that is necessary is to restate the cost-push hypothesis in terms of a more disaggregated model.

Consider n different categories of labour and $(n-1)$ wage differential ratios $W_2/W_1, W_3/W_1, \ldots W_n/W_1$ where the wage rate[1] of the first category is taken as a *numéraire*. Define

$$\frac{W_2}{W_1} = \beta_2, \frac{W_3}{W_1} = \beta_3, \ldots, \frac{W_n}{W_1} = \beta_n$$

(note that $\beta_1 = 1$). Clearly

$$W_i = \beta_j W_j (i, j = 1, 2, \ldots, n).$$

If the set of differentials β_2, β_3, . . . , β_n is generally regarded as just and equitable by all of the participants in the wage bargain, then there will be no tendency for one group to make a wage claim so as to improve its relative position on the scale of differentials. On the other hand if one group, dissatisfied with its own relative position in the pecking order, unilaterally attempts to leapfrog some other groups, this will set in motion a chain reaction among *all* other groups in an effort to restore what was generally considered to be a fair structure of differentials. *All* money wages will tend to move in sympathy with that of the dissatisfied group. Such behaviour bears a close resemblance to the simple model outlined above since the inflationary impulse arises from the fact that the *ex ante* and *ex post* values of at least one element of the vector $(1, \beta_2,$ $\beta_3, ... , \beta_n)$ are out of line.

3.2   Particular models of cost inflation

In the models of pure cost inflation such as the one sketched in section 3.1, the process of price determination is regarded as a non-economic operation. It is the outcome not of the market process implicit in text-book price theory, but of some sort of trial of strength between competing economic groups. The existence of extensive monopolistic or quasi-monopolistic powers in the hands of large corporations and big unions renders the study of the inflationary process by reference to competitive models of price determination a futile exercise. If this view of the world is correct it follows that attempts to explain inflation by examining the aggregate relation of supply to demand will be fruitless.

3.2.i   *The Ackley model of administered prices*

A less extreme position is espoused by Ackley (Ackley, 1958; 1959; 1961) who, following Duesenberry's highly mathematical exercise (see Duesenberry, 1950), sought to demonstrate how cost and demand factors would interact to produce price inflation. Like Duesenberry, Ackley considered two sorts of market for goods, services and factors, the first comprising those markets in which prices are competitively determined by the forces of supply and demand and the second comprising those markets in which prices are administered 'according to some rule or judgement'. The former group of markets would include the markets for the large number of basic raw materials and also the important market for agricultural products. The latter group of markets would encompass the vast bulk of industrial submarkets. If all markets, including the labour market, set prices according to the mark-up principle, the presence of aggregate excess demand would not in itself force up prices. On the other hand, as soon as we allow some prices to be competitively determined, the possibility of a demand-induced inflationary spiral becomes more immediate. According to Ackley, this could occur in two ways. Firstly, if, as he assumes, the prices of many raw materials are market-determined, the prices of those goods which involve these scarce materials in their production will also rise. Secondly, since he also assumes, quite reasonably, that the prices of agricultural products are market-determined, any scarcity of such products due to an aggregate excess of demand over supply would force up the price of foodstuffs. Both these effects will have a considerable impact on the cost of living and, since Ackley assumes that 'the money wage is, of all prices, one of the most clearly administered', there will be upward pressure on the money wage rate. This will put further pressure on prices and the spiral continues indefinitely. The sensitivity of the price level to variations in the pressure of aggregate demand clearly depends upon two factors. The first is the extent to which the prices of goods, services and factors are market-determined. The second is the incidence of demand pressure: if most of the excess demand is experienced by markets in which prices are administered, prices will show little tendency to rise.

It follows from the logic of Ackley's model that at least one of the following conditions must be satisfied if a steady inflationary process is to be set in motion:

either (a) there must be persistent excess demand for the goods and services produced in the competitive sector of the economy which is subsequently generalised via the mark-up mechanism to other, non-competitive, sectors;
or (b) there must be sustained upward pressure upon the wage rate (in the case of wage-push) or the profit rate (in the case of profit-push): a pure cost inflation of the Holzman type would result in which 'the demands of labour and the mark-up practices of business cannot be harmonized by sufficient productivity increases'. The eventual outcome of this mechanism is described symbolically in equation (3.4).

The upshot of the Ackley model is that excess aggregate demand will only produce upward pressure on the price level to the extent that it is experienced in the competitive sectors of the economy. Otherwise the only process that remains which is capable of generating inflationary pressure is the pure cost-push mechanism outlined in Section 3.1.

3.2.ii The Wiles model

In a recent *tour d'horizon* on the state of economic theory, P. Wiles (1973) has singled out the problem of inflation as being the most eloquent demonstration of the inability of contemporary economic theory to come to grips with the realities confronting modern economies. Although he deliberately set out to provoke public debate and despite the lack of rigour contained in certain misdirected attacks on the monetarist position, Wiles has performed a valuable service in advancing a version of the cost-push hypothesis which underpins much of the current discussion of inflation in influential political and journalistic circles.

The analytical basis for the Wiles model is contained in two propositions:

(a) 'The main function of prices is not to be resource-allocators but cost-coverers' (Wiles 1973);

(b) wage costs, by far the most important component of total costs, are determined, not by market forces, but by the whim and fancy of trade union leaders.

From these two premises follows the inevitable conclusion that the rate of change of prices will be determined by the rate of change of money wages which, in turn, will depend upon the frame of mind of trade union leaders. According to this line of reasoning, the level and rate of change of prices will be determined, not by the actions of the monetary and fiscal authorities, but by trade union fiat. The idea that we live in a world of Walrasian *tâtonnement* in which there is a continual tendency for markets to clear, albeit gradually, is dismissed by Wiles as being patently unreal.

Although this view of the inflationary process does possess some intuitive appeal, several questions need to be answered before it can be considered as a serious explanation of current events and not merely a series of unsubstantiated *ad hoc* observations. Firstly, what is there in the Wiles thesis to explain the recent alarming acceleration in the rate of inflation not only in the United Kingdom, but throughout the western world? Secondly, what role is played by the monetary authorities in the inflationary process?

To the first question Wiles replies that three distinct developments have occurred in all western economies which lead inevitably to an intensification of the struggle between competing income groups for increased income shares. Firstly with the growth in communications both within and between countries, wage claims have become based upon a much broader set of criteria. Gone are the days when most wage claims were based upon the actual situation within a trade or upon money wage concessions made in comparable trades. Demonstration effects make international comparisons in wage demands increasingly dominant so that the money wage rate is, to all intents and purposes, simply a figure 'picked out of the air'. A second possible cause of the recent upsurge in wage claims is the extension of New Left irrationalism from university campuses into the arena of collective bargaining. A third and possibly related cause is the fact that left wingers have replaced right wingers at the head of many trade unions.

To the second question regarding the role of the monetary authorities during times of inflation Wiles replies that they will validate and underwrite all increases in the price level no matter what their source; the main objective of the monetary authorities is to maintain full employment and in attempting to achieve this goal they will be forced into pursuing an accommodating monetary policy. In this respect Wiles has adopted a view of monetary policy which is not far removed from that of many neo-Keynesians: the monetary authorities will not step in to dampen an inflationary spiral for their main concern is with the maintenance of full employment and (perhaps) low interest rates. The supply of money should therefore be regarded, not as exogenous as in monetarist theories, but as endogenous. The supply of money is a direct function of the level of money income.

3.2.iii   Jackson, Turner and Wilkinson

In a recently published monograph, Jackson, Turner and Wilkinson (1972) have turned their attention to a highly important question: do trade unions cause inflation? A large number of important issues are raised and hypotheses floated in this monograph. A consideration of some of these points will have to be postponed to chapter 6 while discussion of most of the rest will be omitted completely. Nevertheless it may be useful at this stage to summarise one important argument which emerges from the work of these authors which has a direct relevance to the study of cost inflation.

The authors start by examining the inflationary experience of the whole world and note that the countries of the world may be classified into two distinct groups. The first group, by far the largest, comprises those countries undergoing 'normal' or 'equilibrium' inflation of around 3% or 4% each year. The second group, all of which are situated in Latin America, is suffering from rates of inflation in excess of 30% each year. This latter group of countries is said to be experiencing *strato-inflation*. The authors attach great significance to the statistical clustering of inflation rates around 3% in the first group and 30% in the latter group. The fact that no country over the period 1948-71 'has had an annual inflation rate between 9.6% and 21.6%' constitutes, in their view, strong *prima facie* grounds for believing that 'normal' inflation and strato-inflation are different in kind.

Having divided world inflationary experience in this manner, Jackson, Turner and Wilkinson proceed to formulate two separate explanatory models to correspond to the two distinct types of inflation. For 'normal' inflations they propose a model which, in essence, is of the wage-leadership type: the national rate of inflation will be determined by the rate of increase in money wages in some 'key' group. The Jackson, Turner and Wilkinson variant on this approach is to maintain that the key sector will be the one which enjoys the fastest rate of productivity growth. The consequent rate of increase in money wages in the key sector will be generalised by institutional factors to the rest of the labour market, even to sectors where no increase in productivity has occurred. (For a more substantial treatment of this class of model the reader is referred to chapter 6.)

Of more direct relevance to the study of theories of cost inflation is their examination of the experience of strato-inflationary economies. Once an inflationary process of considerable magnitude has been set in train by some initial shock, it becomes vital for individual economic groups to defend their living standards at all costs. The initial inflationary impulse may have been imparted by an expansive monetary policy, a devaluation of the currency or simply by political mismanagement. Nevertheless once it becomes generally appreciated that the initial rise in prices is not a once and for all phenomenon and is likely to be replicated into the indefinite future, a social conflict will break out which governments have found to be almost impossible to extinguish. All attempts to bring the rate of inflation below 10% have required such political upheaval that they have generally been abandoned after a year or so.

The ferocity of the social conflict between competing groups provides the major feature which distinguishes strato-inflations from 'equilibrium' inflations:

> *In the equilibrium-inflationary economies, social and industrial conflict is mostly about the distribution of the yearly (marginal) additions to the national product: the basic distribution of income, whether between social classes or economic groups remains relatively stable from year to year. But in the strato-inflations, social conflict centres on the basic distribution of income itself.* (Jackson, Turner and Wilkinson, 1972)

In support of this conjecture they cite as an example the fact that, during the 1960s, the incidence of recorded strikes in Chile (one of the strato-inflationary economies) was ten times higher than that in Britain as was its rate of inflation.

One of the great weaknesses in the Jackson, Turner and Wilkinson thesis is their failure to come to grips with the mountain of theoretical and empirical literature built up by economists in the Chicago tradition which seeks to demonstrate that the Latin American inflations can best be explained by a fundamentally monetarist model. The six strato-inflationary economies do indeed suffer from greater social conflict than the highly industrialised economies. Although in part it may be a result of lower absolute living standards in these countries, such social unrest is also, according to monetarists, a *consequence* of the inflation which was generated by a political inability or unwillingness to exercise sufficient control over the rate of monetary expansion.

The debate between monetarists and what may be called institutionalists has been raging for many years and has yet to be resolved satisfactorily, for there is a severe problem of interpretation of econometric results on Latin American inflations. Discussion of this rather complex matter must be deferred to chapter 8.

Moreover the recent experience of the United Kingdom and Japan, to take but two examples, must cast some doubt upon the contemporary relevance of the rather convenient clustering of inflation rates in industrialised countries around 3%. At the time of writing, the predicted annual rate of inflation for the UK is 20% and the actual rate of inflation of Japan is currently running at more than 22%. Are Britain and Japan on the verge of becoming strato-inflationary economies? If so, what has produced this state of affairs? What is the precise mechanism which drives an economy from a situation of 'normal' inflation down the perilous path to strato-inflation? The recent alarming acceleration in the rates of inflation in western economies has rendered obsolete many of the statistical distinctions contained in the Jackson, Turner and Wilkinson monograph.

3.3 The distinction between demand-pull and cost-push inflation: a preliminary view

In this section we shall be concerned with providing a preliminary answer to one question: is it possible to devise a test which will distinguish between demand-pull and cost-push theories of inflation?

The question has obvious relevance to the selection of the appropriate set of policy instruments for tackling inflation. If purely institutional factors are responsible for causing inflation, as the extreme cost-push position implies, then the only way of conquering inflation is completely to revamp the framework of wage and price setting. The only solution to a problem which stems from the inadequacy of institutions lies in the abolition or reform of those very same institutions, e.g. through prices and incomes policies. Adherents of a demand-pull explanation of inflation would tend to disagree. Any long term solution to the inflation problem must be built upon the solid foundation of demand restraint. In this respect, Keynesians and monetarists find themselves in rare agreement so that income-expenditure and monetarist models may be lumped together in their diagnosis of the source of inflationary pressure in a closed economy. (The same does not apply to the diagnosis of the inflationary experience of open economies.) When it comes to prescribing remedies for the inflationary malady however this small measure of agreement becomes heavily diluted. Keynesians would in general plump for a policy of demand restraint engineered through a restrictive fiscal policy and supplemented in the short term by a prices and incomes policy. On the other hand monetarists would, quite predictably, tend to prefer a regime of monetary control in which the rate of monetary expansion is *gradually* reduced to a rate compatible with the growth in real income. Nevertheless, if we assume that a reasonable indicator of the pressure of demand is the unemployment rate (see chapter 4), the income-expenditure and monetarist models produce the identical prediction that a fall in the unemployment rate produced by expansive monetary/fiscal policies should be correlated with a rise in the rate of inflation. The same is true, *mutatis mutandis*, for a rise in the unemployment rate produced by a contractionary monetary/fiscal policy.

This consideration led Samuelson and Solow (1960) to propose the following experiment in an attempt to distinguish demand from cost inflation:

> *If a small relaxation of demand were followed by great moderations*
> *in the march of wages and other costs so that the social cost of a*

stable price index turned out to be very small in terms of sacrificed
high-level employment and output, then the demand-pull hypothesis
would have received its most important confirmation. On the other
hand, if mild demand repression checked cost and price increases not
at all or only mildly, so that considerable unemployment would have
to be engineered before the price level updrift could be prevented,
then the cost-push hypothesis would have received its most
important confirmation.

The methodology of this approach is to examine whether the demand-pull prediction stands up to empirical scrutiny and, should it fail to do so, to deduce, *faute de mieux*, that cost-push factors were responsible for inflation.

Nor would the situation be much improved if monetarists were to produce a series of statistical equations purporting to demonstrate the dependence of the rate of inflation upon the rate of monetary expansion. The more sophisticated among cost-push theorists, while accepting the statistical association between these two variables, would simply reverse the direction of causation and assert that strong inflationary pressure leads to supportive expansions in the supply of money.

It should be clear by now that, at a high level of aggregation, a number of insuperable hurdles are encountered in testing the cost-push thesis. This is due principally to the immeasurability of most of the cost-push variables, such as the degree of social conflict. Apart from the rather negative statement that one would expect to find little or no inverse correlation between the rate of inflation and the unemployment rate, no immediate test of the cost-push diagnosis is readily forthcoming.

It may be helpful at this stage to dispose of some of the more facile tests of the cost-push hypothesis which have been proposed over the years. (For a useful discussion of many of the fallacies which abound in this area of economics, the reader is referred to Samuelson and Solow, 1960.) For example it has often been naively believed that cost and demand inflation could be distinguished by examining which rose first, wages or prices. If wages rose first, this constituted evidence in favour of cost inflation, and if prices rose first, it pointed to the presence of demand pressure. Quite apart from the almost insuperable problem of selecting a suitable base period for the analysis, such an approach is futile since it is quite possible that the initial impact of a higher level of aggregate demand is felt in the labour market first of all and is subsequently transmitted to the goods market, perhaps by some mark-up scheme. Other writers have asserted that, where money wages rise faster than labour productivity, then this is evidence in favour of the cost-push hypothesis. But it has already been pointed out that whether one considers the money wage rate to be an administered price or a market-determined price, one would nevertheless expect money wages to rise in a situation of excess aggregate demand as well as in a situation of autonomous wage or profit push. In fact it would be extremely difficult to conceive of any theory of inflation in which the money wage rate failed to rise. The empirical difficulty of specifying the conditions under which the cost-push hypothesis may be refuted or otherwise becomes less acute, however, when the analysis becomes more disaggregated, as will be seen in chapter 6.

Finally, if any theory of inflation is to be regarded as a serious contender in explaining the current inflation it must be capable of indicating the precise stimulus which produced the recent acceleration in the rate of *world* inflation. It would require the most remarkable of coincidences if, for example, Britain and Japan, two countries with very diverse records in economic performance and in industrial relations, were to begin almost simultaneously to suffer from a degree of social conflict which just happened to produce more or less the same rate of inflation. When considered on an international level, the cost-push hypothesis lacks much of the credibility which other models, most notably the monetarist hypothesis, are able to command. In particular, the Humean price-specie-flow mechanism and the related monetary theory of the balance of payments succeed in providing a viable indication of the factors at work in disseminating inflationary pressure throughout the non-communist world. The problem of world inflation will be dealt with more fully in chapter 8.

Note to chapter 3

1. Note that W_i refers to the wage rate of the ith category of labour and *not* the wage bill. In this minor respect the analysis differs from that of the preceding model.

CHAPTER 4
Wage Inflation and Excess Demand

The income—expenditure model of inflation predicts that price and wage inflation will be induced by excess demand for goods and labour. In this chapter we shall concentrate on the specific relation between wage inflation and excess demand for labour. In the literature of the early 1960s this relation was the centrepiece of the theory of inflation. It was widely held that the rate of inflation was determined in the long run by the level of excess demand for labour (usually measured by the rate of unemployment) while, in the short run, fluctuations in both import prices and productivity growth would combine with excess demand for labour in determining the rate of inflation. Subsequent theory and evidence has put the relation between wage inflation and excess demand into a broader context. In particular the expectations hypothesis has largely discredited the view that a long-run relation of this kind exists. Further, attention has increasingly been focused on the determinants of excess demand as the central issue in inflation theory. Both of these developments have served to diminish the importance of the relation between wage inflation and excess demand as an *explanation* of the inflationary process by relegating it to the role of a vital link in a chain of relations which together constitute an explanation of that process. However because this relation remains an important element in the theory of inflation and because its development in the literature of the early 1960s was uniquely important in advancing our understanding of the inflationary process, it is necessary to consider it in some detail.

4.1 The 'Phillips Curve'

The relation between excess demand in the labour market and wage inflation was essentially an empirical discovery. In a pathbreaking article, published in 1958, A. W. Phillips carried out a statistical investigation of the relation between the rate of unemployment and the rate of change of money wages (Phillips,

1958). Although it is clear that Phillips had in mind the hypothesis that wage inflation was induced by excess demand for labour there is no evidence that he derived his hypothesis from the income-expenditure models of inflation. Essentially Phillips' work consisted of statistical tests of the relation between the level of unemployment and the rate of change of money wages in the UK over the period 1861–1957 with only a vague and unrigorous hypothesis in mind. His results however were quite striking. He obtained, by means of rather unorthodox statistical methods, the graphic relationship shown in fig. 4.1. This relation has come to be known as the 'Phillips Curve'. The fitted curve was taken to indicate the rate of money wage inflation which would occur at different levels of aggregate unemployment, which in turn are proxies for different levels of excess demand for labour. The curve has some interesting aspects. For example it may be seen from fig. 4.1 that at a rate of unemployment of about 5½% wages would remain static. Of more relevance to policy-makers the curve shows that at a rate of unemployment of about 2½% wages would rise at around 2% per annum which is consistent with price stability since the trend growth rate of productivity is also about 2% per annum. The possible policy implications of these findings were quickly recognised. (See for example Paish, 1968). At its crudest the chief implication to be drawn from the curve is that price stability can be achieved if policy can somehow stabilise the level of unemployment at around 2½%. In practice this prescription purports to refer to a long-run situation; it was accepted that in the short run fluctuations in productivity growth and import prices would be reflected in price changes.

The Phillips curve quite clearly had important implications for both the theory of inflation and for economic policy. There was therefore a need to examine its theoretical foundations more rigorously and to subject the data to more sophisticated statistical testing. In this chapter we shall examine certain aspects of the debate which followed the publication of Phillips' article. In later chapters a number of embellishments on the basic Phillips model, together with alternative models, are discussed and the expectations hypothesis is introduced to complete the excess demand/expectations model of inflation.

Fig. 4.1

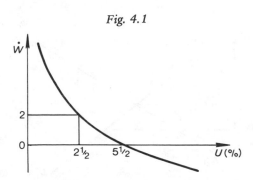

Lipsey on the Phillips Curve. The most significant attempt to give theoretical and
statistical rigour to the Phillips curve concept in the early 1960s was made by
Lipsey (1960). Lipsey chose to begin his theoretical analysis by examining the
behaviour of wage rates in a micro-labour market. Quite apart from the fact that
this approach does not flow from the theory underlying the income-
expenditure models, which might have been considered appropriate in view of
the fact that the empirical result to be interpreted was an aggregate one, there
are distinct problems which arise from being confined to partial equilibrium
analysis and the difficulties of subsequent aggregation. (See Peston, 1971, for
detailed discussion of this matter.) Lipsey's analysis however undoubtedly
carried the debate forward swiftly and remains for many the standard approach.
Let us therefore proceed with an exposition of Lipsey's analysis by examining
first the workings of a micro-labour market.

The micro-labour market. For the moment a micro-labour market will simply be
defined as a market within which labour is more mobile than it is between
markets. Following Lipsey (1960) we may consider a simple excess demand
situation in a labour market, i. In fig. 4.2 the supply and demand curves relating
to a single labour market at some point in time are represented by two straight
lines $N_{si}N_{si1}$ and D_iD_{i1}. The equilibrium wage rate, i.e. the rate which will equate
supply and demand, is OW_{ie}. (Note that while the Phillips relation is in respect
of *money* wages and the unemployment rate, Lipsey's analysis is phrased in
orthodox neoclassical terms so that there is some ambiguity about his approach.
Neoclassical market analysis postulates that it is the real wage which equilibrates
markets. Lipsey does not explicitly refer to this matter but there are two
possible implicit assumptions which permit money wage analysis to be
interchangeable with real wage analysis. First it might be assumed that the price
level is constant throughout so that changes in the money wage are equivalent to
changes in the real wage. Second we might assume that both the demand and
supply curves for labour are expressed in money terms, i.e. are both multiplied

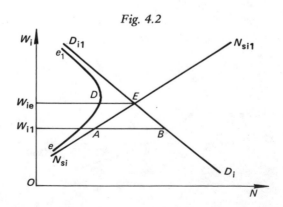

Fig. 4.2

by the price level. Both assumptions are legitimate in the interests of expositional simplicity but require clearer specification where more realistic models are being constructed. We shall return to this matter in later chapters.) Suppose however that the current wage rate was only OW_{i1}. An excess demand for labour would exist in this situation and would comprise AB units of labour. At a wage rate of OW_{i1} a disequilibrium will exist in the market and there will be an upward pressure on the wage rate. In this situation, assuming that the supply and demand curves for labour remain stable over time, the equilibrating function of the wage rate will cause it to rise from OW_{i1} to OW_{ie}. The movement of the wage rate towards OW_{ie} may be called the reaction of the wage to the disequilibrium situation associated with the existence of excess demand in the labour market at wage rate OW_{i1}. At this point it is necessary to consider what will determine the *speed* of the reaction of the wage rate to the existence of a market disequilibrium. The simplest and most intuitively plausible assumption to make is that the speed of the wage reaction is dependent on the ratio of excess demand to total labour supply.

$$\dot{W}_i = f \frac{(D_i - N_{si})}{N_{si}} \qquad (4.1)$$

where

$$\dot{W}_i = \frac{dW_i}{dt} \times \frac{1}{W_i}.$$

Thus the larger is the excess demand for labour, the faster will be the rate of adjustment in the wage rate.

We may call the expression in equation (4.1) a *reaction function* which maps from $(D_i - N_{si})/N_{si}$ to $\dot{W}_i$. The simplest form of reaction is a linear one of the form:

$$\dot{W}_i = a \frac{(D_i - N_{si})}{N_{si}}. \qquad (4.2)$$

This function is illustrated in fig. 4.3.

Fig. 4.3

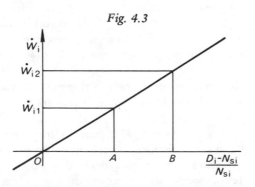

The reaction function simply relates certain rates of excess demand to the corresponding (proportional) speed of the wage adjustment. Thus, when excess demand is equal to OA (say $(AB/W_{i1}A)$ in fig. 4.2) wages will increase at a rate of W_{i1}. This reaction function is valid so long as the speed of the wage response to any given level of excess demand is constant over time. It is useful in that it dispenses with the need for information about the total supply and demand schedules and requires only that the amount which is supplied and demanded at the existing market price is known.

Suppose that the market was in a disequilibrium situation with an excess demand of $OA(OA = AB/W_{i1}A)$, then wages will rise at a rate of W_1 and after some time (which is the reaction period) the wage rate will be equal to OW_{ie} and $\dot{W}_i$ will then be zero. In terms of the reaction function, the market situation will be described by the point of origin and an equilibrium may be said to obtain. This simply means that the supply and demand prices of labour are equal at a wage rate of OW_{ie} and that vacancies (V_c) will be equal to unemployment; i.e.

$$D_i = N_i + V_{ci} = N_{si} = N_i + U_i$$

where N_i is employment. In this situation the wage rate will have risen at a speed sufficient to equilibrate the market and so long as the supply and demand schedules remain stable there will be no further tendency for the wage rate to rise.

Unemployment in the micro-labour market. It is important to note at this point that, so long as any workers change jobs within the micro-labour market and it takes a finite time for them to find a new job, unemployment will be positive while excess demand may be positive. When the market is in equilibrium vacancies will equal the numbers unemployed. When excess demand is positive $V_{ci} > U_i$ and when excess demand is negative $V_{ci} < U_i$. In the former case where $V_{ci} > U_i$ excess demand would be $V_{ci} - U_i$ and U_i would be the number of frictionally unemployed workers. In the latter case where $V_{ci} < U_i$, V_{ci} would be the number of frictionally unemployed workers; i.e. $U_{if} = \min(V_{ci}, U_i)$. These definitions apply only within a single homogeneous labour market where structural unemployment is by definition unable to exist. The curve $e_1 e$ in fig. 4.2 illustrates the frontier of effective employment when frictional unemployment is taken account of. The curve $e_1 e$ is displaced to the left of the frontier $D_{i1}EN_{si}$ by the amount of frictional unemployment, measured by vacancies where $W_i > W_{ie}$ and by unemployment where $W_i < W_{ie}$. When $W_i = W_{ie}$, $DE = V_{ci} = U_i$.

The existence of frictional unemployment is therefore compatible with either positive or negative excess demand in a micro-labour market.

The measurement of excess demand. The demand for labour is difficult to measure in practice and it is therefore difficult to construct a testable relation based on an excess-demand variable since demand is not directly observable. Theoretically the best approximate measure of excess demand might be generated by considering vacancy and unemployment data. Thus we might say that $(V_c - U)/N_s$ is a good approximation for $(D - N_s)/N_s$. However, since it is difficult to obtain reliable data for a vacancy time series in most countries, since many vacancies are simply not notified and therefore not recorded, Phillips and Lipsey employed the aggregate unemployment rate as a proxy measure of excess demand for labour. Certain refinements of this measure will be discussed in the following chapter.

Excess demand and the unemployment rate. Unemployment data are normally easily available in detailed and accurate form and theoretically the unemployment rate will provide an approximate measure of the level of excess demand over certain ranges of excess demand. Consider the relation between excess demand and unemployment.

This relation, illustrated in fig. 4.4, is non-linear to the left of a but linear to the right of a. It is linear to the right of a because excess demand will be negative, i.e. $V_{ci} < U_i$ and the level of unemployment will directly reflect the level of excess demand. At point a, $V_{ci} = U_i$ (for the micro-market i) and excess demand will be zero; i.e. the going wage rate in the market is the equilibrium rate OW_{ie} in fig. 4.2. To the left of a the level of excess demand will be positive; i.e. $V_{ci} > U_i$. According to the analysis of frictional unemployment given earlier, all of the unemployment between O and a will be frictional. Hence the relation described above in fig. 4.4 implies that frictional unemployment will vary with the level of excess demand in a non-linear and inverse fashion. The inverse quality of this relation implies that an increase in the level of excess demand reduces the average period of frictional unemployment by a magnitude great enough to more than offset any increase in the numbers frictionally unemployed.

Fig. 4.4

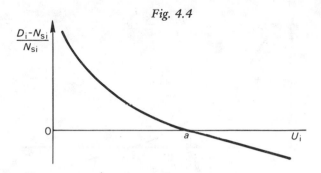

It is now only necessary to combine the two relationships

$$\dot{W} = a \frac{(D_i - N_{si})}{N_{si}}$$

and

$$U_i = f \frac{(D_i - N_{si})}{N_{si}}$$

in order to yield a testable relationship between the rate of change of wages and the level of excess demand. These relations are combined graphically in fig. 4.5. This figure illustrates another form of the market reaction function which is essentially the same as that illustrated in fig. 4.3, the difference between the two being that in fig. 4.5 the unemployment rate is used as an approximate indicator of the true level of excess demand used in fig. 4.3. The formulation of the reaction function illustrated in fig. 4.5 is theoretically inferior to that in fig. 4.3 but yields a testable relation. The main part of this function is non-linear but in the range $U_i > Oa$ will be linear by assumption (i.e. both of the functions combined to yield this reaction function were linear in that range). In functional form this relation will be described by some equation of the general form $\dot{W} = \alpha + \beta U^{-c}; U < a$.

Consider how to interpret this reaction function. At time t_1 we observe that the unemployment rate is Oc and that wages are increasing at a rate of $\dot{W}_{i1}$. This means that the market is in disequilibrium during period t_1 with unemployment (which is an index of excess demand) of approximately $Oa - Oc$, and that wages are rising to equilibrate the market at a rate $\dot{W}_{i1}$. In period t_2 we now observe that the unemployment level has fallen to Ob (excess demand has increased) and that the rate of increase of wages has increased to $\dot{W}_{i2}$. We may say here that over the period shifts in the supply or demand schedules must have occurred at a faster rate than the equilibrating increase in wages and that the disequilibrium has increased as a result. If no shifts in the supply and demand schedules had occurred after the initial disequilibrium in period t_1 was observed, then, of course, in period t_2, $\dot{W}_i$ would be zero and unemployment Oa, i.e. the disequilibrium would have been eliminated by the equilibrating rise in the wage rate and unemployment and vacancies would be equal at Oa.

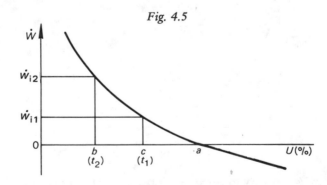

Fig. 4.5

Persistent excess demand. In order to explain the continuous tendency for wages to rise where positive excess demand exists we have been required to conceive of a situation in which the demand curve is displacing more rapidly in time than the supply curve. This is not entirely satisfactory but is an inevitable consequence of partial equilibrium analysis. While it is true that the nature of the continuous inflationary process does involve a persistent growth of labour demand in excess of the growth of labour supply in individual markets it is helpful to recall the analysis contained in the income-expenditure models. That analysis showed that when real expenditure exceeded real output (usually as a consequence of government policy) money wages and prices would inflate. (Persistent inflation can, of course, occur for other reasons, such as those discussed in relation to the expectations hypothesis and cost-push models.) At the macroeconomic level this is a simple concept. However, while it is the case that this process must operate in the micro-markets, it is difficult to conceptualise the disaggregation. With this caveat in mind we shall continue to conceive of persistent excess demand in micro-labour markets as a process of dynamic displacement of supply and demand curves at differential rates.

Aggregating the micro-markets. The foregoing analysis has referred to a single homogeneous labour market. The next step therefore is to consider how we may move from the single market case to a many market case.

Aggregating micro-reaction functions in a satisfactory theoretical manner is always fraught with difficulties and this is especially the case when dealing with labour markets. Professor Peston has admirably summarised the nature of these difficulties in a recent paper (Peston, 1971). Attempts have however been made to aggregate the system of micro-reaction functions in order to supply a basis for analysing the observed relation $\dot{W} = f(U)$. Probably the simplest approach to the aggregation problem is that employed by Hansen (1970), who simply manipulates the Laspeyres wage index. There are however specific problems associated with a general aggregate result of this kind which arise particularly in relation to the *distribution* of excess demand (or unemployment) amongst submarkets. This latter question is well illustrated by Lipsey's (1960) approach to the aggregation problem.

Lipsey's aggregation procedure. Assume that there are only two labour markets in the economy and that mobility within each market is greater than between the markets. Further assume that in each labour market the $\dot{W} = f(U)$ reaction function is identical and that labour supply in each market is equal. Aggregation of the two markets, a and b, is very simple under these assumptions:

$$U = \frac{U_a + U_b}{2} \text{ and } \dot{W} = \frac{\dot{W}_a + \dot{W}_b}{2}.$$

Now, if both markets experienced the same proportional rate of unemployment, aggregate unemployment would be equal to each market rate; i.e. $U_a = U_b = U$. Similarly, since the reaction function is identical for both markets, the rate of change of wages in each market would be the same and would also equal the macro rate of wage increase; i.e. $\dot{W}_a = \dot{W}_b = \dot{W}$. Thus the macro-reaction function would be identical to each of the micro-functions for all situations in which $U_a = U_b$. A different situation would however arise where U_a was not equal to U_b.

Assume that aggregate unemployment, U, is equal to Oa in fig. 4.4. Now by definition

$$\frac{U_a + U_b}{2} = U = Oa.$$

Now let $U_a < U_b$. Taking a simple hypothetical example we may specify that $U_a = Oa - x\%$ and that $U_b = Oa + x\%$. Obviously the average unemployment rate is Oa and U_a is less than Oa by the same number of percentage points as U_b is greater than Oa. Fig. 4.6 illustrates this situation. The reaction function illustrated in the diagram is the micro-function for both market a and market b. If unemployment rates in each market were equal this reaction function would also obtain for the macro-market. It may however be seen by inspection that when average unemployment is Oa but unemployment in market b is Od and in market a is Oc then the average rate of increase in wages will be positive.[1] This is so because the positive rate of increase in wages in market a is numerically greater than the negative rate of reduction in wages in market b and this in turn is a phenomenon which derives from the non-linear configuration of the reaction function to the left of a. The macro-reaction function will therefore not intersect the axis at Oa but instead at some unemployment rate greater than Oa. Thus because the rate of unemployment is unequally distributed between the two micro-markets the macro-reaction function will be displaced upwards. This phenomenon will obviously be true for all situations in which some markets experience an excess demand for labour, that is when structural unemployment exists. It will also always be true for all situations where all markets experience an excess demand for labour. The foregoing analysis suggests therefore that at the macro-level it is not only the *rate* but also the *distribution* of unemployment which determines the location of the macro-reaction function. Thus for any set of micro-markets with identical reaction functions the macro-function which will be traced out to relate the average rate of change of wages as unemployment

Fig. 4.6

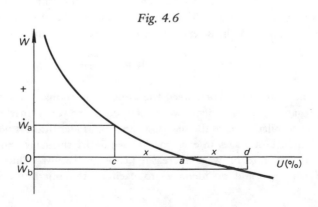

varies will be systematically above the micro-functions when unemployment is unequally distributed. Intuitively it is also obvious that if this is so then the greater the degree of inequality in the distribution of unemployment between the various micro-markets the greater will be the rightward displacement of the macro-function.

The problems of aggregation. We have already noted that Lipsey and others chose to attempt to supply a theoretical underpinning to the Phillips result by first analysing the behaviour of micro-markets under excess demand and then aggregating these to produce a result which is consistent with Phillips macro observation. Aggregation of this kind is highly dependent on the assumptions which must accompany it and is rarely satisfactory. Peston (1971) has pointed to the various difficulties associated with this sort of aggregation. A more satisfactory approach to the whole question of providing a theoretical underpinning to the Phillips finding might have been to analyse it (a macro finding) in terms of income-expenditure theory and then proceed to examine certain of the particular problems which arise as a result of *disaggregation*. This approach would have placed the Phillips result in the mainstream of macro-economic theory from the outset and have the advantage of examining micro-market relations in the context of a macroeconomic system. However, the aggregation procedure employed by Lipsey yields certain predictions based on particular assumptions and these are worth further consideration.

The predictions which aggregation yields. We have already noted that Lipsey's analysis yields the prediction that the location of the macro-Phillips curve will depend on the *distribution* as well as the rate of unemployment. Specifically Lipsey argues that, where all the micro-reaction functions are identical, the macro-reaction function will be displaced above the micro-functions when unemployment rates are unequal. Peston has shown that this is not necessarily the case where the wage index is base-weighted (as in the UK).[2] Further the assumption that the micro-reaction functions are identical is both crucial and unrealistic. It has been demonstrated that (a) the assumption is not true of regional or industrial submarkets for labour (Bowers *et al.*, 1970; Sargan, 1971); and (b) that if it is dropped Lipsey's prediction need not hold (Bowers *et al.*, 1970). In addition there is an implicit assumption in the Lipsey model which derives from confining his detailed analysis to a partial equilibrium model. This assumption is that there is no intermarket mobility of labour in response to either differential intermarket wage rates or unemployment/vacancy ratios. If this assumption were dropped then the distribution of unemployment (and excess demands) between submarkets would itself be a function of changes in the structure of wages and employment and could only be analysed within a dynamic and general model.

Despite these difficulties with the Lipsey model the question of how the distribution of unemployment between submarkets affects aggregate relations is of considerable interest. For example if it could be shown (as Lipsey suggests) that the greater is the inequality in the distribution of unemployment between submarkets, the further to the right will be the macro-Phillips curve, then it would clearly be an object of economic policy to reduce that inequality. There is another matter however for which the distributional hypothesis has relevance. As well as finding a relationship between the rate of change of wages and the *level* of unemployment, $\dot{W} = f(U)$, Phillips found a relation between the *rate of change* of unemployment and wage changes, $\dot{W} = g(\dot{U})$. Diagrammatically this relation appeared in the form of 'loops' around the Phillips curve. Lipsey explained the 'loops' in terms of unequally distributed unemployment in submarkets. Let us however examine the whole mystery of the loops.

The 'Loops'. Phillips noted that in the course of a cycle unemployment would be falling on the cyclical upswing and rising on the cyclical downswing. This is what we would expect if the rate of unemployment is an indicator of the level of demand. He further observed that when unemployment was rising the rate of change of wages was lower than would be expected at that rate of unemployment and that when unemployment was falling the rate of change of wages was higher than would be expected at that rate of unemployment. This phenomenon can best be illustrated by observing a hypothetical cycle and observing the relations sequentially. This done in fig. 4.7.

In fig. 4.7 the average macro-reaction function is shown with eight annual observations, comprising a complete cycle, individually illustrated. Each annual observation is linked to the observation for the following year by a line. Two observations, for years 3 and 6, were made for the same unemployment rate *ON*. Unemployment is falling from year 1 to year 4 and rising from year 4 to year 8. The rate of change of wages in years 1, 2 and 3 is systematically higher than the average for those rates of unemployment as indicated by the reaction function. The rate of change of wages is systematically lower than the average for the years 5, 6, 7 and 8 when unemployment is rising. Hence we have a loop around the macro-function and an apparent relation between $\dot{W}$ and the rate of change

Fig. 4.7

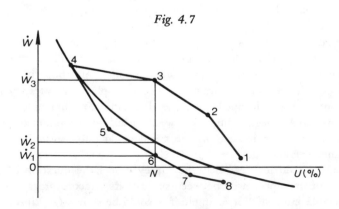

of unemployment, $\dot{U}$. Consider observations 3 and 6. Both observations were made at the same level of unemployment ON at which the macro-function predicts a rate of change of wages of $\dot{W}_2$. Observation 3 occurs when unemployment is falling (demand rising) and the actual $\dot{W}$ is $\dot{W}_3$. Observation 6 is made when unemployment is rising (demand falling) and the actual $\dot{W}$ is $\dot{W}_1$. This implies as well as $\dot{W} = f(U)$ that $\dot{W} = g(U, \dot{U})$. Phillips explains this phenomenon in terms of expectations. He says

> ... *in a year of rising business activity, with the demand for labour increasing and the percentage unemployment decreasing, employers will be bidding more vigorously for the services of labour than they would be in a year during which the average percentage unemployment was the same but the demand for labour was not increasing.*
>
> *Conversely in a year of falling business activity, with the demand for labour decreasing and the percentage unemployment increasing, employers will be less inclined to grant wage increases, and workers will be in a weaker position to press for them than they would be in a year during which the average percentage unemployment was the same but the demand for labour was not decreasing.* (Phillips, 1958)

Lipsey explains the phenomenon of the loops in terms of the relationship between micro-labour markets which experience different unemployment rates and the resultant macro-relationship which will be traced out in the course of a complete cycle. In fig. 4.8 the identical micro-reaction function for two markets, a and b, is shown as a broken line. The observed path of the macro-function over a cycle is shown by the solid line.

Suppose the economy begins with a substantial excess supply of labour in both markets but that unemployment in market a is greater than in market b. Now assume that a cyclical upswing gets under way and that during the upswing demand in market b grows by a greater proportion than in market a. We start with unemployment of $1a$ and $1b$ which yields the macro-observation 1. In the

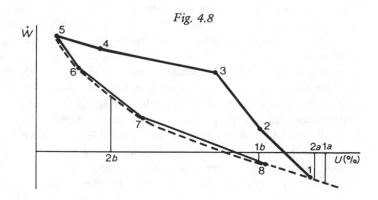

Fig. 4.8

first period of the upswing unemployment in market b falls to $2b$ (positive excess demand) and unemployment in market a falls to $2a$ (excess supply). The macro-observation is 2 which indicates that average wage rates are rising although there is still (possibly) a net excess of supply for labour in the economy as a whole. (We may ignore problems of weighting the average rate of wage change by employment levels since they do not affect the essential analysis.) Similarly, as we proceed to periods 3, 4 and 5, the level of excess demand is in each period higher in market b than in market a. This means that the macro-relation which will be traced out will for each period be displaced to the right of the micro-reaction function. If both markets experienced the same level of excess demand in each period of the upswing then the macro-relation would coincide with the micro-relation. However, because market a always exhibits greater unemployment than market b on the upswing the macro-relation will be held to the right of the micro-relation, which traces market b's behaviour, by the heavier unemployment level in market a in each period. Hence the north-eastern bound of the loop is simply a macro-relation which is an average of two micro-market relations which respond to increasing demand with a time-lag which results in an unequal distribution of unemployment between them.

On the downswing, periods 5, 6, 7 and 8, Lipsey simply assumes that the lagged response disappears and that both markets will begin the downswing at approximately equal levels of excess demand in period 5 and experience a uniform rate of increase in unemployment through to period 8. The macro-relation for the downswing therefore approximates to the micro-function.

The 'loop' is therefore the actual macro-relation and the observed relation between $\dot{W}$ and U is no more than an average relation running through the centre of the loops given some degree of inequality in the distribution of unemployment between the micro-markets. The implied Lipsey relation therefore is not that $\dot{W} = f(U, \dot{U})$ but instead that $\dot{W} = j(U, q_u)$ where q_u is a measure of the intermarket dispersion of unemployment.

Lipsey's explanation of U-dot and the loops is ingenious but unsatisfactory in many respects. First, Lipsey does not explain why time-lags in adjustment should apply on the upswing of the cycle but not on the downswing. Second, the assumption that reaction functions in submarkets are identical is important to the argument and probably unrealistic. Third, wages in each submarket are assumed to respond to excess demand in that market and this assumption is crucial. This is an implausible assumption in view of the institutional character of wage fixing arrangements in the UK. Trade union wage policy is rarely related to conditions in submarkets and, where earnings rather than wage rates are the issue, criteria of comparability, productivity related wage claims etc. tend to stifle the independent adjustment process in submarkets. (Lipsey himself has stressed that it is *wage rates* which are the relevant variable.) For these reasons Lipsey's hypothesis does not seem to be adequate. Hines (1971) — and also Hansen (1970) — has proposed a more satisfactory interpretation of the mystery of the loops. (For a more formal statement of Hines' hypothesis, see

Appendix 2 of this chapter.) Hines shows that vacancies and unemployment are related in a non-linear way. Thus when excess demand for labour is rising, vacancies will rise more rapidly than unemployment. Conversely, when excess demand is falling, unemployment will rise more rapidly than vacancies. Hence when the unemployment rate is used as a proxy for the level of excess demand it will mis-state the level of excess demand. The nature of this mis-statement will be such that for any given level of unemployment employers, bidding for labour on the basis of the level of excess demand, will bid harder for labour when unemployment is falling (for the reasons given by Phillips) than when it is rising. The effects of their bidding (if it is successful) will be to reduce unemployment by less than it reduces vacancies when excess demand is rising. This process will produce loops of the kind identified by Phillips. Thus in situations where excess demand is changing, the rate of change of unemployment is a valid proxy along with the level of unemployment for the level of excess demand for labour. This seems to solve the mystery of the loops.

Price changes. Phillips also observed a relation between changes in the cost of living and the rate of change of money wages. He postulates a 'threshold effect' in this relation. Basically Phillips suggests that it is only when the cost of living rises more rapidly than money wages (as a result of an increase in import prices) that this factor will influence the rate of change in wages. Where money wages are rising more rapidly than the cost of living then '. . . employers will merely be giving under the name of cost of living adjustments part of the wage increases which they would in any case have given as a result of their competitive bidding for labour' (Phillips, 1958). In other words he appears to suggest that when demand factors induce rises in wages greater than the rise in the cost of living there is already full compensation for price rises provided for in the wage rise but that when a reduction in the real wage is threatened by a faster rate of increase in the cost of living than in wages then a cost of living adjustment on top of what would be induced by demand pressure will be added to wage rates. The evidence provided by Phillips on this hypothesis is very much of the nature of casual empiricism and is not particularly convincing.

The Phillips model therefore postulates three basic relations between the rate of change of money wages and its determinants. The rate of change of money wages is predominantly determined by the level of unemployment but also by the rate of change of that level and also by the rate of change of the cost of living when this rate exceeds the rate of change of wages which would be induced by demand pressures.

4.2 The empirical evidence

The foregoing analysis proposed by Hansen (1970) and Lipsey (1960) involves simply proceeding from conventional microeconomic analysis to yield a macroeconomic hypothesis which is testable. The basic hypothesis is that $\dot{W} = f(U)$ where U is the national average percentage of unemployment and $\dot{W}$ is the rate of change of money wage rates. U is implicitly an indicator of the level of excess demand in the economy as a whole. The relation to be tested will be a stable one over time so long as the distribution of unemployment does not change.

Phillips' test. The first test of this type of hypothesis was carried out by A. W. Phillips and the results were published in 1958. Phillips used some rather unorthodox statistical procedures to carry out his test and was later criticised by a number of economists for so doing. However, Phillips postulated the following basic relationship:

$$\dot{W} = a + bU^{-c} \qquad (4.3a)$$

which may be rewritten:

$$\log (\dot{W} - a) = \log b - c \log U \qquad (4.3b)$$

Equation (4.3b) is linear in the logarithms and therefore easier to handle in testing. Since for observations where $\dot{W} < a$ the logarithms would have to be negative, and because there is no such thing as a negative logarithm, direct testing of all observations individually was impossible. Phillips was obliged therefore to group observations in class intervals based on the level of unemployment and found mean values for $\dot{W}$ and U for each group. The curve was then fitted to these observations by trial and error. His observations covered the whole period 1861–1957 but were broken down into three main time periods, 1861–1913, 1913–48 and 1948–57. The basic fitted relation emerged as:

$$\dot{W} + 0.9 = 9.638 \, U^{-1.394} \qquad (4.4)$$

or

$$\log (\dot{W} + 0.9) = 0.984 - 1.394 \log U \qquad (4.4a)$$

There are no standard tests of the statistical significance of the overall fitted relation nor of the coefficients in the Phillips study. However, it was clear by inspection of the scatter diagrams which he prepared that the fitted relation was significant. Diagrammatically the curve was of the form shown in fig. 4.1.

This then represents an actual macro-reaction function of the kind which Lipsey theoretically predicted would exist. The basic relationship shown in fig. 4.1 was quite satisfactory for each of the time periods under consideration although it performed less well in one or two sub-periods and in the period 1948–57. Although this is the basic relation established by Phillips, he did of course incorporate the variables U-dot and price changes in his model.

Lipsey's test. The analysis in the earlier part of this chapter is derived from Lipsey's paper and is considerably more sophisticated than the rather general assertions of the implied relations contained in the paper by Phillips. However, let us now consider briefly the statistical results obtained by Lipsey using much the same data as used by Phillips.

Lipsey's results may be summarised as follows:
The postulated relationship is given by the equation

$$\dot{W} = \alpha_1 + \alpha_2 U^{-1} + \alpha_3 U^{-2} + \alpha_3 \dot{U} + \alpha_4 \dot{P}.$$

The best fit was given by the equation:

$$\dot{W} = -1.21 + 6.54 U^{-1} + 2.26 U^{-2} - 0.019 \dot{U} + 0.21 \dot{P}; \quad R^2 = 0.85.$$

This equation shows that variations in U, $\dot{U}$ and $\dot{P}$ explain 85% of the variance in $\dot{W}$. The squared partial correlation coefficients were $U, 0.78$; $\dot{U}, 0.50$; $\dot{P}, 0.17$. These indicate that variations in U explain 78% of the variance in $\dot{W}$ while $\dot{U}$ removes a further 50% of the variance not associated with U and $\dot{P}$ removed a further 17% of the variance not associated with U and $\dot{U}$.

The period 1923–57. The parameters of the equations set out above were estimated on data relating to the period 1862–1913. The application of these equations to data for the subsequent period yielded some interesting results and these are set out briefly below.

(i) The basic equation which explains the variance in $\dot{W}$ in terms of U, $\dot{U}$ and $\dot{P}$ continues to perform well throughout the period;

(ii) the variables U and $\dot{U}$ prove to be considerably less significant in explaining the variance in $\dot{W}$ after 1923 and especially so in the period 1947–57.

Fig. 4.9

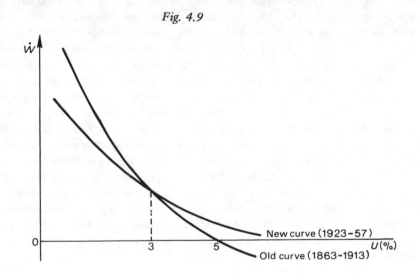

In general the fitted macro-function relating $\dot{W}$ and U, which was the basic relation postulated by Phillips, changes over the period. For levels of U greater than 3% the new relation lay above the old one but for values of U less than 3% the new curve lay below the old one. This shift is illustrated in fig. 4.9.

It should be noted here that while the general explanatory power of the three-variable model did not deteriorate in the postwar period the explanatory power of U did deteriorate significantly. Indeed the predictive power of the equation in the later years of the period depended more on the $\dot{P}$ variable than any other. This change has some interesting implications and we shall consider these in a more general context in chapters 5 and 7.

Tests of the inter-market unemployment distribution hypothesis. A prediction of the Lipsey model is that the greater the inequality in the distribution of unemployment between submarkets, the greater will be the rate of wage inflation for a given level of average unemployment. Various tests of this hypothesis in different guises have been made. There are however a number of practical difficulties involved in devising a test. Firstly, of course, there is the problem of defining a 'labour submarket'. Certain researchers have chosen to define a submarket in *regional* terms and devised tests accordingly. (See Brechling, 1974; McKay and Hart, 1974; Archibald, 1969; Thomas and Stoney, 1972.) Only Thomas and Stoney (1972) have claimed satisfactory results. Other work has concentrated on *industrial* labour markets (Sargan, 1971) but again has not produced conclusive results. We have tested a variant of the model in which specific institutional criteria are incorporated and an *occupational* definition of labour submarkets is used with modest success (Mulvey and Trevithick, 1974). The second difficulty probably explains why no one has found empirical support for the Lipsey hypothesis. That is that the hypothesis depends crucially upon certain assumptions which may or may not be met in practice. We noted earlier that Peston (1971) and Bowers *et al.* (1970) have shown that the predictions of the Lipsey model are only accurate when there exists a particular configuration of micro-reaction functions and a particular distribution of unemployment associated with them. Since it is virtually impossible to sort out the expected behaviour of the model from the actual structure of micro-reaction functions and unemployment which exists, a straight test of the Lipsey hypothesis is more likely to test the validity of its assumptions than its predictive power. The fact that virtually all of the empirical models based on the hypothesis have little predictive power therefore suggests that the hypothesis is based on unrealistic assumptions. There need be no mystery here — it is quite possible that the shape of submarket Phillips curves is associated in practice with a distribution of unemployment which will have the effect of neutralising the Lipsey effect. (See Appendix 1 to this chapter for a formal discussion of the general issues involved.)

4.3 Summary and conclusions

We began by noting that income-expenditure models of inflation predict that wage inflation will occur in response to the existence of excess demand for labour. Phillips, proceeding from a vague analogy with the adjustment process in the product market, empirically derived a non-linear relation between the rate of change of wages and the level of unemployment standing as a proxy for excess demand for labour. In addition he suggested two subsidiary hypotheses: (a) that the rate of change of unemployment affects employers' expectations and therefore the rate of wage change; and (b) that price changes over a certain threshold also affect the rate of change of wages. The main prediction of Phillips' work therefore was that there would exist a trade-off between wage inflation and the level of excess demand for labour.

Lipsey supplied a theoretical underpinning for Phillips' work by considering an adjustment mechanism which would function within a micro-labour market and then proceeding to aggregate the micro-markets. As well as vastly improving the statistical specification of the Phillips curve, which permitted more detailed analysis of its properties, Lipsey attempted to explain the phenomenon of the loops and advanced an additional prediction of the model: that the distribution of unemployment between submarkets as well as its overall rate would affect the rate of change of wages.

The central question which we must ask in order to draw a conclusion from this analysis is whether or not the case for the existence of a trade-off between wage inflation and excess demand for labour has been established. The answer must be a qualified one — the evidence overwhelmingly suggests the existence of a short-run trade-off between wage inflation and excess demand for labour. So far as the existence of a long-run trade-off between inflation and excess demand is concerned the evidence presented here is inconclusive. While it is true to say that the trade-off relation appears to have existed for a very long period of time, it is of significance that the rate of change of prices assumed a very significant role in the explanation of wage changes during the postwar period when price inflation was rapid and, latterly, accelerating. Indeed, as Parkin *et al.* (1973) have shown, the model only retains its predictive capacity after 1967 if a sophisticated variable approximating expected changes in prices is included. It is therefore possible to suggest tentatively at this stage that *expectations* of price changes may be an important determinant of the rate of inflation along with the level of excess demand for labour and, as will be shown in chapter 7, this casts serious doubts on the existence of a long-run trade-off relation.

Appendix 1 The validity of the intermarket unemployment distribution hypothesis

We have noted that the Lipsey wage-inflation model involves fairly orthodox disequilibrium microeconomics for the most part but yields a prediction about the location of the aggregate Phillips curve (and an explanation of U-dot) which depends on the intermarket dispersion of unemployment. A crucial assumption which underlies this prediction is that the micro-markets in the economy have *identical reaction functions*. The evidence, so far as it relates to geographically defined micro-markets, tends to suggest that this is not so. What then if we assume non-identical micro-reaction functions in various micro-markets. Consider the two market cases illustrated in fig. 4.10.

The curves AA and BB are the micro-reaction functions of market A and market B respectively. Unemployment in market A is initially at U_a and the rate of change of wages in that market is therefore $\dot{W}_{a1}$. Unemployment in market B is initially at U_b and the rate of change of wages in market B is $\dot{W}_{b1}$. The national average rate of unemployment is U_n and the national average rate of change of wages is $\dot{W}_{n1}$. Assume now that unemployment in market A is increased to U_n and that unemployment in market B is decreased to U_n leaving the national average unemployment rate unchanged at U_n. Now, ignoring weights, it is visually obvious that the rate of change in wages in market B

Fig. 4.10

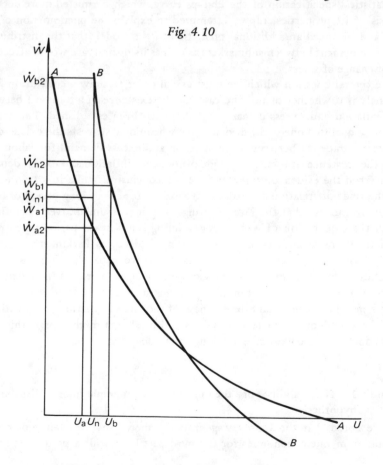

increases by more than the rate of change of wages in market A is reduced and therefore that the national average rate of change of wages $\dot{W}_{n2}$ is greater than $\dot{W}_{n1}$. Hence in this case an *equalisation* of the unemployment rates in the two micro-markets caused an upward displacement of the macro-observation. This is in contrast to the prediction of the Lipsey dispersion hypothesis. It is clear however that a result consistent with Lipsey's hypothesis could have been obtained if we had selected differently sloped functions or different points on the functions used to carry out our test. We may say, however, that the general prediction of the Lipsey hypothesis does not survive the relaxation of his assumption that micro-reactions are identical for all submarkets. More specifically we may say (for the linear case) that a change in the distribution of unemployment will increase $\dot{W}_n$ when:

$$| \Sigma_r W_r a_r \lambda_r | > | \Sigma_r W_r a_r \lambda_r |$$

$$\lambda_r < 0 \qquad \lambda_r > 0$$

and reduce $\dot{W}_n$ when the inequality is reversed, where W_r is the ratio of the rth market's labour force to the total labour force, where a_r is the slope of the Phillips curve for the rth market and where λ_r is the change in the unemployment rate in market r (Bowers *et al.*, 1970).

Appendix 2   A formal statement of Hines' hypothesis of the 'Loops'

Hines has very succinctly set out a highly plausible interpretation of the phenomenon of the loops. The remainder of this Appendix is largely a quote from Hines (1971). Since in any labour market that is not frictionless (i.e. unemployment cannot be zero) we would expect the vacancy rate (V_{c1}) to be positively related to the level of excess demand (E), the unemployment rate (U) to be negatively related to E and V_c and U to be inversely related over the cycle, we may say that when $\dot{E} \neq 0$, $\dot{V}_c = \dot{U}$.

> *Specifically, $\dot{V} > \dot{U}$ when E is rising and $\dot{V}_c < \dot{U}$ when E is falling so that $|\dot{E}| > |\dot{U}|$ whenever $E_t \neq E_{t-1}$. This implies that E will be higher (lower) when U is falling (rising) than when it is rising (falling) for any given level of U, i.e. E is underestimated when U is falling and overestimated when U is rising. But this means, as Phillips argued, that if employers bid for labour on the basis of the level of excess demand, they will bid more for labour when U is falling than when it is rising for any given level of U. To the extent that such bidding is successful, it reduces both U and V_c. However, given that the relationship between V_c and U is non-linear, it reduces U by less than it reduces V_c. Hence $\dot{W}/W$ will be greater when U is falling than when it is rising for any given level of U. Moreover, the mis-statement*

of E *by* U *varies in a manner which is determined by the non-linearity in the relationship between* V_c *and* E, U *and* E *as well as by the pattern of cyclical variations in* E. *Define the mis-statement of* E *by* U *as* M.

$$M = \frac{\partial V_c}{\partial E} \dot{E} \quad \dot{M} = \frac{\partial^2 V_c}{\partial E^2} \dot{E} + \frac{\partial V_c}{\partial E} \ddot{E} \text{ where } \frac{\partial^2 V_c}{\partial E^2} > 0 \text{ but tends to a limit}$$
of zero.

Assume that on the upswing of the cycle $\dot{E} > 0$, $\ddot{E} > 0$ *for* E < 0 *and* $\ddot{E} < 0$ *for* E > 0. *Assume that the upswing and the downswing are symmetrical. It is then readily seen that there will be anti-clockwise loops whenever* E *is not constant. Thus if vacancy statistics are not available so that* E *is not directly measurable, in non-stationary situations,* $\dot{U}/U$ *is a valid proxy with* U/L *for the level of excess demand.* (Hines, 1971, pp. 146–7)

Notes to chapter 4

1. Theoretically we should use employment weights in calculating the rate of change of average wages. However, since such weights would reinforce the effect noted above, they are omitted in the interests of simplicity. However, the use of *wage bill* weights introduces problems for Lipsey's hypothesis. (See Peston, 1971.)

2. A base-weighted wage index weights changes in each employment sector by the size of the wage bill in that sector.

CHAPTER 5

Wage and Price Inflation

The central hypothesis advanced by the Phillips/Lipsey model of wage inflation is that wage inflation is a function of excess demand for labour. We have noted that a short-run relation of this kind is well supported by the evidence but that the existence of any long-run relation is called into question by the expectations hypothesis. Let us for the moment concentrate on the proposition that there exists a short-run trade-off between wage inflation and excess demand for labour as indicated by the level of unemployment.

Phelps Brown (1971) has criticised the Phillips/Lipsey model on two general grounds. First, he has argued that the model is oversimplified since it assumes that the labour market functions in much the same way as a product market. He disputes that this is the case. He points to the differences in the nature of supply and demand, the methods of price fixing and the essentially human characteristics of the labour market which he considers makes the strict analogy with the product market invalid. Second, Phelps Brown is unhappy with the *ceteris paribus* assumption which he says underlies the model. The relation $\dot{W} = f(U)$ is the critical determinant of wage inflation *when the values of all other possible influences on the rate of wage inflation are given*. This assumption has been widely challenged and a vast body of literature, almost entirely empirical, has been devoted to proposing alternatives to the Phillips/Lipsey model.

In section 1 of this chapter we shall consider Phelps Brown's first point of criticism by briefly examining the predictions of a specifically labour market adjustment process under conditions of excess demand. In section 5.2, we shall review some of the principal hypotheses which set out to assert the independent determining influence on wage inflation of economic variables other than the level of unemployment. In section 5.3 we shall examine the view that the Phillips relation has ceased to hold since 1966 and in section 5.4 we shall proceed from the *wage* equation to the *price* equation.

5.1 The labour market and wage inflation

The strict analogy between the behaviour of the labour market and that of the product market which characterises the orthodox model is clearly unsatisfactory. The problem of explaining why frictional unemployment varies with the level of excess demand, which was referrred to in the previous chapter, raised a complex issue of labour market analysis which had to be solved in an arbitrary way. This is an example of how specific labour market relations intruded into the orthodox model; most of the remainder are assumed away by recourse to product market analysis. Can we then construct a more realistic model of the labour market under changing economic circumstances and will such a model explain the Phillips relation?

Stock and flow models of the labour market.[1] In recent times a number of models of the labour market which dispense with many of the usual assumptions of competitive market analysis have been formulated (Holt, 1971b; Phelps, 1971c; Mortensen, 1971). The main characteristic of these models is that they view the labour market in terms of stocks and flows of labour, and decision-making within the market occurs in the context of risk, uncertainty, imperfect information, search costs and the subjective aspirations of workers and employers.[2] Probably the best known such model is that of Holt and the main theme of his work is briefly traced out below.

Holt's model. Holt views the labour market as consisting of four basic stocks of labour and numerous flows between each of these stocks. The stocks are employment, unemployment, vacancies and non-participants. The flows include quits, lay-offs, new hires, recalls, new entrants, exits and retirements. Stocks and flows are interdependent since a flow into or out of a stock will influence the size of the stock and the size of the stock will in turn influence the size of the flows into and out of the stock. The two critical stocks in the model from the point of view of wage determination are those of unemployed workers and unfilled vacancies, $\bar{U}$ and $\bar{V}_c$. The stock of unemployed workers depends on the inflow rate of quits and layoffs and the outflow rate of new hires and recalls. The stock of vacancies depends on the inflow rate of new hires and recalls and the outflow rate of quits and the growth of new vacancies. It is clear that these stocks are interdependent in that their size is determined by the same basic flows. But in addition the stocks interact to influence the flow rates which determine their size. Thus the size of the vacancy stock will obviously influence the quit rate; when $\bar{V}_c$ is relatively large the quit rate will increase and vice versa. Similarly the size of the unemployment stock will influence the quit rate; when $\bar{U}$ is relatively small the quit rate will tend to be high and vice versa. In the same way all of the flows which determine the size of $\bar{U}$ and $\bar{V}_c$ will themselves be influenced by the size of the stocks. This may appear to be a hopelessly intractable set of interactions which leads us no further forward in understanding the dynamics of the labour market. There is however an additional facet to the model.

The search hypothesis. The various flows which determine the stocks $\bar{U}$ and $\bar{V}_c$ depend on variables other than just the size of the stocks. For example when $\bar{V}_c$

is large and $\bar{U}$ is small, workers who are already employed may consider the situation opportune to seek a better job. They may therefore either quit to search or search on job. Search, in either case, involves costs and is characterised by certain wage aspirations on the part of workers and employers which are in turn affected by the duration of unemployment and vacancies on average. In general the longer the duration of unemployment (or search) the lower the aspired wage of the worker, and the longer the duration of vacancies the higher the aspired wage offer of the employer. For both parties aspired wages are best expressed in probability terms and we may denote the offer-acceptance probability by the term B_{oa} which depends on such things as the average of the previous wages of the workers and the vacancies, the rates at which worker and employer aspiration wages change over time and the average durations of unemployment and vacancies. B_{oa} may be defined as the average probability that a contact between an unemployed worker and matching vacancy will result in an offer which is accepted. The total potential number of contacts between unemployed workers and vacancies is $\bar{U} \cdot \bar{V}_c$ and the total number of contacts per period of time will be $(\bar{U} \cdot \bar{V}_c/A_m)$ where A_m is the average market searchtime involved in encountering and exploring any contact. The expected flow of hires and recalls per period of time is obtained by multiplying by B_{oa} and this gives us an absolute turnover expression:

$$f = \frac{\bar{U} \cdot \bar{V}_c \cdot B_{oa}}{A_m} \tag{5.1}$$

where f is the flow of new hires and recalls per period. This may be rewritten:

$$\bar{U} \cdot \bar{V}_c = \frac{f \cdot A_m}{B_{oa}} . \tag{5.2}$$

The right-hand side of this equation is likely to be constant in the short term. A_m is likely to be invariant with the level of activity. Both B_{oa} and f are determined by factors which vary inversely with each other as the level of activity changes (e.g. average duration of unemployment and vacancies, quit rates and lay-off rates etc.) and these will tend to cancel out, leaving both B_{oa} and f constant except for trend effects on f. Thus $\bar{U} \cdot \bar{V}_c$ is likely to be constant over time. We may now write equation (5.2) in terms of rates rather than absolute values:

$$U \cdot V_c \cdot = \frac{F \cdot A_m}{B_{oa}} \tag{5.3}$$

where U is the unemployment rate, V_c is the vacancy rate and F is the turnover rate.

The rate of change of wages. Consider now the way in which wages might be expected to behave as the vacancy and unemployment stocks vary as a result of changes in the average duration of vacancies and unemployment. We have already noted that Holt postulates that the workers' aspired wage is a declining function of the average duration of unemployment and that the employers' wage offer will be an increasing function of the average duration of vacancies. In general the longer (shorter) is the average duration of unemployment the lower (higher) will be the wage aspiration of the worker and the higher (lower) will be the stock of unemployment. In general the longer (shorter) is the average duration of vacancies, the higher (lower) will be the wage offer of employers and the larger (smaller) will be the stock of vacancies. Now the stocks $\bar{U}$ and $\bar{V}_c$ will vary with the level of activity and so will the various flows into and out of these stocks. Let $\theta = V_c/U$ which is the ratio of the vacancy rate to the unemployment rate. Wage changes will depend on the ratio θ since it is determined by the average duration of unemployment and vacancies which in turn determine wage aspirations. Hence we may say that $\dot{W} = g(\theta)$. Now by manipulating equation (5.3) we obtain:

$$\frac{V_c}{U} = \frac{F \cdot A_m}{B_{oa}} \cdot U^{-2} \tag{5.4}$$

Substituting (5.4) into $\dot{W} = g(\theta)$ yields a Phillips-type relation:

$$\dot{W} = g\left(\frac{F \cdot A_m}{B_{oa}} \cdot U^{-2}\right), \ g'(\theta) > 0 \tag{5.5}$$

While Holt's model predicts a Phillips-type of relation between the rate of change of money wages and the unemployment rate, it does so by means of a rather more elaborate analysis than that of Lipsey. The critical element in the wage change process in the Holt model is that changes in the average wage level are generated 'by countless individual offer and acceptance decisions as workers and vacancies flow through the market, as employers grant on-the-job wage increases to inhibit this flow and as unions push for wage increases to hold their relative positions' (Holt, 1971b). Hence the Holt model, which incorporates a complex series of behavioural relations specific to the labour market, suggests that although the orthodox market analysis used by Lipsey is oversimplified the end result is similar. It is of interest in this regard that Holt's complete model also predicts that the greater the degree of inequality in the distribution of unemployment between submarkets the further to the right the trade-off relation will lie. In addition an explanation of the 'loops' emerges from the Holt model since changes in employment will be inversely correlated with changes in unemployment and positively correlated with an increased offer level when the demand for labour increases.

The foregoing is a highly simplified attempt to outline the main theme in Holt's model and every conceivable shortcut has been employed in the interests of brevity. The model itself is sophisticated and complex and could not be adequately dealt with here. Hence the summary given above is intended only to indicate that a model specific to the labour market predicts a Phillips relation and therefore that criticism of the product market analogy in analysis of the trade-off may be justified to the extent that it ignores many characteristics specific to the labour market, but nevertheless the contention that the balance of supply and demand in the labour market is a determinant of wage changes remains valid.

5.2 The Phillips relation, measurement problems and alternative explanatory variables

There is a good deal of evidence that a Phillips-type relation has held for most developed economies. Studies carried out in North America and Continental Europe demonstrate some such relationship although wide differences in the strength, slope and location of the curve exist between countries (OECD, 1970). The USA is an area of particular interest in this regard. A number of early attempts to relate $\dot{W}$ to U for the US economy yielded rather poor results, suggesting the presence of only a weak inverse relationship. This was especially the case for the postwar period (see Bhatia, 1961). But later studies using refined data (Simler and Tella, 1968) and refined definitions of the variables (Perry, 1966) do appear to evidence a reasonably strong Phillips relation, including the postwar period. It appears however that the Phillips curve does not fit US data as closely as that of the UK; that the US Phillips curve tends to be stable for short time periods only; that the US Phillips curve lies somewhat to the right of the UK one and that during the postwar period it has tended to shift inwards towards the origin. These differences have been variously accounted for by differences in the distribution of unemployment between structural and demand-deficient components, the institutional structure of wage fixing in the US and differences in the structure of the labour force (see Bowen and Berry, 1963).

The measurement of excess demand. In empirical work it is convenient to assume that U is a good approximation for $(D - N_\text{s})/N_\text{s}$ since unemployment data are easily available and normally reliable. However, certain researchers have expressed dissatisfaction with this measure and have experimented with alternatives. Ideally one would wish to have available comprehensive and reliable data on both unemployment and vacancies. From these a $(V_\text{c} - U)/N_\text{s}$ series could be calculated and would presumably be an accurate indicator of the level of excess demand for labour. The most significant problem in this respect is that the recorded vacancies data are generally thought to be unreliable mainly because they are not comprehensive. Unemployment data have also been held to be unreliable since recorded unemployment data do not take account of various types of 'hidden' unemployment (persons willing and able to work who are not registered as unemployed) and labour hoarding. It is not appropriate in a book of this kind to dwell on problems of data and measurement so we shall simply record briefly the main refinements which have been made.

Unemployment and vacancies. Dow and Dicks-Mireaux (1959) chose, despite the inadequacies of the recorded vacancy data, to construct a measure of excess demand utilising both vacancy and unemployment data for the postwar years in the UK. Using this series they obtained quite a good fit for the relation

$$\dot{W} = \frac{f(V_c - U)}{N_s}.$$

It should be noted however that Dow and Dicks-Mireaux interpret their result in terms of a hypothesis which postulates that the level of excess demand has semi-political effects on the 'climate of wage negotiations'. This is a theme that has been taken up by Phelps Brown (1971), E. S. Phelps (1971) and others. However, as Burton (1972) points out, if the climate hypothesis was correct we should not expect to find any evidence of the existence of micro-trade-off relations in submarkets. There is evidence however which suggests that such micro-relations do exist for regional, industrial and even city labour markets (see Hines, 1969).

Vacancy rates. Vacancy data have been used in place of unemployment data in some studies (Bowers *et al.*, 1970). Theoretically we would expect vacancies to be related non-linearly to unemployment and therefore to be an equally adequate proxy for the level of excess demand. (See Hansen, 1970, for an analysis of the expected relationship between vacancies and unemployment.) The practical difference between them in empirical work is simply a matter of the reliability of the recorded date. Since the unemployment data are generally thought to be more reliable than the vacancy data as a proxy for excess demand it was only when the unemployment variable seemed to lose its explanatory power (after 1967) that serious experiments with the vacancy data were carried out. Bowers *et al.* reported good results in estimating the wage equation for the UK using the vacancy rate as a proxy for excess demand. Later work has however tended to suggest that the period 1966-9 (the last three years observed by Bowers *et al.*) may have been subject to special influences which affected the ability of the unemployment rate to proxy excess demand and others have re-established the greater explanatory power of the unemployment rate (as against the vacancy rate) when post-1969 observations are included (see Parkin, Sumner and Ward, 1974). We shall return to the question of why the unemployment rate appeared to lose its explanatory power in the UK wage equation between 1966 and 1969 in section 5.3.

Augmented unemployment variables. The ideal unemployment series with which to proxy the excess demand for labour is one which measures the actual numbers of persons who are effectively not in employment but who are willing and able to work. Several studies have attempted to estimate the 'hidden unemployed' who are not registered as unemployed. Simler and Tella (1968) made estimates of this kind for the US. Taylor (1970) has made similar estimates for the US. The results of augmenting the unemployment data in this way have had mixed results in improving the explanatory power of unemployment in the wage equation. While Simler and Tella found the fit was improved for the US, Perry (1971) found hidden unemployment to be insignificant. Taylor (1970) found the augmented unemployment variable did not perform better in the US wage equation than the straightforward unemployment variable. This suggests that hidden unemployment is related to registered unemployment in some fairly stable way over time. Taylor (1972) has introduced a different augmentation of the registered unemployed into the wage equation for the UK. He has made estimates of the rate of labour hoarding by employers (i.e. labour retained by employers but which is surplus to current requirements) and has added this to the rate of registered unemployment. This augmented unemployment variable performs well in explaining the rate of change of *earnings* corrected for overtime but does not perform any better than registered unemployment as a regressor in the *wage rate* change equation.

A conclusion. In most empirical tests of economic models one is required to rely on variables which are only approximate indicators of the theoretically specified variable. The models tested are therefore only as accurate in explaining or predicting phenomena as the variables they employ are correctly specified and measured. Measuring excess demand for labour is a particularly difficult task and a good deal of effort has rightly gone into discovering the most refined proxy variable available. But while those refined proxies have, for certain time periods, particular countries and changing institutional backgrounds, improved on the power of the rate of registered unemployment in explaining wage changes, the most consistently successful proxy remains that of registered unemployment, as the most recent studies available to us confirm (see Parkin, Sumner and Ward, 1974). We may now consider the question of which measure of wage changes is the appropriate dependent variable in the wage equation.

Wages, earnings and wage drift. So far we have used the term 'wages' in a loose way. Wages may refer to negotiated wage rates (minimum or standard, time or piece) or to actual earnings (hourly or weekly) and certain issues arise in relation to which definition we use when we talk about wage inflation. The main such issue concerns the economic nature of the relationship between wage-rate changes and earnings changes. One school of thought (see Hines, 1964) holds that earnings inflate continuously in response to the continuous pull of excess demand and that the periodic process of collective bargaining simply serves to consolidate the wage drift so generated in inter-bargaining periods into negotiated wage rates. Another school of thought (see OEEC, 1961) contends that wage drift tends to 'float' on top of negotiated wage rates, since it tends to be a largely institutionalised additive to basic rates, and that the rate of earnings inflation is mainly determined by wage rate inflation. Empirical tests have produced mixed results which suggest a certain amount of 'consolidation' and a

certain amount of 'floating' in the wage-rate/earnings-change relation. (It should
be noted here that the 'consolidation' versus 'floating' drift controversy is not
coincident with the 'demand-pull' versus 'cost-push' controversy since it is quite
likely that changes in wage drift will not reflect fully the current level of excess
demand for labour and collective bargaining may therefore produce changes in
wage rates which are essentially demand induced (OEEC, 1961). A sophisticated
study was carried out by Dicks-Mireaux and Shepherd (1962) for the UK (wage
drift is not a significant phenomenon in the USA) and they found evidence of a
significant consolidation effect but by no means as strong an effect as estimated
by the OEEC study (1961). In a recent study Ashenfelter and Pencavel (1974)
have argued that the determinants of weekly earnings change in the UK since the
war have been wage-rate changes together with increased overtime working. On
balance the evidence seems to point to a situation in which wage rates rise in
response to the pressure of demand and that earnings rise as a result.
Institutional factors are however undoubtedly involved in this process also,
although their effects may be fairly constant elements (see Dicks-Mireaux and
Dow, 1959). In a general way it is probably acceptable to agree with Lipsey
(1960) that ' . . . although *a priori* reasoning can suggest many reasons why rates
and earnings may not move together, they do in fact stay, over a very long
period of time, remarkably close together, so that any theory which explains one
will go a long way to explain the other'. There has also been disagreement over
the appropriate specification of the wage-change variable, resulting in part from
the earnings versus wage rates controversy, but also involving issues of
measurement.

Various reservations, both on theoretical and statistical grounds, have been
made to the use of wage-rate data. Peston (1971) has argued that the (demand)
'price of labour' is properly measured by earnings plus national insurance
contributions, SET, etc. and (presumably) less REP. Ashenfelter and Pencavel
(1974) have suggested that the wage index must take account of the fraction of
workers receiving wage increases in each period. Taylor (1972) has pointed out
that the relation between earnings change and wage-rate change has differed over
different time periods. The main point here is that, in empirical tests of the
wage-inflation/excess-demand hypothesis, we require a dependent variable which
measures the price of labour; no single variable is self-evidently the right one, but
wage rates appear to have served as an adequate proxy in practice. It remains the
case however that disagreement on this issue exists and there is therefore a need
to ensure that the data series chosen as the proxy for wage inflation is
appropriate to the particular model tested and this may, of course, require a
wage-change variable which is more elaborate than the basic wage-rate index.
(For a discussion of these points see Taylor, 1972, and Ashenfelter and Pencavel,
1974).

The ceteris paribus *assumption*
We noted at the beginning of this chapter that the 'pure' Phillips relation
implicitly assumes that, with given values of the influences on wage changes

other than the unemployment rate, the rate of change of wages is determined by the level of excess demand, measured by the rate of enemployment. This assumption has been challenged and the central role of other independent variables in the wage-change equation asserted. We shall consider certain of these variables in this chapter.

Profits and wage changes. A number of studies have indicated that the level (and changes in the level) of profits is a significant explanatory variable in the wage-change equation (see Bowen, 1960). The most common interpretations placed on the profit variable are that (a) it indicates the balance of bargaining power in the labour market (Bowen, 1960; Kaldor, 1959); (b) that profits-push inflation has evoked a detensive wage response (Ackley, 1958); and (c) that profits and wages will rise together when there is excess demand in both goods and labour markets. It should be said at the outset that the studies which indicate an association between wage changes and a profit variable normally do not include a price-change variable and the inclusion of such a variable generally reduces the significance of the profit variable (Bowen and Berry, 1963). Further, Lipsey and Steuer (1961) for the UK and Bodkin (1966) for the United States have found only a weak association between wage changes and profit variables. It should therefore be borne in mind in any discussion of the role of a profit variable that its statistical credentials are by no means impeccable.

The bargaining power hypothesis depends on the notion that when profit levels are high trade unions will feel that a favourable opportunity exists to press for higher wages, since these can be financed out of high profits with a minimum of employers' resistance. At the same time the opportunity cost (in terms of lost profits) to the employer of facing a strike is greatest when profits are high and his ability to buy off a dispute is in any case enhanced by high profits. Hence we might expect a large number of wage claims to be advanced by trade unions and successfully negotiated when profits are high and a small number to be advanced with less success when profits are low. A variant of this hypothesis, advanced by Kaldor (1959), links profit rates with productivity growth and investment levels but retains the bargaining power approach where unions are 'eager' to press claims when industry is prosperous and employers are 'willing' and 'able' to meet these. Neither approach seems particularly plausible; the former since profits are presumably an endogenous variable, determined by demand factors, productivity, concentration ratios, etc., all of which imply a proxy role for profits rather than an independent causal role. If for example profit levels were a proxy for excess demand in both goods and factor markets then the so-called bargaining power hypothesis could be relegated to an intermediate step in a process in which the unions and employers read the market signals correctly and act through the appropriate institutions accordingly. If on the other hand profits are closely linked to labour productivity then a different interpretation, such as that advanced by Kuh (1967), which we shall consider shortly, might be appropriate.

The remaining possibility is that an independent profits-push initiates a defensive wage push by labour. This notion is often based on opinions regarding the price-fixing behaviour of the US steel industry which involves a price-fixing process governed by a 'profit target' which is periodically raised. Machlup (1960) finds little evidence that this has been a significant feature of US experience in the postwar period. In view of the market power enjoyed by many firms in the US, if this phenomenon is not significant there it is unlikely that it is anywhere else.

We are inclined to be highly suspicious of the role attributed to profit variables in the wage determination equation, partly because of their statistical ambiguity and partly because there is no convincing theoretical interpretation of the part which they might play in the wage/price change process. Kuh (1967) has argued that profits are a proxy for productivity change and that the latter is the causal influence on the rate of change of the money wage level. (See also chapter 6.)

Productivity and wage changes. Kuh has advanced a theoretical and statistical analysis of the relation between the money wage level and the value of the average product of labour. His statistical results are good, but no better than those obtained for many more orthodox models.

Kuh begins by deriving an expression to explain the equilibrium wage *level* from the Cobb—Douglas production function. In equilibrium the real wage rate, W/P, is equal to the marginal product of labour, $\partial X/\partial N$, where X is total physical product and N is the input of man hours. In the Cobb—Douglas case the average product of labour, X/N, is related to the marginal product of labour by a multiplicative constant, a. (Consider a Cobb—Douglas production function of the type $X = A \cdot N^a \cdot K^b$ where $a + b = 1$. The marginal product of labour is: $\partial X/\partial N = a \cdot A \cdot N^{a-1} \cdot K^b$; the average product of labour is $X/N = A \cdot N^{a-1} \cdot K^b$; therefore $\partial X/\partial N = a. (X/N)$.)

$$W/P = a(X/N) \qquad\qquad (5.6)$$

or

$$W = a(PX/N). \qquad\qquad (5.7)$$

Equation (5.7) tells us that the equilibrium wage level is a constant function of the average *value* product of labour. It is clear from (5.7) that when the demand for labour rises, either because P or X rises relatively faster than N, wages will also rise so long as the supply of labour is inelastic with respect to the wage level (as Kuh assumes). Kuh also accommodates the observed relation between wage changes and the unemployment rate into his hypothesis, arguing that the unemployment variable will reflect bargaining power and that there will tend to be an inverse cyclical relation between the average product of labour and the unemployment rate. This relation, while non-linear, will tend to be fairly weak because the employed and the unemployed are viewed as being largely non-competing groups in the labour market. However, the central hypothesis advanced by Kuh is that wage changes will be caused by changes in the average product of labour in the long run and that other influences, such as unemployment, will simply cause fluctuations around the long-term trend. The basic equation generated by Kuh is of the form:

$$\dot{W} = B(PX/N)\alpha \cdot U^{-\beta} \tag{5.8}$$

where B, α, and β are parameters. Kuh's interpretation of the basic Phillips relation is therefore quite different from that of the orthodox models. Any relation between U and $\dot{W}$ is short-term and indirect in nature and distinctly subordinate to the relation between wage changes and average value product.

Kuh also claims to explain the observed association between the rate of change of wages and profits by arguing that profits will be closely associated with the average product of labour. Thus, under a mark-up assumption concerning price fixing, we may say that profits will move in sympathy with:

$$Z = PX/WN \tag{5.9}$$

where Z is the mark-up on wage costs, and Z will therefore be an indicator of the profit position. This proposition would relegate the profit variable to the role of a proxy for average value product.

The Kuh model purports to be a radical departure from the conventional theory of the Phillips curve but depends on a number of rather restrictive assumptions. In the first place almost all of the problems relating to labour supply are assumed away in a quite unrealistic manner; thus Kuh assumes labour supply to be inelastic with respect to the wage rate, the employed and unemployed are assumed to be non-competing groups in the labour force, etc. Secondly, the impact of technological change on the average and marginal products of labour, an issue of some complexity, is side-stepped by the two assumptions of a Cobb—Douglas function and neutral technological change. Thirdly, the direction of causality in the model is ambiguous, and the assertion that profits are merely a proxy for average value product of labour is no more persuasive than Bowen's (1960) assertion of the reverse. Finally, in addition to the theoretical shortcomings of the Kuh model, the statistical validity of the wage-change/productivity-change relation is also in considerable doubt. Dicks-Mireaux (1961), using UK data, was unable to find a statistically significant role for the productivity-change variable in his wage equation.

Prices and wage changes. Econometric studies have established a fairly strong association between changes in wages and changes in prices. This association might indicate that $\dot{W} = f(\dot{P})$ or that $\dot{P} = g(\dot{W})$ or that $(\dot{W}, \dot{P}) = m(\lambda)$, where λ is some third variable, and the correct identification of the recorded association depends on some direct evidence of the line of causality or a persuasive theoretical interpretation. For the moment we shall consider only the hypothesis that $\dot{W} = f(\dot{P})$ and postpone discussion of the other hypotheses until section 5.3.

In the literature of the early 1960s, which preceded the proposition of the expectations hypothesis, the significance of price-change variables as regressors in the wage equation was generally rationalised in terms of trade union policies which had as an objective the protection of the real wage. According to Dow (1956) '. . . the norm is for money wages and salaries to compensate for previous price increases; and that variations in money incomes due to other influences can be described in terms of variations about this norm'. There is every reason to suppose that this view is a valid description of the situation which existed throughout much of the postwar period and occasionally in earlier times also. If we accept that this is so however we cannot avoid compromising the long-run validity of the excess-demand/wage-inflation relationship. If the Phillips relation is simply 'a variation about the norm' of a wage/price interaction there is a need to reconsider that relation in such a context. It is precisely this that we shall undertake in chapter 7 when the expectation hypothesis is considered. For the moment however let us confine ourselves to two brief observations about the wage/price relationship as revealed by a number of studies in the early 1960s.

First let us return to a theoretical consideration raised in the previous chapter in relation to Lipsey's model. We noted (on pp. 42–3) that Lipsey's model describes a *money* wage adjustment process which does not correspond with the more conventional *real* wage adjustment process embodied in neoclassical theory. At the same time we observed that Lipsey's empirical model employed price-change variables as regressors in the wage equation and that he found that the explanatory power of these price variables progressively increased over time and, in the postwar period, became the predominant determinant of wage infla- tion. We may take these points together and suggest a tentative hypothesis. Lipsey's regression equation may be simplified to:

$$\dot{W} = f(U) + \alpha\dot{P} . \qquad (5.10)$$

Rearranging terms gives:

$$\dot{W} - \alpha\dot{P} = f(U) \qquad (5.11)$$

The left-hand side of equation (5.11) is an expression which approaches a measure of the rate of change of the real wage rate. The coefficient α on the rate of change of prices was empirically found to be less than unity by Lipsey and others which means that the left-hand side of (5.11) fell short of measuring real wage changes by (approximately) the amount that α was less than unity. In the pre-First Wórld War period α was only equal to 0.21; however, in the post-Second World War period α was equal to 0.69. The point here is that over the years the price-change variable has increased its coefficient very considerably and that in the most recent period the relationship actually tested by Lipsey was coming close to the theoretically expected neoclassical hypothesis that the real wage will be responsive to excess demand for labour. It would be misleading to attach too much importance to this phenomenon, not least because an adequate specification of the rate of change of the real wage may require a more sophisticated price deflator than $\dot{P}_t$. However, as we shall see in chapter 7, there is a persuasive case for believing that a short-run relationship may exist between real wage change and excess demand for labour.

Secondly let us note certain of the statistical results which have been obtained for the relation $W = f(P)$ and also consider the problems involved in testing the relation. The statistical problems are largely to do with the simultaneous nature of the wage/price-change relation and the time-form of the relation. The main problem is to find a method of testing the wage-chage—price-change association in such a way as to reveal the significance of the particular line of causality postulated. In some instances wage-determination models have employed a price variable which is incapable of revealing any particular line of causality and indiscriminately picks up a 'feedback' effect. In others, lags have been used to specify particular lines of causality but these suffer from the need to specify an *a priori* time-form of the lag system. Probably the most reliable method of estimation is by simultaneous estimation of a wage-change and price-change equation by means of two-stage least-squares regression since this method avoids biased regression coefficients. Such a study has been undertaken by Dicks-Mireaux (1961) and he estimates that the short-term effect on wages of a current change in prices is about one-third of the price change for the postwar UK. Dicks-Mireaux takes this result to indicate that the wage—price spiral will be convergent (in the absence of excess demand and imported inflation). This is so because his equation estimates that the impact of price changes on wage changes and wage changes on prices is in both cases less than unity. The spiral therefore would unwind in time. This conclusion may be usefully compared with the predictions of the expectations hypothesis which we consider in chapter 7.

Is the ceteris paribus *assumption valid?* The independent explanatory power of price, profit and productivity variables in the wage equation has been asserted in a number of studies and we have briefly considered some of these here. The issue at stake here may well be one of choosing between variables which are proxies for roughly the same determining factor or are responsive to it. This is perhaps inevitable when one is dealing with a system of relations between endogenous variables and where there is no clear theoretical or statistical basis for accurately describing the system. As Leijonhufvud (1968) has observed, 'The "hypotheses" tested seem all too often to be of the type: "It seems reasonable to suppose that, by using variable x as an additional or substitute independent variable, a better regression result should be obtained". When the theoretical under-pinnings are no more ambitious than that, there is almost no basis on which to compare results, and new studies seldom knock old ones out of consideration.' We might therefore say that two variables, profit and unemployment, are open to the interpretation that they vary in sympathy with the level of excess demand in the labour market. Changes in productivity may indicate changes in the demand for labour. The effects of institutional factors, some of which we shall consider in detail in chapter 6, may be reflected in certain of the variables considered and also may be picked up in the constant term in the wage equation.

It therefore seems possible to draw a fairly firm conclusion on the matter. Both on theoretical and empirical grounds the case is established for accepting that a short-run trade-off between money wage inflation and excess demand for labour exists and is the central mechanism of inflation in the labour market. Further, the unemployment rate has been and remains the most efficient proxy for excess demand for labour. By way of immediate qualification of these conclusions we should also say that the excess demand model of wage inflation requires to take explicit account of the theoretically expected short-run adjustment process postulated by orthodox neoclassical theory — that excess demand for labour will be related to real wage adjustment. We have already hinted at the role which a price-change variable may have in identifying this relationship, and in chapter 7 we shall fully explore an excess-demand model of wage inflation augmented by expected price changes which is consistent with the neoclassical hypothesis.

So far as the validity of the *ceteris paribus* assumption is concerned then we may simply say that, so far as the short run is concerned, it is a legitimate device for revealing the independent determining power of the level of excess demand on the rate of wage inflation. In the long run, as we shall see, the *ceteris paribus* assumption is irrelevant. The only practical importance of resolving this question is, of course, to attempt to identify control variables from the policy point of view. Hence it is of importance to policy-makers to recognise that a short-run trade-off between excess demand and wage inflation exists. In particular it may be of considerable importance to identify particular numerical values of unemployment and wage change which lie on the trade-off as labour market indicators of policy targets. It is necessary to bear in mind here that anti-inflation policy is not directed towards the manipulation of the unemployment rate but instead towards the management of the *determinants* of excess demand (as well as other things).

5.3   The 'breakdown' of the Phillips relation

Some time around the end of 1966 the Phillips relation appeared suddenly to have lost almost all of its explanatory power. This phenomenon was observed in almost all the major industrialised countries but was most marked in the UK. This development caused a good deal of consternation amongst economists at the time, since they appeared to have lost one of the tidiest economic relationships in an otherwise untidy world. There was therefore in the late 1960s a need to discover the nature of the breakdown of the Phillips relation and to find an alternative way of explaining the theoretically expected relationship between domestic excess demand and wage inflation. A good deal of work on both of these questions has been undertaken and the debate on inflation has simultaneously been carried far beyond them.

It is useful to distinguish these approaches at this stage under three main headings. First, a number of studies attempted to account for the apparent demise of the Phillips relation by investigating changes which had occurred in the relations between certain labour market variables in the late 1960s. Essentially this work examined the hypothesis that unemployment ceased to be an adequate indicator of the level of excess demand for labour. Second, price expectations were introduced as an argument in the wage equation along with the unemployment rate to yield an 'expectations-augmented excess-demand model' of wage inflation. This model purports to explain the inflation of 1966–71 largely in terms of expectations effects while still holding that unemployment remained the best indicator of excess demand for labour (see Parkin, Sumner and Ward, 1974). In this model therefore the short-run trade-off relation between wage inflation and unemployment is held never to have disappeared. Third, the monetarist view of the inflationary process, under the regime of fixed exchange rates which obtained generally until 1971, emphasises that inflation is an international phenomenon caused by changes in the world supply of money. This approach permits only the most limited role to domestic variables in explaining inflation rates and would therefore view the British Phillips relation as a rather minute cog in a very large machine. As it happens quite exceptional international monetary developments (mainly related to American attempts to finance the Vietnam war by means of budget deficits and the coincident emergence of the Eurodollar market) did occur in the mid-1960s and these would be expected by the monetarist school to swamp domestic labour market relations such as the Phillips curve.

These are three of the main approaches to accounting for the decline in the explanatory power of the Phillips relation after 1966. They are not mutually exclusive, indeed the latter two are invariably contained within the same general model. Since the expectations-augmented excess-demand model is dealt with in detail in chapter 7 and the monetarist approach to inflation closely analysed in chapter 8, we shall confine ourselves here to a brief consideration of the hypothesis that changes in labour market variables altered around 1966 and loosened the relation between unemployment and excess demand.

The shift in the relation between vacancies and unemployment: 1966–70. The first, and perhaps most superficially attractive, endogenous factor which might serve to explain the breakdown of the conventional wage-determination equation is the evident shift in the relationship between unemployment and vacancies which occurred in the UK after 1966 (Bowers *et al.*, 1970). This hypothesis would hold that for some unexplained reason the unemployment rate ceased to indicate accurately the level of excess demand for labour after 1966 and that the vacancy rate was a more reliable indicator of excess demand after 1966. This hypothesis can, of course, be tested, and indeed the vacancy rate performs considerably more satisfactorily than the unemployment rate as an explanatory variable in the wage equation for the years 1966—9. However, in 1970 and 1971 this model seriously underpredicts the rate of wage inflation, so seriously indeed as to suggest that it had virtually no relevance in those years. The inescapable fact which emerges from this evidence is that there was not a general domestic excess demand for labour in the ordinary sense after 1969 yet a wage explosion occurred in 1970 and wage inflation was also exceptionally rapid in 1971. Two questions therefore must be asked: (a) why did the orthodox Phillips relation, $\dot{W} = f(U)$, cease to hold from 1967 onwards? and (b) how are we to explain the experience of wage inflation in 1970 and 1971 when even the refined predictive model, $\dot{W} = g(V_c)$, loses all explanatory power in those years?

1967—9. We have noted that by substituting V_c for U in the orthodox (multi-variable) wage equation permits an excess-demand type of explanation of the wage inflation of this period. We do require however to consider why vacancies quite suddenly became a more accurate indicator of the level of excess demand than the unemployment rate in these years. Bowers *et al.* made a thorough investigation of a variety of possible explanations of this phenomenon in 1970 and their findings are briefly reported below. The shift in the relationship between the unemployment rate and demand (measured by vacancies) can be fairly precisely dated as occurring in the last quarter of 1966. This shift occurred in all regions and in all industries. The shift was coincident with (a) a sharp rise in unemployment; (b) a reduction in the dispersion of regional unemployment; and (c) a sharp rise in labour turnover which was sustained throughout the period. There are a variety of possible explanations for each or all of these phenomena, including ' . . . the introduction of earnings-related unemployment benefit; redundancy payments; selective employment tax; incomes policy; general "structural change"; devaluation induced structural change; "shake-out" ' (Bowers *et al.*, 1970, p. 58). The authors, after considering each candidate in detail, plumped for a structural-change explanation in which they suggested that shifts in both the aggregate demand and supply curves for labour have occurred in such a way as to generate increased *structural unemployment*. (Structural unemployment exists when there are both un-employed workers and unfilled vacancies but where the unemployed are not qualified to fill the vacancies). Thus the (tentative) conclusions drawn by Bowers *et al.* were that a domestic excess demand is the best explanation of the events of 1967—9 and that the relatively high unemployment rates in those years are probably accounted for by increased structural unemployment. The causes of the demand and supply shifts which might have led to this increase in structural unemployment are not entirely clear. Selective employment tax, regional policy, technological change in certain industries, the effects of devaluation and the rundown of public investment are all possible explanations of the demand shift effect. Incomes policy and workers' expectations of future employment prospects, giving rise to an increase in voluntary quits, might go some way to explaining the supply shift effect. Finally it is interesting to note that the observed increase in labour turnover after 1966 would, according to the Holt model, predict a shift in the Phillips relation away from the origin (since the *F* component in the constant term in equation (5.5) would be increased). In fact when the Holt model is tested,

$$\dot{W} = a_0 + a_1 \frac{V_c}{U}$$

it predicts well until 1966 and thereafter breaks down (for UK data).

After 1970. While the 1970 Bowers *et al.* model may permit the domestic excess-demand hypothesis to survive the experience of wage inflation between 1967 and 1969 it patently does not offer a ready explanation of subsequent experience. The wage and price explosion which began in the late 1960s, and is still gathering momentum in 1974, has occurred against the background of historically high rates of unemployment and low rates of unfilled vacancies. Bowers *et al.* have reconsidered their 1970 analysis in an article published in 1972 (Bowers *et al.*, 1972). In this later paper the principal finding is that, despite the shift in the relation between unemployment and vacancies, unemployment continued to be an adequate indicator of excess demand for labour. The change in the unemployment/vacancy relation is attributed partly to an increase in the ratio of recorded to true vacancies — a consequence of improved recording procedures in the vacancy data. Hence the shift in the unemployment/vacancy relation is not entirely mirrored by a shift in the relation between unemployment and excess demand; it also reflects a shift in the relation between recorded vacancies and excess demand. The central finding of this study — that unemployment remains a good proxy for excess labour demand — is supported by work undertaken in the Manchester University Inflation Workshop. A study by Parkin *et al.* (1974) concludes that the unemployment rate is still the best indicator of excess demand for labour, although the model tested is augmented by expectations variables and these contribute the bulk of the equation's explanatory power. Nevertheless Parkin, in a later paper (1974), finds the evidence sufficiently convincing to argue that the short-run trade-off between wage inflation and unemployment remains effective but that the proximate cause of the recent wage explosion was expectations.

It is worth noting that the short-run trade-off between inflation and excess demand is a domestic mechanism which relates positive domestic excess demand with positive rates of wage inflation. The studies quoted above, which reassert the relevance of the short-run trade-off in recent UK experience, are therefore paradoxical in that they accept that the recent wage explosion has occurred against a background of domestic *excess supply* of labour (i.e. unemployment has been in excess of the level indicated by the intercept of the Phillips curve on the horizontal axis). Augmenting the wage equation by expectations variables does not remove this paradox because these are themselves generated out of inflation resulting from excess demand. Thus the models of Bowers *et al.* and Parkin *et al.* cannot refer to a closed economy or to an economy with floating exchange rates. Parkin (1974) however points out that the model is consistent with a fixed exchange rate economy since world excess demand can be transmitted into the domestic economy by way of both import and domestic prices. In order to generate an inflation in this way the international inflationary pressures must be sufficient to outweigh the deflationary pressure of domestic excess supply. Until 1971 fixed exchange rates did prevail and the model is therefore relevant until that time. After 1971 however the situation changed and floating exchange rates have become prevalent in the major industrial economies. Theoretically this development should permit countries to follow policies more independently of the international economic environment than previously. Hence the insulation from worldwide inflationary tendencies which a floating exchange rate supplies to individual economies ought severely to reduce the impact of imported inflation and make a situation in which positive inflation coexists with excess labour supply impossible in all but the very short run. It remains to be seen however what will now emerge in practice in this regard since international capital flows appear to be capable of interfering with the free exchange rate adjustment process and therefore of introducing a degree of 'fixity' into the exchange rate system. These matters are developed in detail in chapter 8 and we may simply conclude this section by accepting Parkin's judgement that the Phillips curve did not disappear after 1966 but is alive and well and living under the shadow of world inflationary pressures (Parkin, 1974).

5.4   The price equation

So far we have concentrated our attention on the wage-change equation but now we must consider the determinants of price changes. It was noted earlier that many models of the inflationary process appear to assume a passive price-change mechanism, where prices adjust in response to increases in unit costs, and there are two general versions of this model.

The pure mark-up model. The first version of this model postulates that prices are fixed by summing unit prime costs and adding a fixed percentage mark-up to cover overheads and the profit margin. Dow (1956) employs such a model and the main independent variables are changes in unit labour costs and import prices, both lagged and weighted. The change in the unit labour costs variable is calculated as changes in average money wages deflated by changes in output per man, which implies that prices will be responsive both to changes in the trend of the ULC (unit labour cost) index, as well as to short-run fluctuations, due to cyclical factors, around that index. This is a significant point since a model utilising such a variable implies that the mark-up is on all *non-capital costs* rather than simply on *prime costs*. Nield (1963), as we shall see, makes an explicit distinction between these two possibilities.

In any case the mark-up model takes the following general form on the assumption that the relative share of profits in the value of output is constant:

$$\dot{P}_{t+1} = \alpha_o + \alpha_1 \dot{W}_t - \alpha_2 \left(\frac{\dot{X}}{N}\right)_t + \alpha_3 \dot{P}_{m\,t} \qquad (5.12)$$

where $\dot{P}$ is the rate of change of prices, $\dot{W}$ is the rate of change of money wages, $\dot{P}_m$ is the rate of change of import prices and $(\dot{X}/N)$ is the rate of change of average output per man. Hines (1964), Dicks-Mireaux (1961) and Klein and Ball (1959) have tested variants of this basic equation. In all cases the fit tends to be good.

The 'normal cost' model. Nield (1963) has adopted a slightly different approach to the construction of a price equation. Instead of accepting the pure mark-up hypothesis he has postulated the idea of 'normal-cost pricing'. Normal-cost pricing is a process of price fixing based on the cost of some notional 'normal' output level rather than on actual current costs. Thus when output and costs fluctuate in response to cyclical or other short-term factors, prices will not be adjusted. If on the other hand the costs of producing the 'normal' level of output change, prices will be adjusted accordingly. The most significant source of change in normal costs is likely to be the trend of unit labour costs which are jointly determined by money wages per man hour and the trend of output per man hour. This implies that in the price equation the long-term trend of unit labour costs, rather than the simple money wage deflated by an output per man variable, should be included. This yields the following basic equation:

$$P = \alpha_o + \alpha_1 \beta_1 (ULC) + \alpha_2 \beta_2 P_m; \ \beta_1 + \beta_2 = 1 \qquad (5.13)$$

where P is the price *level* (wholesale), ULC is the trend value of unit labour costs and P_m is the import price level (material and fuel). β_1 and β_2 are weights. Nield tested three extended forms of equation (5.13) using manufacturing index number series employing a complex system of geometrically declining weights to take account of all previous values of each series. (The weights therefore ensure that the more distant in time any observation is, the less will be its impact on the value of the observation.) The three equations tested permitted a distinction to be made between productivity change resulting primarily from technological change (the trend of the ULC index) and changes in productivity resulting from short-term changes in demand (fluctuations around the trend of the ULC index). His results indicated that:

(a) the effect of changes in output per man on prices is symmetrical;
(b) only changes in the trend of the ULC index affect prices;
(c) short-run changes in productivity do not affect prices, probably because they reflect labour hoarding and dishoarding effects at different points in the cycle.

Interpreting the constant term. The constant term in equation (5.12) may allow for the possibility that short-term cost adjustments will not be immediately reflected in price changes but that profit margins will be maintained in the long run on average. Dicks-Mireaux (1961) suggests that this might be the result of some constant upward pressure on the price level or be associated with lags in the price adjustment to cost changes. In the case of Nield's equation (5.13) this explanation cannot hold and it is likely that the constant term in (5.13) reflects the influence of some additional cost factors which are relatively fixed in relation to unit costs.

The Nield study yields an equation which is economically more satisfactory than those based on a simple mark-up hypothesis and subsequent writers have tended to opt for the normal-cost model. Such models generally perform very well statistically and it is noteworthy that, over the period when the Phillips wage equation lost most of its predictive power, the price equation continued to predict well *given the behaviour of wages.* This fact serves to illustrate that it was the wage equation specifically which had deteriorated in recent years, not empirical models of inflation as such.

Demand and price changes. We have already mentioned the possibility that $(\dot{W}, \dot{P}) = f(\lambda)$ where λ is some third variable. An obvious candidate for the third variable in relation to price inflation is excess demand in the goods market, just as excess demand in the labour market was an obvious possible determinant of wage inflation. However, surprisingly little attention has been given to this possibility. It is true that various studies have hinted at this type of relation (see Dicks-Mireaux, 1961; Nield, 1963; Klein and Ball, 1959) but few have examined it in detail. The principal reason why such a possible relation has largely been ignored is probably the wide acceptance of mark-up and normal-cost hypotheses of the price-fixing process.

Williamson (1967) developed a hypothesis first advanced by Kalecki (1954) which accommodates both the mark-up hypothesis and the influence of demand in the determination of the price level. The basic idea in the Williamson/Kalecki model can be illustrated by a simple first order difference equation:

$$P_{jt} = \alpha P_{jt-1} + \beta C_{jt} \qquad (5.14)$$

where P_j is the weighted average of the prices of all the firms in an industry and C_j is the weighted average of the average prime costs of all of the firms in the industry. α and β are the weighted averages of the price and prime cost coefficients of all the firms in the industry. Equation (5.14) gives an expression for the industry equilibrium price. If however prime costs rise, a new equilibrium price will not be attained immediately but only after a process of convergence which will be decribed by the time path of the industry's price level which in turn is given by the solution to (5.14).

The process by which equilibrium is gradually restored and the profit margin regained is of course dependent on relative price effects within the industry.

When costs rise the industry price level will rise by some fraction of the cost increase immediately. This price rise causes an upward adjustment of each firm's demand curve and permits further price rises. This process will continue until a new equilibrium price is established and profit margins within the industry are restored. The actual equation tested by Williamson is very like that used by Nield except that the constant term is omitted and a lagged price variable included.

Williamson's model performs quite well when tested for British manufacturing industry and has the advantage over the others of incorporating into a normal-cost price equation the influence of demand pressure without requiring a direct measure of the excess demand for goods.

'Friction' models of price inflation. Explicit in Williamson's model is the notion of non-instantaneous adjustment to a disequilibrium price situation on the part of the individual firm. Further the model implicitly relates the adjustment process undertaken by each firm to adjustments occurring in each other firm in the industry. Propositions similar to these have been the focal point of a number of rather elaborate studies of price dynamics under conditions of friction (see Phelps and Winter, 1971; Carlson, 1972; Barro, 1972). These latter models do not derive from those of Kalecki and Williamson but are clearly of the same gender.

The Phelps/Winter (1971) model is microeconomic and refers to a situation of atomistic competition. The essential element of friction which is incorporated into this model, and which distinguishes it from the Walrasian model, is that because information is not perfect and not costless, each firm in an atomistic market is at each point in time a transient monopolist. This amounts to little more than saying that, because a firm's customers will not in practice desert it quickly and completely when its price rises above that of its competitors (nor will the firm attract its competitors' custom quickly and completely by reducing its price), the firm may be thought of as facing a highly inelastic demand curve at each moment in time rather than the perfectly elastic demand curve assumed in perfect competition theory. In such a situation each firm may fix its price at any point in time as though it were a monopolist, within a margin of the industry mean price determined by expectations of customer behaviour and the price-fixing behaviour of other firms. Behaviour of this kind is consistent with the profit-maximising assumption since it is short-run present value which is being maximised, taking account of the cost of price adjustment and the costs of holding prices at a level different from the industry mean. Barro's (1972) analysis refers to monopoly proper but yields a similar type of adjustment process since the margin of price deviation from that prescribed in the frictionless case is bounded by the same sort of adjustment costs.

Clearly, in a situation of excess demand for the industry's product, 'a Phillips-like relation between the output level (relative to capacity) and the rate of price increase results if each firm continuously adjusts upward its price as it learns that it is not experiencing a net loss of customers from its higher price and as money wage rates keep pace with the general price level' (Phelps, 1971). Phelps points out however that in the long run, as expected trends catch up with perceived trends, such a Phillips relation will float upwards and become vertical (see chapter 7).

Finally Parkin (1974) has proposed a price-inflation model which is derived by analogy from the wage-inflation model constructed by Parkin *et al.* (1974). This model incorporates expectations variables and in its aggregate form holds that the rate of price inflation is dependent on the level of excess demand (for goods), the expected rate of change of unit costs and the expected rate of change of the general level of prices. Thus, as in the Phelps/Winter model, there will be a short-run trade-off between excess demand for goods and the rate of inflation but no such long-run trade-off will exist. It should be noted here that, while Phelps and Winter believe they have made a 'landing on the non-Walrasian continent' by introducing adjustment costs into their model, the same cannot be said of Parkin whose model is strictly analogous to the standard expectations-augmented trade-off relation in the labour market.

The models compared. We have examined three types of price-adjustment model in this section and it is now useful to consider how each fits into the inflationary process. First we have the simple mark-up model which postulates that prices are fixed by adding a fixed percentage mark-up on unit prime costs. The main point about this model is that price inflation will only occur, and will occur in proportion to, an inflation of unit prime costs. Second, the 'normal-cost' model, which postulates that prices will be marked up on the basis of long-run costs, would at first sight be capable of explaining price inflation only where the trend of money wage increases exceeded the trend of productivity change or where the trend of import price changes is upward. This implies that short-run excess demand for goods or factors will not influence price inflation. However, as Parkin (1974) has pointed out, excess demand for labour may very well affect the long-run cost trend and therefore influence the rate of inflation.

Both the simple mark-up hypothesis and the normal-cost hypothesis rely on a model involving only one inflationary gap — a factor gap — and are therefore quite inconsistent with the sophisticated two-gap model of Hansen (see chapter 2). Our third class of price-adjustment models embraces the Kalecki/Williamson approach and the Phelps/Winter model. These models all explicitly allow for demand factors to influence the rate of price inflation directly. The Kalecki/Williamson approach limits the influence of demand factors to an accommodating role in permitting the industry to move from one equilibrium price, defined in terms of a percentage mark-up, to another equilibrium price, also defined in terms of the same percentage mark-up, when unit prime costs increase. The Phelps/Winter model on the other hand expressly yields a short-run trade-off between the degree of capacity utilisation and the rate of change of prices. This latter model therefore is quite consistent with the two-gap macroeconomic model of inflation. It is also a model which has an inherent plausibility which the others lack. It is based on assumptions of friction in the goods market – an assumption most economists would readily accept in relation to the labour market – and demonstrates that, by a process which appeals to commonsense and casual observation, it is perfectly reasonable to view the production agents in an atomistic market as exercising 'transient' monopoly power in respect of price making. Since each such producer enjoys such power the atomistic market becomes something approaching competition amongst monopolists with each producer's actions validating those of his competitors. With excess demand in the goods market – a phenomenon as likely as excess demand in the labour market – the trade-off relation in the short run is simply between capacity utilisation and price inflation. Parkin (1974) reaches this same conclusion by augmenting the excess-demand model with expectations variables. The Parkin model however, because it does not incorporate the 'frictions' which permit even competitive firms to act as monopolists, yields different predictions under different types of competition, the price/excess-demand trade-off being particularly sensitive under monopoly and relatively insensitive under a high degree of competition.

Empirical evidence. There are no *a priori* means of settling which is the appropriate model of price inflation. Nor are empirical tests likely to be conclusive since the main difference between one- and two-gap models of the inflationary process is unlikely to be often apparent (i.e. unemployment is likely to vary in sympathy with the degree of capacity utilisation). But for what it is worth we may note that the following results have been obtained from tests of the various price equations. The simple mark-up hypothesis, as we noted earlier, has tended to produce a good fit for the UK but, if unemployment and capacity utilisation are highly correlated, this does not tell us a great deal. The normal-cost model has been subjected to rigorous testing by Godley and Nordhaus (1972) and they find strongly in favour of the normal-cost hypothesis and strongly against the excess-demand hypothesis. They do not however distinguish between the prices of tradeable and non-tradeable goods, or, alternatively, between international and domestic excess demand. The excess-demand hypothesis has been tested for the UK by Solow (1969), for the USA by Laidler (1973) and for the 'Group of Ten' industrial countries by Duck *et al.* (1975), with mixed results. For both the USA and the Group of Ten the excess-demand variables perform quite well when tested in an expectations-augmented model. For the UK, Solow finds that excess demand is a good explanatory variable but this result must be contrasted with the strongly negative findings of Godley and Nordhaus (1972).

The empirical results are therefore very mixed: they seem to support all three hypotheses in some measure. While we cannot therefore reject any of these hypotheses we may note that the price-inflation/excess-demand hypothesis is one which requires to be viewed in an international rather than domestic context — either by distinguishing between tradeable and non-tradeable goods or by viewing excess demand in an international context — and that where this has been done the results are reasonably favourable (Duck *et al.*, 1975). The Phelps/Winter model, although the authors do not say so, seems to be most relevant to the case of non-tradeable goods. This is because the information and adjustment frictions are considerably more likely to apply in a wholly domestic market than in one which is open to international competition.

5.5   Conclusions

In this chapter we have reviewed four of the main themes which have occupied the attention of economists in the wake of the Phillips/Lipsey literature. Two other major topics of interest — the influence of trade unions on inflation and the expectations hypothesis — are examined in detail in the following two chapters. Let us now attempt to draw some conclusions about the topics reviewed in this chapter.

The first topic dealt with concerned the adequacy of an essentially product market model to explain the process of adjustment in the labour market. It is certainly the case that the labour market is different in many important respects from the product market and that Lipsey's analysis does not adequately take account of this. Holt's labour market model demonstrates however that a result similar to that derived by Lipsey can be derived from a sophisticated analysis of the labour market which incorporates all the main distinguishing characteristics of such a market. The second issue reviewed concerned the validity of the short-run trade-off between wage inflation and unemployment as an independent mechanism in the labour market. In our brief survey of alternative independent influences on the rate of wage inflation we skimmed across a vast literature on the subject and concluded that, so long as unemployment is a valid proxy for excess demand in the labour market, the short-run trade-off is a valid and independent mechanism in the labour market. Indeed we might well agree with Laidler (1971) when he observes of the debate which spawned such a vast literature, 'in my judgement at least, nothing of basic importance was added by this literature to the fundamental contributions of Phillips and Lipsey'. The third issue considered was the apparent breakdown of the Phillips relation after 1966. Many explanations of this phenomenon were advanced but the most recent evidence available to us seems to suggest that the 'breakdown' never really occurred at all. It is too soon to be conclusive about this matter but on balance it is reasonable to accept that the most recent evidence is persuasive enough to re-establish the fact of the short-run trade-off. Our fourth topic concerned the determinants of price inflation. The essential matter at issue is whether price inflation is a passive response to changes in unit costs or a process which may be directly caused by excess demand for goods. We considered three basic types of price-determination model and the empirical evidence which has attempted to discriminate between them. Although there is no sure theoretical way of discriminating betwen the different models we are inclined to the view that those which permit excess demand for goods to exercise a determining role in price inflation are most realistic. The evidence which has emerged from various empirical studies is often ambiguous and has produced conflicting results. There is therefore little but prejudice available to us presently in deciding which view to adopt.

Notes to chapter 5

1. It should be noted that this section is in no way intended as a complete summary of the models and the reader is urged to consult the original articles cited.
2. However, those of Phelps (1971) and Mortensen (1971) specifically introduce price and wage expectations into the analysis and discussion of these is deferred to chapter 7.

CHAPTER 6

Trade Unions and Inflation

So far we have spoken of wage inflation without reference to the actual machinery by which wages are actually fixed and changed. That machinery consists of a variety of institutions both voluntary and statutory. Almost half of the labour force in the UK, and about a quarter in the USA, are members of trade unions and their wages are fixed in collective bargaining between the unions and employers. Moreover many of those employees who are not members of trade unions effectively have their wages fixed in accordance with the outcome of collective bargaining by way of convention, third-party decision or defensive employer tactics. While there is no way of estimating the extent to which collective bargaining determines wage rates in practice, it is safe to say that a majority of wages are effectively determined by the outcome of collective bargaining. We must now therefore recognise that wage inflation is largely the result of the outcomes of a series of collective bargains.

To recognise that wage inflation is largely the outcome of a collective bargaining process is not to suggest that the bargaining process itself affects the process of inflation. The market requires that there be some kind of administrative machinery (however atomistic) whereby market-determined wage adjustments are translated into actual pay changes and wage offers. There is no reason to suppose that such machinery will necessarily affect the process of wage inflation. Collective bargaining is however a rather special form of machinery for fixing pay since it is intended to reduce or eliminate the competitive element in the supply of labour and affect the market adjustment process as a result. Consequently trade unions have often been conceived of in economic theory as monopolistic organisations and the analysis of wage determination under trade unions has incorporated this conception.

Bargaining models. A great variety of 'bargaining models' of wage determination under trade unions have been constructed and they normally have a large number of common characteristics. Normally bargaining models confine themselves to analysis which is based on comparative statics, partial equilibrium and frictionless markets. (There are of course exceptions.) Further, these models normally assume that bargaining occurs within economic bounds derived from the bilateral monopoly model. Within these bounds the theory of games has often been employed to describe the settlement process, but in other treatments non-game theoretic analysis has been used. All these models have a common theme: joint maximisation of distributable gains in proportion to the potential costs of disagreement. Thus bargaining models tend to assume narrow economic objectives in bargaining, the central importance of the strike or lock-out threat and cool calculation by both sides of the costs, probabilities and likely outcomes of disagreement. A good survey of bargaining models has been written by de Menil (1971).

For the purposes of analysing the impact of trade union activity on wage inflation we believe that such models have only the most limited relevance. Parkin (1974) has suggested that the predictions of the bargaining models conform with those of the expectations-augmented/excess-demand hypothesis. Thus we have the obvious proposition that 'in a general inflation a proportionate marking up of all prices and wage rates will keep real wage rates approximately constant' (Johnston, 1974). This is certainly in line with the predictions of the expectations-augmented/excess-demand model 'that wage change will be homogeneous of degree one in money "price" changes' (Parkin, 1974). However, the most important prediction of bargaining models is that 'rational economic calculation on the part of the employers can lead to wage increases in response to union demands even though there has been no change, or even an adverse change, in the level of excess demand that a conventional Phillips curve analysis regards as an essential pre-requisite for a wage change' (Johnston, 1974). This latter prediction is, of course, entirely in line with the cost-push theory of inflation which was discussed in chapter 3. We shall however discuss the influence of trade union activity on wage inflation within a broader context than that permitted by bargaining models while recognising that, within their rather strict limitations, such models are useful microeconomic devices for analysing certain of the mechanics of cost inflation. In section 6.1 therefore we shall consider a general theoretical approach to trade union activity in the labour market and in section 6.2 go on to consider the available empirical evidence which permits a limited evaluation of aspects of that theoretical background.

6.1   Trade unions and the labour market

In order to contain our analysis of the role of trade unions in the labour market within the general excess-demand model which has been developed in previous chapters, it is convenient to begin by considering an aggregate reaction function relating wage changes to the level of excess demand. This device permits us to examine four specific hypotheses about trade union influence in a simple way. Assume a linear market reaction function of the type

$$\dot{W} = aE, \ E = \frac{D - Ns}{Ns}$$

where E is the level of excess demand for labour. Four possible (representative, but by no means exhaustive) cases by which the activity of trade unions may affect the rate of wage inflation are:

(a) that the trade union does not affect the market adjustment process so that

$$\dot{W} = aE,$$

with or without trade union activity in the market;

(b) the trade union biases the reaction function above the level at which it would be located in the absence of the union so that

$$\dot{W} = aE + z, \ z > 0;$$

(c) the trade union biases the market reaction function so that

$$\dot{W} = bE + z, \ b < a \text{ and } z > 0;$$

(d) the trade union biases the reaction function so that

$$\dot{W} = cE, \ c < a.$$

Each of these may be conveniently illustrated in a single diagram (fig. 6.1). It should be noted here that cases (b) and (c) postulate that trade union activity influences the rate of wage inflation *independent of the level of excess demand for labour*, i.e. $f(0) \neq 0$. Case (d), in contrast, postulates only that trade unions will affect *the speed of adjustment*, i.e. $f(0) = 0$. It should also be noted that where the effect of trade union activity is to shift the supply curve of labour so as to alter the level of excess demand, the reaction function will not be biased.

Fig. 6.1

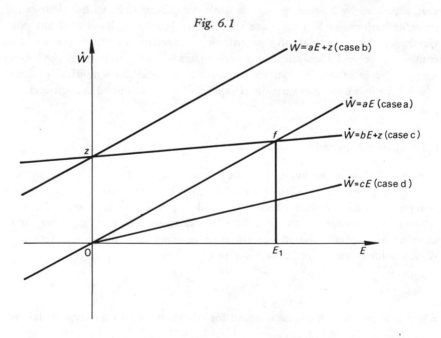

Fig. 6.2

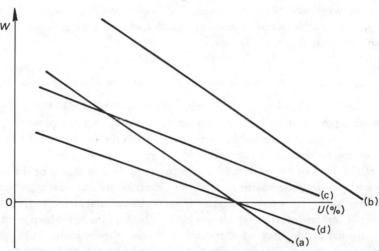

These reaction functions may be translated into Phillips curves (linear for convenience) so long as the relation $U = f(E)$ holds and is the same in each case, as is so in fig. 6.2. Case (a) simply states that the activities of trade unions in the wage-fixing process are neutral and that the trade union only 'rubber stamps' the wage adjustments determined by market forces. Case (b) states that trade union activity generates an inflationary bias in the labour market so that, for all levels of excess demand, the rate of wage inflation will be higher than that which would result from the reaction of the market alone by a constant amount z. The inflationary bias so generated by the trade union may be attributed to its exercise of 'market power' or 'the collective bargaining advantage' in the wage-fixing process. Case (c) is somewhat different from (b) in that the trade union is only capable of biasing the reaction function upwards over a certain range of excess demand levels, OE_1, in fig. 6.1, and biases it downwards for other levels of excess demand, $E > E_1$. The logic of this case is that while the trade union may be able to accelerate the speed of wage adjustment at low levels of excess demand through the exercise of market power, a point will be reached at which the trade union will actually dampen the rate of wage increase because its bureaucratic nature, and its need to operate through the periodic and time-consuming process of collective bargaining, prevent it from securing a rate of wage increase as rapid as a very tight market would yield. Case (d) is, on the face of it, an intuitively unlikely one but must be taken seriously since none other than Professor Friedman (1951) has suggested it. In reality case (d) is an extension of case (c), holding that bureaucratic trade unions operating through the process of collective bargaining will have the effect of dampening the rate of wage increase at *all* levels of excess demand for labour.

Each of the cases listed above is theoretically plausible but there is no way of evaluating their relative merits on theoretical grounds alone, since economic theory has little conclusive to say about the impact of trade unionism on the process of wage determination. The need is therefore for empirical evidence to assist in choosing between competing hypotheses and a brief summary of the available evidence is given in section 6.2.

6.1.i　The nature of trade union market power and the choice of indicators

Two of our hypotheses suggest that trade unions may be able to bias the market adjustment process in such a way as to secure a more rapid rate of wage increase than would result if trade unions were absent from the market for at least some levels of excess demand and are capable of generating wage inflation independent of the level of excess demand (cases (b) and (c)). For this to be the case we must attribute to trade unions the ability to exercise 'market power', which may be defined simply as a power deriving from organisational action to fix prices at a level in excess of that which could be obtained in the absence of such organisational action. But what factors determine the existence and degree of union market power? Clearly, from the definition of market power given above, it must be that it is *collective* rather than *individual* wage-fixing processes which might introduce a bias into the market adjustment process. The advantages which the collective unit may possess over the individual in wage fixing may include:

(a) the ability to articulate wage demands with a greater degree of skill, aggressiveness and with more perfect market knowledge;
(b) the ability to threaten or undertake collective industrial actions against an employer (as against the individual's quit threat);
(c) the political and institutional, as well as economic, motivations which shape trade union wage policy (as against the predominantly economic motivation of the individual).

Similar categories of possible advantages of collective bargaining have been discussed by Holt (1971a), Levinson (1966) and others, so that we need only briefly elaborate on them here.

'Power' and 'militancy'. The collective bargaining advantage, as outlined above, is a hybrid concept which makes no specific distinction between the *objective capacity* to exercise market power and the *subjective propensities* to translate that potential into realised power. Purdy and Zis (1974) have recently highlighted the need to make such a distinction between 'power' and 'militancy'. In the discussion of the collective bargaining advantage which follows it will be seen that that advantage embraces both 'power' and 'militancy' within it. This is admittedly unsatisfactory but probably inevitable. It is unsatisfactory because a failure to make a clear theoretical distinction between power and militancy makes it very hard to devise testable models of union influence. It is inevitable since we simply have no theory which is capable of making this kind of

distinction into an operational concept. These points are well illustrated by Purdy and Zis. They recognise fully the need to conceptualise trade union activity in terms of the sources of power, the means of power and the results of power but are unable to offer more than a tentative and rather abstract approach to analysing these. This is no criticism of Purdy and Zis. They have rightly drawn attention to an important *lacuna* in the literature and have made some imaginative suggestions as to how it might be approached but have not, as yet, developed an adequate theory for doing so.

We shall therefore proceed with a general discussion of the main features of the collective bargaining advantage. We note and accept the view that there is a distinction between power and militancy in trade union activity and that this is relevant both to the theory of trade union influence and to the construction of empirical models. The relevance of this distinction will be apparent as we proceed, both in this section and in section 6.2. (The reader should consult Purdy and Zis (1974) for a full discussion of this topic.)

Union influence on non-union wages. One point of importance in any discussion of the impact of union activity on wage inflation is that trade union activity may very well influence the growth of non-union, as well as union, wage rates. For example it seems likely that employers of non-union labour who wish to prevent the unionisation of their labour force will be inclined to ensure that their employees' wages rise at a rate sufficient to prevent the development of a union/non-union wage differential large enough to create a demand for unionisation. Also it is probably the case that when third parties (arbitrators, etc.) are involved in determining non-union wage rates they will be influenced by the development of union wage rates. Hence we cannot measure the impact of union activity in the labour market in terms of the union/non-union wage differential without reservation.

The collective bargaining advantage: information and expertise. Point (a) above (p. 90) refers to the capacity of a trade union to gather and marshal information relevant to a wage demand and to have access to greater skill in utilising this information in the bargaining process than would be available to the individual. This advantage simply derives from the fact that trade unions have greater resources and more specialised bargaining expertise than does the individual.

It is of interest to consider how trade unions might, because of their superior access to and use of information, influence the relative importance of market variables in the wage-determination process as against the influence on these of individuals. Thus we might reasonably expect that trade unions will have access to more accurate and up-to-date information on the profitability of companies, the changes in productivity which are taking place and the behaviour of consumer prices than will the individual. Further, the trade union is, in consequence of its particular expertise in wage bargaining, better able than the individual to identify opportune circumstances for advancing wage claims and to phrase these claims in terms of persuasive economic argument. For example trade unions are probably more conscious of real wage adjustments than are individuals and this will lead them to take greater account of price changes (past, present and expected) than will individuals. It is also likely that trade unions know a good deal more about company profitability and productivity developments than do individuals and are therefore better able to evaluate the strength of employer resistance to wage claims at any point in time. For the individual, knowledge of market circumstances relevant to his ability to improve his wages is likely to be confined to immediate and impressionistic information which will probably be difficult to use effectively in support of a wage claim. Hence it is possible that the statistical significance which has been attributed to variables such as productivity, profitability and price changes in varying degrees and at different points in time may be partly explicable in terms of variations in the strength and emphasis of trade union activity over time. There is some evidence which would support this hypothesis and this will be discussed in section 6.2.

In contrast to the view outlined above there are some who have argued that the collective bargaining advantage is actually negative at some or all levels of excess demand for labour. This argument holds that when wages are being drawn up by market forces the intervention of the trade union, because it must prepare a case for a wage increase and present it through formal procedures, will be involved in time-consuming processes which will prevent it from securing a rate of wage increase as rapid as the market alone would yield. The Friedman version of this hypothesis (case (d)) argues that such an effect will occur at all levels of excess demand while the Meidner and Rehn hypothesis (see Hansen, 1970) restricts the union 'damping' effect to high levels of excess demand only (case (c)). It is rather difficult to find a satisfactory theoretical justification for the damping hypothesis. While it is probably true that trade union negotiated wage rates react more slowly to market forces than non-union wage rates in excess demand situations (because collective bargaining is a periodic and time-consuming process) this simply produces a lagged union wage reaction function. Such a lag in the union response to market forces will not however produce a biased reaction function. Consider the case of a single labour market in which the relation $\dot{W}_{mt} = ae_t$ holds when the labour force is not unionised. Suppose now that a trade union organises the labour force and indulges in the time-consuming process of collective bargaining such that in each time period the rate of wage increase is a reaction to some past level of excess demand, e_{t-1}. The wage equation for the market is now $\dot{W}_{ut} = ae_{t-1}$ and the difference between the market and union rates of wage increase is $\dot{W}_{mt} - \dot{W}_{ut} = a(e_t - e_{t-1})$, which will be consistently positive only when excess demand is a monotonically increasing function of time, a highly unlikely situation. The case for the full or restricted damping hypothesis must therefore rest on grounds other than a trade union induced lag in the wage-adjustment process.

The collective bargaining advantage: strikes versus quits. Point (b) (p. 90) implies that the coercive effects on employers of a threatened or actual strike are greater than those of the threatened or actual quit of an individual. Holt (1971a) has expressed this aspect of the collective bargaining advantage as equal to $\max(S - pQ, 0)$ where S is the ratio of the cost of a strike to the company and the union respectively, Q is the ratio of the cost of a quit to the company and the individual respectively and p is a constant which reflects any difference between the propensity of the union to strike and the individual to quit. Holt argues that the collective bargaining advantage will be greatest at high levels of unemployment, and will decline as unemployment falls. The basic argument in support of this contention is that the quit-cost ratio rises relatively faster than the strike-cost ratio as the labour market tightens. Holt's hypothesis suggests that the union/non-union wage differential will be *negatively* correlated with strike activity. This is because the union/non-union differential will tend to fall as the labour market tightens and the collective bargaining advantage is reduced. In this situation unions will feel 'oppressed' and the narrowing of the differential will '. . . pose a threat to the union as an organization' (1971a, p.89), since all of this is likely to occur against a background of high industrial profits.

We would therefore expect unions to engage in strike activity to a greater extent in times of low unemployment than in times of high unemployment and there is some evidence to support this conclusion (see Mulvey, 1968 and Pencavel, 1970). While there is some empirical evidence to support some of Holt's propositions, the overall hypothesis is, as Holt admits, somewhat speculative.

In contrast to Holt's hypothesis a number of authors have chosen to stress the importance of trade union rank and file militancy in determining the level of strike activity at different levels of unemployment (see for example Ashenfelter *et al.,* 1970; Ashenfelter and Johnson, 1969; Godfrey, 1971). These argue that the level of strike activity will be *positively* correlated with the union/non-union differential. The logic of this argument is simply that trade unions will tend to actually use the strike weapon most frequently when unemployment is low and that this will be *effective* in increasing the union/non-union wage differential. Holt's position is, at least superficially, less plausible since he is forced to the paradoxical conclusion that 'it may be true that when there are the greatest number of strikes, unions are having their smallest effect on wages — the strikes in considerable part are gestures of complaint' (1971a). It is of course possible to conduct tests which can assist in choosing between these two hypotheses and we shall consider these in section 6.2.

While there is an obvious intuitive appeal in viewing strike activity as the principal manifestation of union power and/or militancy it may well be that this is a superficial and therefore partial approach. Purdy and Zis (1974) have argued persuasively that 'cut-price' industrial actions, such as overtime bans, go-slows, withdrawals of co-operation etc., may be equally important forms of trade union sanction. Further, as Purdy and Zis and others have pointed out, strikes vary in frequency, duration and worker involvement; they are seasonally correlated; they often have nothing ostensible to do with wage claims; and they have become, in certain firms and industries, accepted by both sides as inevitable rituals. For these reasons the notion that the incidence of strikes is a clear-cut indicator of trade union power or militancy is unacceptable. As a theoretical approximation to the ultimate economic sanctions which can be employed in wage bargaining, 'strikes' and 'strike threats' (defined broadly enough, e.g. to include 'cut-price' actions) may be useful, but there remain many difficulties in making strikes a measurable indicator of union power or militancy in empirical work.

The collective bargaining advantage: political variables. In his classic study, Ross (1948) advanced the hypothesis that the primary determinants of trade union wage policy were 'political' rather than economic. While not everyone would agree entirely with Ross's proposition there are few who would deny that trade unions respond to political pressures which are more or less independent of the economic environment in formulating and pursuing their wage policies. The kind of political pressures which might influence the behaviour of the trade union derive essentially from its institutional characteristics. Thus the survival of a trade union may depend on its ability to match the economic performance of its rivals; the survival of its leadership may depend on negotiating agreements which are primarily designed to contain factionalism within the union membership; and there may be a positive desire on the part of union leaders to pursue a wage policy which will extend the power of the union or enhance the power of the leadership within the union. Examples of how all of these factors have played a significant role in determining the outcome of wage negotiations are given in Levinson (1966) and Ross (1948). The importance of taking account of the political aspect of trade union power is to emphasise the distinction between the wage policy of the collective as against the individual bargaining unit. Individuals may be expected to bargain on a 'rational' economic basis; trade unions, in so far as they also respond to political pressures, may be found to behave quite irrationally in economic terms. The effects of politically induced 'irrationality' in union behaviour will often involve negotiating agreements which yield lower gain—cost ratios than could have been achieved if political considerations had not intruded, but will nevertheless tend to drive up wage rates more rapidly than would be the case if political pressures had been absent. (The classic example of this situation is where the union incurs massive costs, through strike action etc., in order to secure a very small increase in its members' wage rates. The small increase in wages may however be politically imperative in terms of comparison with the achievements of other unions.) This 'political' aspect of the collective bargaining advantage probably reflects the sources of 'militancy', as distinct from power, to a greater extent than the other aspects.

Some other aspects of bargaining power. In addition to the sources of trade union bargaining power outlined above, mention must be made of certain other specific factors which are also relevant in this regard.

(a) *Concentration ratio*: some authors (e.g. Ross and Goldner, 1950; Bowen, 1960; Segal, 1964) have stressed the importance of the *degree of monopoly* or concentration ratio in the product market as a determinant of trade union power to drive up wage rates. Holt (1971a) phrases this argument in terms of the ease by which firms may pass on increases in labour costs to consumers in the form of higher prices. In general a high concentration ratio will be associated with a low price elasticity of demand and vice versa. We might therefore expect industries with low concentration ratios to be characterised by weak unionism, low profits and low rates of wage increase and those with high concentration ratios to be characterised by strong unionism, high profits and a rapid rate of wage increases.

(b) *The transfer mechanism and wage leadership*: the existence of wage transfer mechanisms has been recognised since Ross (1948) talked of 'orbits of coercive comparison' and Dunlop (1950) of 'wage contours'. Essentially a wage transfer mechanism is created by a tendency for trade unions to pursue wage policies designed to maintain or establish relationships (horizontal and vertical) between the wages of workers in different employments (see chapter 3). The transfer mechanism has been variously described as 'pattern bargaining', 'a demonstration effect', 'a comparison effect', 'comparability effects' and so on, and appears to be a feature, in varying degrees, of the collective bargaining system of most countries. The concept of the transfer mechanism is essentially within the category of political aspects of trade union activity but we are considering it separately since it underpins a distinct hypothesis of trade union impact on wage changes, that of wage leadership. The wage leadership hypothesis concerns the influence of a 'key bargain' on the wage rates of all of the employment sectors embraced by the transfer mechanism. Basically the hypothesis postulates that some particular group of workers will strike a 'key bargain' which will then be imitated by other groups of workers in order to re-establish the *status quo ante* in the relations between the wage rates of the groups involved. The process by which the terms of the key bargain are generalised, the transfer mechanism, is invariably connected either with trade union attachment to notions of horizontal and vertical equity in wage fixing or with situations in which inter-union competition makes it imperative for each union to be seen to perform at least as well as its rivals. This is an essentially political process, leading to upward adjustments of a large number of wage rates in response to some key bargain which may or may not have been struck according to criteria common to the whole employment group embraced by the transfer mechanism. An interesting question here is what determines the key bargain. It may very well be the case that the key bargain reflects the economic circumstances of the particular employment in which it was struck, for example a local excess demand for labour (Mulvey and Trevithick, 1974) or a productivity agreement (Jackson *et al.*, 1972), while its generalisation into other sectors reflects only the institutional or political force of the transfer mechanism. We shall return to this question with some tentative answers in section 6.2. The hypothesis outlined here is one which we have examined (Mulvey and Trevithick, 1974). Alternative versions of the same basic theme have been advanced by others (Seltzer, 1951; Levinson, 1960; Sargan, 1971; Hines, 1971; Brechling, 1972; Phelps Brown, 1971; Eckstein and Wilson, 1962; Thomas and Stoney, 1972).

6.1.ii   Trade unions, wage inflation and the union differential

So far we have discussed some of the factors which might be expected to create a positive union/non-union wage differential. For our purposes it is necessary to consider how that differential will behave over time. Consider the basic wage equation in an economy in which some workers are unionised and others are not:

$$W = (1 - \alpha)W_n + \alpha W_u, \quad \alpha > 0 \text{ and constant} \tag{6.1}$$

where W, W_n and W_u are the average wage rate, average non-union wage rate and average union wage rate respectively and α is the proportion of the labour force earning union wages. Now let the union wage differential be λ so that:

$$W_u = W_n(1 + \lambda), \quad \lambda > 0. \tag{6.2}$$

Substituting equation (6.2) into equation (6.1) gives:

$$W = W_n(1 + \alpha\lambda). \tag{6.3}$$

Differentiating (6.3) with respect to time gives:

$$\dot{W} = \dot{W}_n + \left(\frac{\alpha}{1 + \alpha\lambda}\right)\frac{d\lambda}{dt}. \tag{6.4}$$

Now let us return to the assumption that $\dot{W}_n = aE$, which is the competitive (or non-unionised) market reaction function listed under case (a) on p. 88. We may now rewrite equation (6.4) in the following form:

$$\dot{W} = aE + \left(\frac{\alpha}{1 + \alpha\lambda}\right)\frac{d\lambda}{dt}. \tag{6.5}$$

Similarly if we assume that $\lambda > 0$ and constant and differentiate equation (6.3) with respect to time we obtain:

$$\dot{W} = aE + \left(\frac{\lambda}{1 + \lambda k}\right)\frac{d\alpha}{dt}. \tag{6.6}$$

We may derive certain simple conclusions from these relations about how the rate of wage inflation will respond to change in the union/non-union wage differential and the proportion of the labour force unionised:

(a) when $(d\lambda/dt) > 0$ and α constant, or $(d\alpha/dt) > 0$ and λ constant then $\dot{W} > aE$ and will correspond to case (b) in fig. 6.1;

(b) when λ and $\propto$ are both constant then $\dot{W} = aE$ which corresponds to case (a) in fig. 6.1.

This simply means that there are two routes by which trade unions can introduce an inflationary bias into the adjustment process in the labour market; by increasing the union/non-union wage differential or by increasing the proportion of the labour force in receipt of the union wage. This much is obvious. We must now briefly consider how to interpret these conclusions in terms of the impact of trade union activity in the labour market.

The union/non-union differential. Equation (6.5) tells us that in order that the trade union may bias the market adjustment process in an inflationary manner the union/non-union wage differential must increase over time, i.e. $(d\lambda/dt) > 0$. It is clear that the effect of the collective bargaining advantage could be to widen progressively the union/non-union differential, as a consequence of the application of any aspect of that advantage, and thus bias the market adjustment function in an inflationary way. Direct evidence on the behaviour of the union/non-union differential is confused and contradictory (see for example Ross and Goldner, 1950; Douglas, 1930; Levinson, 1951; Cullen, 1956; Maher, 1965; Garbarino, 1950; Slichter, 1952; Lewis, 1963). What does however tend to emerge from these studies, particularly that of Lewis, is that at different periods of time the union/non-union differential has varied considerably (from 0—5% in the 1940s to 25—40% in the early 1930s in the US, Lewis, 1963) and that it appears in a general way to vary inversely with the level of demand. In a very general way this would tend to support the type of hypothesis listed under (c) in fig. 6.1 and is consistent with Holt's (1971a) hypothesis. This leads us to the question of how to design appropriate empirical tests of the impact of the union on the rate of wage inflation. Essentially what is required to formulate a testable model of the impact of the union on the process of inflation is some measure of trade union 'pushfulness'. As we have already noted the collective bargaining advantage comprises several elements, only some of which are in any sense measurable. For this reason a variety of proxy indicators of trade union militancy have been employed in empirical work, the main ones being:

(a) the proportion of the labour force organised in unions (Vanderkamp, 1966; Pierson, 1968);
(b) strike activity (Ashenfelter *et al.*, 1970; Ashenfelter and Johnson, 1969; Godfrey, 1971; Ward and Zis, 1974; Taylor, 1972);
(c) industry profitability (Bowen, 1960);
(d) concentration ratios (Segal, 1964);
(e) subjective estimate of militancy (Dicks-Mireaux and Dow, 1959);
(f) the rate of change in the proportion unionised (Hines, 1964).

Indicators (b), (e) and (f) purport to be proxies for trade union militancy. Indicators (a), (c) and (d) are more of the nature of circumstances which facilitate the effective exercise of any given degree of militancy, i.e. 'power' variables. Let us then briefly review the empirical evidence on the impact of trade unions in the inflationary process.

6.2 Empirical evidence on the impact of trade unions in wage inflation

6.2.i Percentage unionisation

An intuitively attractive approach to estimating the effect of trade union activity on the rate of change of wages by means of a unionisation variable is to divide labour markets into 'strongly' and 'weakly' organised groups, estimate a Phillips curve for each group and compare the coefficients on the unemployment variables. An early study of this type for the USA by McCaffree (1963) indicated support for hypothesis (c) in fig. 6.1, but subsequent studies for the USA and Canada have obtained results which may be interpreted as support for hypothesis (b) (Vanderkamp, 1966; Pierson, 1968). Pierson (1968) carried out a study of the US manufacturing sector in which she divided the sector into strongly and weakly organised industry groups. She then estimated Phillips curves for each group and observed that the coefficient on the unemployment variable, U^{-1}, was larger for the strongly organised group than for the weakly organised group. This result indicates that the Phillips curve for the strongly organised group is displaced above the curve for the weakly organised group at all levels of unemployment (as curve (b) is displaced above curve (a) in fig. 6.2). A similar type of study has been carried out for Canada by Vanderkamp (1966). Vanderkamp used a simultaneously estimated wage/price equation system, and obtained a larger coefficient on the strongly organised Phillips curve than on the weakly organised Phillips curve. In addition Vanderkamp was able to explain the rate of change of wages better in the strongly organised group than in the weakly organised group:

$$R^2(SO) = 0.89 \quad \text{and} \quad R^2(WO) = 0.52.$$

This type of cross-section study is probably the closest approximation practicable to the ideal test, which would be to compare the location of the micro-Phillips curves in markets which are alike in all respects save that some are unionised and some are not. The Pierson and Vanderkamp studies may however be criticised on the grounds that they assume that the effects of union activity can be distinguished by considering markets differentiated only by relative degrees of organisation (the usual threshold is 40% unionisation); Levinson (1966) would argue that the compared sectors may be distinguished by characteristics which predispose them to have both different wage-change/ unemployment trade-off relations and different degrees of unionisation, such as different entry characteristics. Moreover the findings of Pierson and Vanderkamp conflict with those of McCaffree (1963) which indicated support for hypothesis (c) in fig. 6.1.

It is interesting to note that both the Pierson and Vanderkamp studies revealed that when the rate of change of prices was included as a regressor in the cross-section studies it entered the equation for the strongly unionised sector with a larger coefficient than in the equation for the weakly unionised sector. This finding lends some support to the notion, outlined in section 6.1, that trade unions can ensure a fuller and more rapid reflection of changes in prices in current wage changes than is possible in a non-unionised market. This conclusion also emerges, in a more direct way, from a recent study of the UK by Thomas (1974). The capacity to do this presumably reflects the superior information and expertise advantage of the collective unit over the individual unit in collective bargaining.

Strike activity. In section 6.1 it was noted that there is disagreement between various authors on the relation between strike activity and the behaviour of the union/non-union differential. Holt (1971a) argues that the union/non-union differential will fall as unemployment falls and that strike activity will increase as unemployment falls; hence we would expect an inverse relation between strike activity and the union/non-union differential. In contrast other authors (Ashenfelter *et al.*, 1970; Ashenfelter and Johnson, 1969; Godfrey, 1971) have argued that falling unemployment will be associated with an increasing differential and increasing strike activity. These relations lead one to expect a positive correlation between the differential and strike activity. There is insufficient evidence on the behaviour of the differential over the cycle to discriminate between these two hypotheses but it is certainly the case that most empirical work employing a strike activity variable as a regressor in the wage equation finds a significant positive correlation (Taylor, 1972).

In a recent study Ward and Zis (1974) have tested wage equations employing various strike and other militancy regressors for five European countries. Ward and Zis make it clear that they are highly sceptical about the validity of using strike variables as a proxy for union militancy and their study is designed to examine the extent to which strike variables can explain the international wage inflation of recent years. In order to ensure that the strike variables used are unrestricted by *a priori* hypotheses, strikes are entered as regressors by frequency, days lost, workers involved and as a composite of all three. The countries covered are the UK, Belgium, Netherlands, France, Italy and Germany and the data refer to the period 1956—71. As additional regressors the rate of unemployment is used to proxy excess demand for labour and a price-change variable (lagged by one quarter) is used to proxy price expectations. Only one of the strike variables — strike frequency — turns out to be generally significant, and even it is not significant for all the countries examined. The authors conclude from their results that the trade union militancy hypothesis, as proxied by strike variables, is not substantiated except possibly in Italy and France.

As so often in empirical work of this kind we are left with a series of conflicting results. In part this derives from the differences in model and variable specification, time periods chosen for examination and the country being considered. In addition however the models tested have virtually no theoretical underpinning and are therefore prone to be mis-specified. For example we have seen that there are two, directly contradictory, hypotheses concerning the expected sign on the strike variable. Moreover Ward and Zis introduce their paper by declaring that there are two, directly contradictory, possible lines of causality in the model: union militancy (measured by strikes) may cause wage inflation, or wage inflation may cause strikes. Empirical tests, and crude ones at that, are hardly likely to establish very reliable conclusions when conducted in a theoretical vacuum of the kind described. We must therefore accept that no firm conclusion can be drawn from the evidence reviewed here but note that the great majority of studies employing a strike activity regressor in the wage equation have found it to enter with a significant coefficient.

Industry profits (see also chapter 5). Studies which have employed as regressors in the wage equation the profit level together with some indicator of union activity and the concentration ratio have, for individual industries, proved to have a high degree of explanatory power and the profit variable was normally significant (Ross and Goldner, 1950; Segal, 1964; Bowen, 1960). But since the explanatory power of each of these variables taken by itself is low, it was generally assumed that it was 'the *combined* result of strong union power aided by and functioning within a profitable and concentrated product market environment that together explain the more favourable wage movements' (Levinson, 1966). Levinson however has shown that, by substituting a concept based on the entry characteristics of an industry for the more usual concentration ratio, the profit variable becomes relatively unimportant as an explanatory variable in the industry wage equation for the US. We shall consider Levinson's work next but for the time being remain unconvinced that the bargaining power hypothesis is necessarily the proper interpretation to place on wage equations which incorporate a statistically significant profit variable.

Concentration ratios. The concept of the concentration ratio of an industry relates primarily to the degree of monopoly in the product market. Certain studies have found the concentration ratio to be a significant explanatory variable in the industry wage equation when profits and unionisation are included as regressors (Ross and Goldner, 1950; Bowen, 1960; Segal, 1964). Almost all such studies have used US data. Other authors have disputed the relevance of the concentration ratio, notably Levinson (1966), and have argued a rather more complex case for a relation between market structure and union power. Levinson's hypothesis is simple, emphasising the *entry characteristics* of an industry in place of the more general concept of the degree of monopoly. Thus he says,

> *... To the extent that the structure of the industry facilitates the establishment of new firms outside the union's jurisdiction, the union's ability to maintain control over the labor force in the industry will be gradually eroded and with it, the union's ability to press aggressively for wage increases. Conversely, if the market structure of the industry makes such entry difficult, the union's jurisdictional control,* once established, *is better protected and its power position maintained.*

He further argues that the correlation between wage increases and the concentration ratio simply reflects the fact that the entry characteristics of an industry will be associated with its concentration ratio. His findings lend considerable support to this hypothesis. Whichever is the proper interpretation of the significance of the concentration ratio/ease of entry variable (and we prefer Levinson's interpretation) it is clearly very plausible to conclude from the findings of the studies cited that trade unions do affect the rate of wage inflation according to the structure of the product market. Since, according to Levinson's hypothesis, imperfections in the product market are directly associated with the degree of trade union power in the labour market, we may say that the competitive labour market reaction function does not necessarily describe the adjustment process in markets which are imperfectly competitive in products. While the evidence suggests an upward bias of the reaction function it does not help us to discriminate between cases (b) and (c) in fig. 6.1, only to discount case (d) and to limit strictly the relevance of case (a).

Subjective estimates of trade union militancy. Since any attempt to measure trade union aggressiveness quantitatively is at best a process of rough approximation, certain authors have simply chosen to make subjective judgements as to the degree of trade union militancy which was evident in various periods of time. Such a procedure is open to charges of being unscientific, arbitrary and self-fulfilling. There can however be little doubt that judgements made about the aggressiveness of trade unions, which are necessarily impressionistic but founded on an appraisal of all the available evidence, might very well provide an approximate measure of militancy every bit as accurate as those based on partial and selective measures which claim greater objectivity. Thus Dicks-Mireaux and Dow (1959) constructed an index of trade union militancy consisting of five steps beginning with 'marked restraint' and ending with 'marked pushfulness' and found this variable to have been statistically significant in explaining the rate of change of wages in the UK during the years 1946–56. It is of interest in this context to note that it was necessary to employ a dummy variable to take account of trade union militancy in May 1968 in France in a study of French wage inflation (OECD, 1970). It is easy to take issue with the use of essentially impressionistic and subjective indicators of trade union militancy such as those cited above but, given the vast problems involved in obtaining any precise and objective measure of that elusive quality, there is every reason to regard them as seriously as any other measure and to accept the findings of Dicks-Mireaux and Dow as further evidence of a trade union effect on the rate of wage inflation.

The rate of change of the percentage unionised. In a celebrated article in the *Review of Economic Studies* in 1964 and in some subsequent work, A. G. Hines produced rather spectacular econometric evidence that the rate of change of the percentage unionised was a highly significant explanatory variable in the wage equation for the UK over a long time period but especially in the postwar period (Hines, 1964; 1969; 1971). He hypothesises that this association reflects trade union pushfulness manifest in simultaneous trade union recruitment campaigns and wage demands. Hines' work has been subject to prolonged and vigorous criticism by a number of authors.

The debate has been a curious one. On the one hand most of Hines' critics seem to be inspired by a profound incredulity regarding his hypothesis. It seems to many that it is simply not plausible to hypothesise that trade unions actually initiate recruitment campaigns in order to build up their membership in preparation for negotiations over wage demands. This scepticism is further reinforced by the minute variations which have actually taken place in trade union membership in the UK since the war. On the other hand, Hines' critics have to contend with the fact that the unionisation variable enters almost every equation tested with a highly significant coefficient and appears virtually immune to statistical attack. But it remains the case that a substantial body of literature exists which has as its object the refutation of Hines' work and we must therefore consider it here. It would be inappropriate however to dwell on the detail of this criticism at any length and we may therefore simply and briefly list the main points of criticism.

(a) The statistical validity of the Hines model has been questioned by some authors. Thomas and Stoney (1970) have argued that the model may be mis-specified. Considered as a stochastic difference equation system the model is dynamically explosive and this limits the use of standard significance tests. Purdy and Zis (1973) have redefined the change-in-unionisation variable in order to bring it more closely into line with Hines' own hypothesis, redefined the wage and price variables to make them consistent with each other and re-estimated the equation using annual rather than quarterly data. Their findings reduce the significance of the change-in-unionisation variable but it nevertheless remains significant. Taken together these findings suggest that the statistical significance of the Hines model is less than that claimed by Hines himself, but they do not alter the fact that his change-in-unionisation variable, however defined or measured, remains significant in the wage equation.

(b) The hypothesis underpinning Hines' result has come in for sustained criticism. It may be immediately objected that his findings merely reflect the influence of changes in the proportion of the labour force in receipt of the union wage. Equation (6.6) shows that, if the union/non-union wage differential is positive, an increase in the proportion of workers in receipt of the union wage will raise the average wage. This is an alternative to the Hines hypothesis and is not self-evidently connected with union militancy. A second possibility is that workers will tend to join unions as a defensive measure (to ensure that they are in benefit) when a strike seems likely. In so far as wages do in fact rise in situations where workers are inclined to take such defensive actions, the result will be consistent with Hines' results. Whether the change in unionisation so recorded is a meaningful proxy for trade union militancy or not is hard to say. (Presumably the wage outcome would be the same whether or not workers defensively join the union, so that we are really measuring workers' expectations of militant action, and, if so, surely there are better ways of approximating this effect.) Thirdly, the postulated line of causality in the Hines model is ambiguous. Is it not a more plausible hypothesis than that advanced by Hines to suppose that when trade unions secure increases in wages, *for whatever reason,* the union may attract an increase in its membership? Because data on union membership is available only on an annual basis it is not possible to refute this hypothesis. Fourthly, Burrows and Hitiris (1970) and Godfrey (1971) have argued that variations in the percentage unionised in the UK since the war have been too minute to reflect changes in union pushfulness. This point is slightly dubious in view of the very large absolute increases and decreases in union membership which appear to have occurred in many unions (see Hunter, 1974). Fifthly, Purdy and Zis have devoted a large part of two papers (1973; 1974) to attempts to discredit Hines' model (on the basis of statistical objections and alternative hypotheses of the kind noted above) without a great deal of success. Statistically the Hines result is extraordinarily robust and, since the theory underlying it is so ambiguous, his own hypothesis is not easily knocked out of contention by its competitors. Ultimately it becomes a matter of judgement as to which hypothesis one chooses to accept in the present state of knowledge. We are prepared to speculate that the Hines hypothesis is too implausible to accept and prefer the alternatives which do not rely on any trade union militancy explanation.

Lastly, it is of interest to note that the change-in-unionisation variable has been found statistically significant for the USA (Ashenfelter *et al.,* 1970) but not for the Netherlands (Ward and Zis, 1974), while for Germany it is significant but enters the equation with a negative coefficient (Ward and Zis, 1974). (Data problems preclude tests for most other European countries.)

The transfer mechanism and wage leadership. Trade unions can affect the rate of wage inflation by creating a 'wage transfer mechanism' based on criteria of horizontal and vertical equity in the structure of relative wages. Such a mechanism implies the existence of 'wage leaders' and 'wage followers' in the labour force. Numerous efforts to substantiate this intuitively plausible hypothesis have been made for both the USA and the UK (see Sargan, 1971;

Brechling, 1972; Eckstein and Wilson, 1962; Thomas and Stoney, 1972; Seltzer, 1951; Mulvey and Trevithick, 1974; Jackson *et al.*, 1972; Levinson, 1960). In general these studies have yielded findings which tend to support some type of wage-leadership—transfer-mechanism hypothesis in a wide variety of contexts. In particular Seltzer (1951) and Levinson (1960) have produced convincing evidence of a wage-leadership process in the US steel and automobile industries. Similarly Eckstein and Wilson (1962) have found that, for a group of inter related US heavy industries, including automobiles and steel, wage leadership and 'wage rounds' could be clearly identified. In those studies however the key bargain was always taken as given and its determinants remained unknown. This in itself is not from our point of view an important *lacuna,* since it is the institutional and political phenomenon of the transfer mechanism which supplies the vehicle by which the trade union may influence the rate of wage change independent of the level of demand. It is of interest however to consider what the determinants of the key bargain may be. A local excess demand situation (Mulvey and Trevithick, 1974), a productivity agreement (Jackson *et al.*, 1972), particular aggression on the part of some trade union or some such special circumstances are all possible candidates for the occasion of a key bargain. In a study which we carried out, relating to the Republic of Ireland, it was found that the rate of unemployment amongst a group of skilled manual workers (the rate of unemployment amongst electricians being the proxy) together with a shift dummy (to take account of wage-freeze effects) explained 87% of the variation in the rate of change of average hourly earnings (Mulvey and Trevithick, 1974). This finding lends considerable support to the hypothesis that because excess demand persisted in certain occupational labour markets in Ireland, while excess supply characterised the aggregate labour market, the overall rate of wage inflation was related to the conditions prevailing in the tightest markets through a wage-leadership—transfer-mechanism effect. These findings were, of course, specific to the circumstances of Ireland and may or may not be relevant to the situation in other countries. It is in fact unlikely that a single group or a single cause is persistently involved in a wage-leadership process in most European or North American countries. What appears to be more likely is that at various points of time circumstances will favour the negotiation of a key bargain in some employment sector, and this will be generalised to some, or all, other sectors by way of a transfer mechanism, but the leading sector will vary over time and the circumstances favouring the key bargain will differ in different cases. This is an area of some importance in understanding the internal mechanism by which trade unions influence the inflationary process and much work remains to be done in relation to the phenomenon of wage leadership.

6.3   Conclusions

The empirical evidence we have briefly surveyed in this chapter is a somewhat confusing mixture. The hypotheses tested, the variables employed in the tests and the levels of aggregation vary from study to study, yet each would claim to be a statistical investigation of the impact of trade union activity on the process of wage determination. What then can we conclude from this mixture of findings? Firstly, we may tentatively draw from the evidence presented the broad conclusion that trade union activity does, in certain circumstances at least, appear to introduce an inflationary bias into the labour market. This is a general finding which emerges in some measure from almost all the studies considered, but one which does not deny the possibility that the impact of the union may be negligible or even negative under certain circumstances. For example many studies have found that when the level of labour demand is low (unemployment high) trade unions generally can ensure that wages continue to inflate (or at worst prevent wages from falling) and increase the union/non-union differential (see in particular Lewis, 1963). There is however a genuine doubt as to the effective impact of the union when labour markets are tight (see Thomas, 1974) and there is no way of distinguishing between hypotheses (b) and (c) in fig. 6.1 on the basis of the available evidence. All that we can say is that the evidence is broadly consistent with both hypotheses (b) and (c) and inconsistent with hypotheses (a) and (d).

In addition to this general conclusion we may also say that the evidence suggests that the significance of the price-change variable in the wage equation varies directly with the degree of unionisation and that product market variables, such as entry characteristics and perhaps concentration ratios, affect the degree of influence of trade unions in the labour market. The existence of transfer mechanisms and the impact of key bargains too is evidently another aspect of the impact of the union on the process of wage inflation.

While these conclusions are significant they are of a highly general nature and as a result tell us little about the precise mechanics of the inflationary impact of trade unions. In particular we can know little, from the available evidence, of the nature and effects of the 'militancy' aspect of trade union behaviour. The pure militancy effect might be defined as a subjective quality in trade union activity which, given the values of the objective power variables such as percentage unionisation, influences their impact on the process of wage determination. An extreme example of this effect is the extraordinary upsurge of trade union militancy in France in May 1968. Less extreme examples might be found in UK experience in 1971–72 and in various continental countries in the late 1960s. What appears to have occurred in these instances is that some surge of aggression within the trade union movement developed and was not obviously related to any of the conventional criteria which we commonly suppose determine the power of trade unions. Only subjective measures of trade union militancy such as that employed by Dicks-Mireaux and Dow (1959), and possibly strike variables, get anywhere near taking account of this factor. This is an aspect of trade union behaviour that requires to be researched further, since it has clear relevance for the policy-maker. Further, since this unquantifiable element is barely taken account of in most of the empirical work cited, we may record a reservation as to the significance of the findings of these studies.

CHAPTER 7

Expectations and Inflation

Up to this point, it has been assumed that the trade-off relation between unemployment and inflation would be reasonably stable in both the short run and the long run. A once and for all shift in the relation could indeed occur (due for example to a change in the relationship between unemployment and aggregate demand), but it was considered to be only a temporary nuisance from the point of view of prediction: the theoretical underpinning remained intact.

In contrast an influential school of thought has recently emerged which argues that the introduction of a hypothesis concerning the role of expectations in the process of inflation yields the prediction that the Phillips curve will display a chronic tendency to upward or downward displacement over time if the government tries to maintain a level of unemployment at a rate other than the 'natural' rate. Such a prediction has obvious and crucial implications for economic policy. The belief that it is faced with a stable, inverse relationship between inflation and unemployment will clearly convince a government that it has some considerable room for manoeuvre in deciding upon its preferred combinations of inflation and unemployment. Such freedom of action is denied the authorities if the adherents of the *expectations hypothesis*, who deny the existence of a non-vertical Phillips curve in the long run, are correct.

In this chapter we shall be concerned with three basic issues:

(a) the theoretical arguments for and against the expectations hypothesis;
(b) the empirical evidence in support of competing theories;
(c) in an appendix to this chapter we shall examine the implications for economic policy of a vertical long-run Phillips curve. The reason for the relegation of this topic into an appendix is that the techniques involved in the solution of the optimal policy problem are technically difficult. Important though this topic is to policy-makers, not all readers may be disposed to follow the detailed chain of reasoning.

The analysis will be confined to an examination of the role of expectations in generating inflationary pressure within the context of a *closed* economy. In addition, although the expectations hypothesis has been pioneered by monetarists, a discussion of the precise manner in which demand is manipulated in order to achieve some desired unemployment rate is omitted in the interests of simplicity of exposition. Both of these constraints will be relaxed in chapter 8.

7.1 The expectations hypothesis and the natural unemployment rate

In the first part of this section we shall be concerned with the theoretical underpinning of the expectations hypothesis; we shall concentrate principally upon the work of Friedman. Certain Keynesian objections, raised mainly by Tobin, will be raised in the second part.

7.1.i Friedman on the stability of the long-run trade-off relation

Following upon the initial enthusiasm which greeted the largely empirical work of Phillips (1958), Lipsey (1960) and others, there has arisen a growing scepticism concerning the long-run properties of the trade-off relation $\dot{P} = f(U)$. Long before the crude, closed-economy version of the Phillips curve had been exposed to criticism by the facts of national and international experience it had come under increasing attack on basically theoretical grounds from economists working within a more strictly neoclassical tradition. Many writers (Friedman, 1968; Phelps, 1968; Cagan, 1968) contend that if the authorities attempt to maintain a level of unemployment which does not coincide with the 'natural' unemployment rate then the inevitable outcome will be either accelerating inflation or accelerating deflation.

This concept of the natural rate of unemployment plays a central role in Friedman's assault upon the notion that there exists in the long-run a Phillips curve of the conventional type:

> At any moment of time, there is some level of unemployment which has the property that it is consistent with equilibrium in the structure of real wage rates. . . . The 'natural rate of unemployment', in other words, is the level that would be ground out by the Walrasian system of general equilibrium equations, provided there is imbedded in them the actual structural characteristics of the labor and commodity markets, including market imperfections, stochastic variability in demands and supplies, the cost of gathering information about job vacancies and labor availabilities, the costs of mobility and so on. (Friedman, 1968)

In highly simplified terms, the natural unemployment rate, U^*, can be ragarded as the rate which, once certain realistic modifications are made to the basic model, will be consistent with an *employment* rate N_F in fig. 2.1. To this extent it may be regarded as a *full-employment level of unemployment*. If the demand for labour exceeds N_F, the actual unemployment rate will be below U^* and there will be upward pressure on the real wage rate. Similarly deficient aggregate labour demand will produce an actual unemployment rate in excess of U^* and will put downward pressure upon the real wage rate. Only when the actual and natural rates coincide will the real wage rate clear the labour market. From that point onwards real wages will rise in line with labour productivity.

But does not the foregoing analysis closely resemble the theoretical relationship embodied in the Phillips curve? To this question Friedman gives a resounding No. Whereas Phillips' original contribution to the study of wage inflation was couched entirely in terms of *money* wage rates, Friedman maintains that the central object of study should be the behaviour of *real* wage rates at various levels of unemployment. The Phillips procedure of examining how money wage rates respond to varying levels of aggregate demand may not be too misleading when the *average* rate of change of prices has been negligible over a substantial period of time. On the other hand, where the rate of price inflation has been appreciable over some relevant time horizon, the Phillips exercise loses all meaning.

The logic of Friedman's position will be substantially clarified if we modify the original Phillips relation in which the rate of change of money wages, $\dot{W}$, is the dependent variable and substitute $\dot{P}$, the rate of price inflation, in its place. The Phillips proposition therefore becomes

$$\dot{P} = f(x_1, x_2, \ldots, x_n)$$

where x_is are variables such as the rate of unemployment, the rate of change of import prices, the rate of productivity growth, etc. Simplifying still further we may assume that the $f(\ )$ function possesses only one argument, the unemployment rate, so that we may write

$$\dot{P} = f(U). \tag{7.1}$$

Fundamental to Friedman's objection to the existence of a stable trade-off relation of the type indicated by equation (7.1) is the notion that, for each *anticipated* or *expected* rate of inflation, there corresponds a unique trade-off relation: the higher the expected rate of inflation, $\dot{P}^e$, the further to the north-east will be the trade-off relation. This proposition is illustrated in fig. 7.1 in which three different trade-off relations correspond to three different

Fig. 7.1

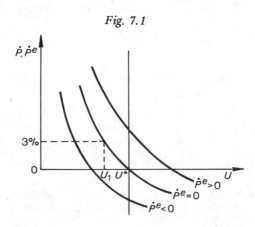

expected rates of inflation. Each curve is an identical copy of all other curves but is displaced in either an upward or a downward direction. For example the highest curve of the three (the one corresponding to a positive expected rate of inflation) is an image of the middle curve (corresponding to zero expected inflation); the vertical distance between the two curves measures the difference between their two expected rates of inflation.

Let us now suppose for the sake of argument that prices have been stable over a long period of time and are generally expected to remain stable. In such circumstances the expected rate of inflation will be zero and the middle curve will be the relevant trade-off relation. If prices are to remain stable, it is clear that the authorities will have to exercise restraint in the use of the monetary and fiscal instruments at their disposal and maintain an unemployment rate U^*. If on the other hand it is assumed that the authorities have a change of heart and decide that the cost of price stability in terms of unemployment is too high, they may use the very same instruments to drive the unemployment rate down to U_1. In the short period the pursuit of such a policy will produce a rate of inflation of, say, 3% which may seem at the time to be an acceptable price to pay for a lower unemployment rate. As prices continue to rise however individuals and groups who have entered into contracts framed in *nominal* terms come to recognise that inflation is depriving them of part of the *real* remuneration which they had anticipated. They will rightly place the blame for such losses upon their failure to anticipate correctly the inflation which had occurred. Gradually people will begin to abandon their erstwhile belief in the stability of prices and will take steps to anticipate future inflation with a view to safeguarding their real living standards.

On the other hand as long as the government persists in maintaining an unemployment rate U_1, such attempts by individuals and groups to anticipate inflation on the basis of their past mistakes can only be self-defeating. Suppose for example that, after assuming that prices would remain stable into the indefinite future, people come to terms with a realised rate of inflation of 3% and begin to adjust all nominal contracts, including wage bargains, accordingly. That is, the expected rate of inflation rises from zero to 3%. In these circumstances the rate of inflation will rise to 6%, for the relevant trade-off relation will be one which corresponds to an expected rate of inflation of 3%. Once again inflation will have been underanticipated by a margin of 3% and once again there will be a tendency to revise expectations in an upward direction. By maintaining an unemployment rate U_1, the authorities will eventually plunge the economy into a headlong decline into hyper-inflation. Only by managing demand in such a way as to maintain unemployment at a level U^* will the authorities be able to prevent any acceleration in the rate of inflation. This unemployment rate is, of course, the 'natural' rate. The upshot of this line of reasoning is that accelerating inflation or deflation can only be avoided by setting the unemployment rate at its 'natural' rate. Inflation can still occur at this rate, depending upon the initial state of price expectations, but it will be taking place at a *constant* rate.

In order to provide a framework for a discussion of the econometric evidence on the expectations hypothesis, it is necessary to translate the preceding verbal analysis into a form more amenable to empirical scrutiny. The existence of a permanent, non-shifting trade-off relation between inflation and unemployment implies the following reduced form relationship:

$$\dot{P} = f(U).$$

On the other hand, the corresponding relationship for the extreme expectations hypothesis is

$$\dot{P} = f(U) + \dot{P}^e. \tag{7.2}$$

Rearranging equation (7.2) will make the expectations hypothesis clearer:

$$\dot{P} - \dot{P}^e = f(U). \tag{7.3}$$

The current rate of inflation can be divided into two parts: that part which is fully anticipated, $\dot{P}^e$; and that part which is unanticipated, $\dot{P} - \dot{P}^e$. The expectations hypothesis states that only *unanticipated* inflation will vary with the unemployment rate. A further implication of this hypothesis is that the only situation in which inflation is fully anticipated is when unemployment is at its natural rate. The natural rate of unemployment may be found very easily (in theory at least): when inflation is fully anticipated, $(\dot{P} - \dot{P}^e) = 0$ so that the natural rate of unemployment is found by evaluating the root of the equation $f(U) = 0$.

But the idea of a *rising* rate of inflation cannot be deduced from the foregoing analysis. It depends upon an assumption, implicit in the verbal account, concerning the formation of expectations. The current expected rate of inflation is supposed to depend systematically upon the actual rates of inflation experienced in the past. Symbolically this may be written

$$\dot{P}_t^e = b(\dot{P}_{t-1}, \dot{P}_{t-2}, \ldots, \dot{P}_{t-n}). \tag{7.4}$$

The exact manner in which the expected rate of inflation depends upon past rates of inflation needs to be spelt out in greater detail. Since expectations are unobservable and unquantifiable in their own right, *a priori* restrictions must be imposed upon the formation of a variable such as $\dot{P}^e$. One convenient and therefore common way of describing the emergence of inflationary expectations is that of *adaptive expectations*. The adaptive expectations model states that the expected rate of inflation in period t is a weighted average of all past rates of inflation. The weights are selected in such a way that greater importance is attached to more recently experienced rates of inflation; more specifically, $\dot{P}_{t-1}, \dot{P}_{t-2}, \dot{P}_{t-3}$ are assigned the respective weights $(1-\psi)$, $\psi(1-\psi)$, $\psi^2(1-\psi)$, etc., where ψ is greater than or equal to zero but less than one; a weighting system which follows this pattern is described as being one of geometrically decreasing weights since the coefficients of the distributed lag equation (7.5) below decline in geometric progression. The adaptive expectations model therefore postulates that expectations are formed according to the following scheme:

$$\dot{P}_t^e = (1 - \psi)\dot{P}_{t-1} + (1 - \psi)\psi\dot{P}_{t-2} + (1 - \psi)\psi^2\dot{P}_{t-3} \qquad (7.5)$$

or

$$\dot{P}_t^e = (1 - \psi) \sum_{j=1}^{\infty} \psi^{j-1}\dot{P}_{t-j}.$$

The assumption that ψ satisfies the property that $0 \leqslant \psi < 1$ is important on two counts. Firstly, it ensures that the expression (7.5) has a finite limit, i.e. that the geometric progression converges. Secondly, it produces the economically meaningful result that the more distant is the rate of inflation, the less is the importance attached to it.

It can be easily verified that the adaptive expectations model described in equation (7.5) is equivalent to the following statement:

$$\dot{P}_t^e - \dot{P}_{t-1}^e = (1 - \psi) (\dot{P}_{t-1} - \dot{P}_{t-1}^e) \qquad (7.6)$$

This description of how expectations evolve is extensively used in the theory of inflation (see, for example, Cagan, 1956, and Solow, 1969) and will be discussed further in section 7.2.

If it can be assumed, as the adaptive expectations model postulates, that the current expected rate of inflation depends systematically upon past rates of inflation and reacts most sensitively to the most recently experienced rates of inflation, then the notion of an acceleration in the rate of price change at unemployment rates other than the natural rate becomes clearer. When the actual rate of inflation exceeds the expected rate of inflation in a given period, as would be the case where the government maintained $U < U^*$, a higher expected rate of inflation will be generated in the subsequent period, leading to a higher *actual* rate of inflation in this period. Since there is no tendency for the unanticipated part of inflation to vanish over time if the government pursues a policy of maintaining unemployment at a level below its natural rate, there will always be a tendency for expectations to be revised upwards in a vain attempt to catch up with the actual rate of inflation. It is this continuous upward revision in the expected rate of inflation which produces the acceleration in the actual rate of inflation. The only situation in which such revision will not occur is when unemployment is at its natural rate.

7.1.ii   Keynesian objections

The fundamental premise which underlies the extreme version of the expectations hypothesis is the contention that the price expectations variable, $\dot{P}^e$, should enter equation (7.2) with a coefficient of unity. Keynesians maintain that this proposition is far from being self-evident either on *a priori* grounds or in the light of the available evidence. If on the other hand it can be demonstrated that the coefficient on $\dot{P}^e$ is significantly less than unity, this will constitute strong evidence in favour of a permanent, non-vertical trade-off relation. For example suppose that the coefficient on $\dot{P}^e$ is ϕ, where ϕ is restricted to the interval $0 \leqslant \phi < 1$. The revised version of equation (7.2) would then read:

$$\dot{P} = f(U) + \phi \dot{P}^e. \tag{7.7}$$

The crucial question which must now be posed is: can inflation be fully anticipated (i.e. $\dot{P} = \dot{P}^e$) over a *range* of unemployment rates? Further manipulation of equation (7.7) will yield an affirmative answer to this question for it can be shown that a permanent, non-vertical trade-off relation will emerge of the type indicated by equation (7.8).

$$\dot{P} = \frac{f(U)}{1 - \phi}. \tag{7.8}$$

Equation (7.8) states that, for an arbitrary unemployment rate selected from within a certain range of values, any divergence between the actual and expected rates of inflation will disappear over time and the eventual rate of inflation will be $f(U)/(1 - \phi)$. Hence it is not only the natural rate of unemployment which is capable of sustaining a constant, fully anticipated rate of inflation: any positive rate of unemployment above a certain minimum value will eventually produce a constant inflation rate (which may, of course, be positive or negative).

The connection between the long-run relation $f(U)/(1 - \phi)$ and the infinite family of short-run trade-offs is depicted in fig. 7.2.

Fig. 7.2

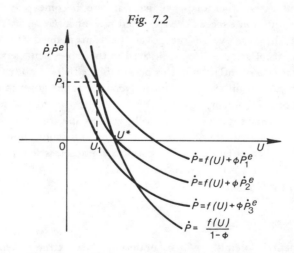

Clearly $\dot{P}_1{}^e > 0$, $\dot{P}_2{}^e = 0$ and $\dot{P}_3{}^e < 0$. Should the government decide to run the economy at some unemployment rate U_1, then eventually the rate of inflation would converge upon $\dot{P}_1$ where inflationary expectations are fulfilled.

But if the above analysis is correct, how are we to interpret a value of ϕ significantly less than unity? The answer lies in the Keynesian nature of the Phillips curve:

> *The Phillips curve idea is in a sense a reincarnation in dynamic guise of the original Keynesian idea of 'money illusion' in the supply of labour. The Phillips curve says that increases in money wages — and more generally, other money incomes — are in some significant degree prized for themselves, even if they do not result in equivalent gains in real income.* (Tobin, 1968)

The ϕ parameter is to be interpreted therefore as the money illusion parameter which was introduced in chapter 2.

Two vital questions of empirical fact remain to be resolved. Firstly, if it can be demonstrated that the expected rate of inflation does in fact depend systematically upon past experienced rates of inflation, what is the speed of reaction of $\dot{P}^e$ to a disequilibrium situation? In the case of adaptive expectations, this amounts to determining the value of ψ. Secondly, what is the value of ϕ? If $\phi = 0$, the original Phillips curve will have been vindicated; if $\phi = 1$, the extreme expectations hypothesis will have been given powerful confirmation; if the intermediate hypothesis is correct and ϕ falls in the interval $0 < \phi < 1$, then it will be valid to deduce that an inverse trade-off relation between inflation and unemployment does indeed exist in the long run, but that it is likely to be considerably steeper than had previously been supposed.

7.2   Empirical evidence on the expectations hypothesis

The central thesis of the Friedman—Phelps analysis is the proposition that $\dot{P}^e$ enters into equation (7.2) with a coefficient of unity. This rests upon the *a priori* conviction that in the long run there is no money illusion and that overall labour market equilibrium is achieved by a gradual convergence of the anticipated real wage rate upon some independent time path determined by the real forces of a market economy. The anticipated real wage rate plays a vital role in allocating labour between different occupations and hence in determining the overall level of employment. Since at any moment in time an upper limit is placed upon the real wage rate by considerations of labour productivity, any divergence between the actual employment rate and the natural employment rate can only be of transitory duration.

An early attempt at testing empirically the Friedman—Phelps expectations hypothesis was undertaken by Brechling (1968). He makes use of the proposition which states that when unemployment is held below its natural rate, inflation will be accelerating; that when unemployment is held at its natural rate, there will be a steady, fully anticipated rate of inflation; and that when unemployment is held above its natural rate, inflation will be decelerating. The advantage of Brechling's test is that it in no way depends upon the manner in which expectations are formed: he is not forced into the position of other researchers who have to assume that expectations are formed according to some scheme such as the adaptive expectations mechanism.

If equation (7.2) is differentiated with respect to time, equation (7.9) is obtained:

$$\frac{d\dot{P}}{dt} = f'(U)\frac{dU}{dt} + \frac{d\dot{P}^e}{dt}. \qquad (7.9)$$

The logic of the expectations hypothesis predicts that $(d\dot{P}^e/dt) > 0$ when $U < U^*$; that $(d\dot{P}^e/dt) = 0$ when $U = U^*$; and that $(d\dot{P}^e/dt) < 0$ when $U > U^*$. Moreover if a hypothetical cycle could be simulated in which unemployment varied cyclically and systematically between an upper bound and lower bound then equation (7.9) would predict that clockwise loops should be observed in the inflation—unemployment plane.

In fact Brechling found that the opposite emerged when the above simulation exercise was performed. *Anticlockwise* loops turned out to be the dominant feature of the model. This squares with many of the early findings on the Phillips curve relation in which, when (dU/dt) was inserted as an additional independent variable, its coefficient tended to be negative, indicating that when unemployment is falling, the rate of inflation will be higher than when it is rising.

Most of the econometric tests of the expectations hypothesis however do not share this reluctance to superimpose an *a priori* scheme upon the formation of expectations. They have in general followed the pioneering work of Solow (1969) in assuming that expectations are formed according to some mechanical rule. In Solow's model the scheme was that of adaptive expectations and its methodology consisted of grafting a time series for $\dot{P}^e$ on to a standard Phillips curve relation and of observing the magnitude of its coefficient ϕ. It will be recalled from section 7.1 that a knowledge of the parameter ψ is necessary before such a series can be generated. In the absence of any independent evidence concerning the speed with which $\dot{P}^e$ is revised in the light of past mistakes, Solow was obliged to construct eleven different series for $\dot{P}^e$ for values of $\psi = 0.0, 0.1, 0.2, \ldots, 1.0$. The exercise then became one of picking out the form of equation (7.10) which proved most satisfactory according to the standard requirements of statistical inference.

$$\dot{P} = f(U), \ldots) + \phi\dot{P}^e(\psi). \qquad (7.10)$$

The best version of equation (7.10) was one in which both ϕ and ψ turned out to be in the region of 0.4, indicating the presence both of substantial money illusion and of a fairly slow speed of reaction of expectations to changes in the actual rate of inflation. These observations led Solow to deduce:

Whatever may be true of Latin-American-size inflations or even smaller perfectly steady inflations, under conditions that really matter — irregular price increases with an order of magnitude of a few percent a year — there is a trade-off between the speed of price increase and the real state of the economy. It is less favourable in the long run than it is at first. It may not be 'permanent'; but it is long enough for me.

In contrast, a similar study by Turnovsky (1972) using Canadian data produced a value of ϕ not significantly different from unity, as did a similar exercise by Saunders and Nobay (1972) who, working on UK data, discovered that ϕ was approximately equal to unity for periods in which prices and incomes policies were not in operation. This latter study introduced a variable which was the ratio of two distributed lag functions to explain the formation of expectations; this bypassed many of the statistical shortcomings of the adaptive expectations mechanism, in particular the danger of *underestimating* the value of ϕ in certain circumstances. Recent work by Parkin, Sumner and Ward (1974) for the UK lends support to this view and indicates that ϕ is probably much nearer to unity than was suspected at first.

Many economists are dissatisfied with the use of distributed lag functions in constructing hypothetical series for variables such as $\dot{P}^e$. Firstly, no matter how general the distributed lag function, there is absolutely no guarantee that expectations are formed in this particular manner. Expectations are highly volatile and just as easily influenced by political events as by past rates of inflation. For example large, highly publicised and hard-fought wage settlements such as followed the British miners' strike in 1973 may play a much more important role in conditioning inflationary expectations than all past experienced rates of inflation. The imposition of rigid, mechanical straightjackets upon $\dot{P}^e$ may be convenient from the point of view of econometric estimation and may occasionally yield plausible results but this is unlikely to tell the full story of how expectations are formed. Secondly, most of the distributed lag approximations to $\dot{P}^e$ are indistinguishable from each other when it comes to their insertion into reduced form econometric regression equations.

These considerations have led economists to experiment with direct data on the state of price expectations. This marks a distinct departure from standard empirical practice, for little confidence has been placed in the past in data derived from questionnaire-type surveys. In particular Carlson and Parkin (1973) have constructed a $\dot{P}^e$ series for the UK based on observations on the percentage of the population who believe it will fall as compared to the percentage who believe it will rise. Using this series they regressed the equation $\dot{P}_t^e = \alpha_0 \dot{P}_{t-1} + \alpha_1 \dot{P}_{t-1}^e$ and found that the adaptive expectations restriction (see equation (7.6)) that $\alpha_0 = (1-\psi)$ and that $\alpha_1 = \psi$ is not rejected. Their most satisfactory hypothesis however turned out to be a *second order* error learning process which had been proposed by Rose (1972):

$$\dot{P}_t^e - \dot{P}_{t-1}^e = (1 - \psi_0)\{\dot{P}_{t-1} - \dot{P}_{t-1}^e\} + (1 - \psi_1)\{\dot{P}_{t-2} - \dot{P}_{t-2}^e\} .$$

The reasonable performance of error learning mechanisms in these studies in which estimates of $\dot{P}^e$ have been arrived at independently has served to restore confidence in their use in econometric studies. Similar results for the United States and Canada have been found by Turnovsky and Wachter (1972) and Turnovsky (1972).

It should be clear by now that there is still a lively debate upon whether the long-run trade-off between inflation and unemployment is vertical or not. If however we were to accept for the sake of argument the Friedman–Phelps contention that $\phi = 1$, what do the empirical studies indicate on the consequent natural unemployment rate? For the UK Parkin, Sumner and Ward (1974) find that it is in the region of 2% while Tobin (1972) quotes a figure for the United States of between 5% and 6%. Regarding the large discrepancy between the values of U^* for the UK and the USA two points should be borne in mind: (a) not only are there measurement differences but there are also considerable differences in the structure of the labour market between the two economies – both of these considerations cast doubt upon the comparability of the estimates; (b) Tobin takes great pains to point out that for the USA the true, full-employment value of U is considerably below the 5–6% figure which results from finding the root of $f(U, \ldots) = 0$ – he cites additional evidence showing that the relevant figure is probably well below 5% although still above the British figure.

Appendix   The expectations hypothesis and economic policy

Writing in the mid-sixties when confidence in a stable Phillips curve was at its peak, Lipsey (1965) proposed the following model in an attempt to show how policy-makers would behave when faced with choosing between the twin evils of inflation and unemployment.

Consider a social utility function in which the level of social utility, μ, varies inversely with both the rate of inflation and the unemployment rate. That is

$$\mu = \mu(\dot{P}, U). \tag{7.11}$$

The problem which policy-makers face is how to maximise equation (7.11) subject to the constraint that $\dot{P} = f(U)$. This is the standard optimisation problem of static equilibrium theory and may be solved by classical maximisation techniques. The outcome of this procedure is illustrated in fig. 7.3. The curves AA' and BB' are just two of the infinite set of concave indifference curves generated by the social utility function $\mu(\dot{P}, U)$. It is evident that those curves situated nearer the origin indicate the enjoyment of a higher level of utility than those situated at a greater distance from the origin. In attempting to reach the indifference curve furthest to the south-west, policy-makers will choose the inflation–unemployment mix $(\dot{P}_{opt}, U_{opt})$.

Fig. 7.3

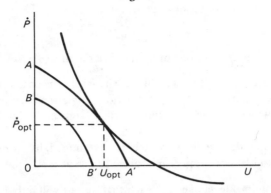

The cardinal assumption of the above analysis is that the constraint remains unaffected by the combination of inflation and unemployment which policy-makers actually select. The choice of a combination ($\dot{P}_{opt}$, U_{opt}) at a particular period of time must in no way prejudice the shape or position of the constraint in any subsequent period. We have seen that it is precisely this assumption which the expectations hypothesis seeks to attack. Unless U_{opt} by some lucky chance turns out to be equal to the natural unemployment rate, the selection of a combination of inflation and unemployment such as the one depicted in fig. 7.3 will serve to shift the constraint in the subsequent period and alter the nature of the problem to be solved. Classical maximisation techniques are unable to cope with problems of this kind so that we must look elsewhere for a solution to the problem.

Fortunately Phelps (1967) has come to grips with the analytical difficulties outlined above by applying certain well known techniques of *intertemporal* optimisation to the problem of finding the optimal inflation–unemployment mix. The remainder of this section will be devoted to an exposition of his model. Subsections (a) to (d) will set out the basic ingredients of the Phelps model; subsection (e) will state the nature of the problem of intertemporal optimisation in terms of these ingredients; and in subsection (f) an attempt will be made at solving this problem and at deriving an optimal rule concerning the utility maximising time path of demand.

(a)   The quasi-Phillips Curve

Phelps starts off with a concept with which we are by now familiar — the Phillips curve — but presents it in a slightly different guise. Instead of concentrating upon the relationship between the rate of change of money wage rates and the unemployment rate, as Phillips and others have done, he focuses attention on the relationship between the rate of change of prices and the level of capacity utilisation, y, the latter being inversely correlated with the unemployment rate. In this form, the strict expectations hypothesis becomes:

$$\dot{P} = g(y) + \dot{P}^e \qquad (7.12)$$

Certain restrictions are imposed upon the variation in $g(y)$:

(i) $g'(y) > 0$, which means that the higher the level of capacity utilisation, the greater is the unanticipated rate of inflation for a given $\dot{P}^e$.

(ii) $g''(y) > 0$, which is the counterpart of a convex Phillips curve where $f''(U) > 0$.

(iii) the upper bound of y is $\bar{y}$, which is determined by considerations of population and labour supply; moreover, $\lim_{y \to \bar{y}} g(y) = \infty$.

(iv) χ is some minimal level of y '. . . such that output will only be large enough to permit production of the programmed investment, leaving no exploited resources for the production of consumption goods'.

The $g(y)$ relationship has another interesting feature: when $\dot{P} = \dot{P}^e$, $g(y) = 0$ and $y = y^*$, i.e. $g(y^*) = 0$; y^* will be recognised as that level of capacity utilisation which will produce a level of unemployment equal to the natural rate of unemployment. These restrictions and properties are illustrated in fig. 7.4. Three hypothetical quasi-Phillips curves are shown in fig. 7.4, each corresponding to a different expected rate of inflation. Curve I corresponds to a positive expected rate of inflation ($\dot{P}_1^e > 0$); curve II corresponds to a zero expected rate of inflation ($\dot{P}_2^e = 0$); and curve III corresponds to a negative expected rate of inflation ($\dot{P}_3^e < 0$).

The statical utility maximising utilisation ratio is $\tilde{y}_1$ when $\dot{P}^e = \dot{P}_1^e$, $\tilde{y}_2$ when $\dot{P}^e = \dot{P}_2^e$ and $\tilde{y}_3$ when $\dot{P}^e = \dot{P}_3^e$. In general the statical optimal utilisation ratio

Fig. 7.4

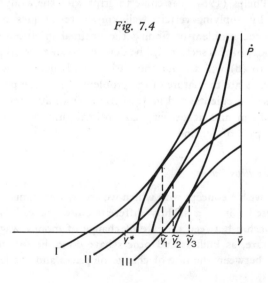

will be a decreasing function of the expected rate of inflation. We shall assume that the initial anticipated rate of inflation, $\dot{P}_0{}^e$, is a datum, so that we may refer to a single statical optimal utilisation ratio $\tilde{y}$.

(b) The adaptive expectations mechanism

We have already encountered this notion in section 7.1 so that little further explanation is necessary, except to rewrite equation (7.6) in continuous form:

$$\frac{d\dot{P}^e}{dt} = a(\dot{P} - \dot{P}^e)$$

$$= a\{[g(y) + \dot{P}^e] - \dot{P}^e\} \quad \text{by equation (7.10)}$$

$$= ag(y)$$

$$= G(y) \tag{7.13}$$

Hence the rate of change of the expected rate of inflation, $(d\dot{P}^e/dt)$, is an increasing function of the utilisation ratio $(G'(y) > 0)$ and the rate of acceleration increases as y increases $(G''(y) > 0)$. Moreover when $y = y^*$, $G(y) = 0$, i.e. when the expected and actual rates of inflation are equal, there is no tendency for individuals to revise their expectations in either direction.

(c) The utility function

At any point of time, utility is assumed to depend upon two variables: (i) the level of capacity utilisation, y, and (ii) the money rate of interest, i. In symbols, this dependence may be written:

$$\mu = \omega(i, y). \tag{7.14}$$

The exact nature of the dependence of μ on y and i needs to be spelt out in greater detail before further analysis of the optimisation can take place.

(i) *The relationship between μ and y.* The fundamental dependence of μ on y is best illustrated by assuming that the money rate of interest does not vary and by constructing fig. 7.5. It is assumed that there are two basic desiderata entering any utility function: consumption and leisure. As y rises towards y^o, consumption rises and undue incursions into the community's leisure time are not made; so that the utility is rising as y rises in this range (in other words the marginal utility of utilisation is positive in this range). As y increases still further however, greater demands will be made upon leisure time. Beyond a certain point, y^o in fig. 7.5, the disutility associated with incursions made upon leisure time by a higher y will outweigh increased utility from higher consumption. To the right of y^o, higher consumption is not worth the sacrifice of leisure required to obtain it.[1] As full capacity is approached, incursions on leisure become intolerable so that as y approaches $\tilde{y}$, the $\omega\,(i,y)_{i=\text{const.}}$ curve tends to minus

Fig. 7.5

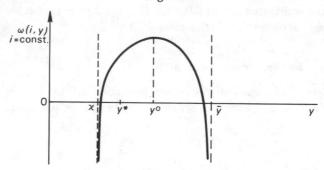

infinity. Similarly as y falls towards χ, the reductions in consumption become more and more alarming so that as y approaches χ, the $\omega(i,y)_{i=\text{const.}}$ curve tends to minus infinity. These assumptions account for the shape of the curve in fig. 7.5.

(*ii*)   *The relationship between μ and* i. We can examine the dependence of μ on i in a similar manner. Assume that the utilisation ratio is constant and examine the variation in μ conssequent upon variation in i (fig. 7.6). If i varies within the range $0 \leqslant i \leqslant \hat{i}$, no diminution in utility will occur as a result of either an increase or a decrease in i. Once i rises beyond a certain interest rate $\hat{i}$ however, further increases in i will bring about a reduction in the level of utility since it will pay to economise on the holding of cash balances by more frequent visits to the bank, etc. Such attempts to economise on the holding of transactions balances will produce disutility for the holder of such balances by reducing his leisure time. As i approaches i_b, which Phelps calls the *barter point*, the monetary system breaks down since the holding of *any* transactions balances becomes prohibitively expensive. If $i \leqslant \hat{i}$, *full liquidity* is said to exist.

Fig. 7.6

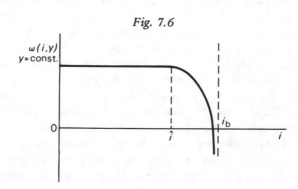

(d)   The real and money rates of interest

The money rate of interest, i, is equal to the real rate of interest, r, plus the expected rate of inflation; i.e. $i = r + \dot{P}^e$. (For further discussion of this relationship the reader is referred to chapter 8.) The real rate of interest is assumed to vary directly with the level of capacity utilisation so that $r = r(y)$. Clearly $r(y) > 0$ and $r'(y) > 0$; a simplifying but not a crucial assumption is that $r''(y) \gtrless 0$. Hence if:

$$i = r(y) + \dot{P}^e,$$

$$\mu = \omega(r(y) + \dot{P}^e, y) = \theta(\dot{P}^e, y) . \tag{7.15}$$

The expected rate of inflation which is just sufficient to permit full liquidity at $i = \hat{\imath}$, given the level of capacity utilisation, is denoted by $\hat{\dot{P}}^e$, where $\hat{\dot{P}}^e$ satisfies the relation $\hat{\imath} = r(y) + \hat{\dot{P}}^e$ for a given y. The greater is y, the smaller the expected rate of inflation which is consistent with full liquidity. We may therefore write $\hat{\dot{P}}^e = \hat{\dot{P}}^e(y)$ where $(d\hat{\dot{P}}^e/dy) < 0$. Of particular interest in subsequent analysis is that value of $\dot{P}^e$ at which there is full liquidity ($i = \hat{\imath}$) *and* equilibrium ($y = y^*$); this value of $\dot{P}^e$ is denoted by $\hat{\dot{P}}^e(y^*)$.

(e)   The nature of the optimisation problem

The dynamic problem to be solved consists of the maximisation of social welfare over time. It involves the determination of an optimal time path for $y(t)$ and hence for $\dot{P}^e(t)$ and $\dot{P}(t)$ also. Social welfare, μ, is the sum of all future utilities from time $t = 0$ onwards. This must be maximised subject to equation (7.13) and the initial condition that $\dot{P}^e(0) = \dot{P}_0^e$ (that is that the initial expected rate of inflation is known). Stated more formally the problem is one of maximising

$$\mu = \int_0^\infty \theta(\dot{P}^e, y) \, dt \tag{7.16}$$

subject to

$$\frac{d\dot{P}^e}{dt} = G(y) \tag{7.13}$$

and

$$\dot{P}^e(0) = \dot{P}_0^e. \tag{7.17}$$

Throughout the remaining analysis we shall assume that the initial expected rate of inflation, $\dot{P}_0^e$, exceeds $\hat{\dot{P}}^e(y^*)$. We shall see later that $\hat{\dot{P}}^e(y^*)$ is the asymptotically optimal expected rate of inflation. In the summary to this section, we shall deal with the situation where $\dot{P}_0^e < \hat{\dot{P}}^e(y^*)$.

(f)   The mathematical solution

First of all the simplifying convention is imposed that the level of utility which corresponds to an expected rate of inflation of $\hat{\dot{P}}^e(y^*)$ and a rate of utilisation of

y^* be set equal to zero, i.e. $\theta(\hat{\dot{P}}^e(y^*), y^*) = 0$. This means that appropriate units of utility measurement are chosen so as to make $\theta(\dot{P}^e(y^*), y^*)$ equal to zero.

Since $(d\dot{P}^e/dt) = G(y)$ and G is a monotonically increasing function of y, we may write $y = G^{-1}(d\dot{P}^e/dt)$. Substituting into equation (7.16) and simplifying the functional notation, the following integral remains to be maximised:

$$\mu = \int_0^\infty V\left(\dot{P}^e, \frac{d\dot{P}^e}{dt}\right) dt = \int_0^\infty V(\dot{P}^e, G)\, dt \qquad (7.18)$$

subject to

$$\dot{P}^e(0) = \dot{P}_0{}^e. \qquad (7.17)$$

This is one of the simplest problems encountered in the calculus of variations and the solution has been well known to economists since the Ramsey–Keynes problem of optimal savings was posed. The necessary condition for a maximum is that

$$V(\dot{P}^e, G) - GV_G(\dot{P}^e, G) = 0 \qquad (7.19)$$

or

$$\frac{V(\dot{P}^e, G)}{G} = V_G(\dot{P}^e, G) \quad \text{where } V_G(\dot{P}^e, G) = \frac{\partial V}{\partial G}$$

This optimal condition must be met at all points in time from $t = 0$ onwards. The value of G which satisfies equation (7.19) at a point in time is the optimal rate of change of the expected rate of inflation and is labelled G_0.

It may be useful to illustrate graphically the $V(\dot{P}^e, G)$ relation. Since we assume that the expected rate of inflation is initially constant at $\dot{P}_0{}^e$, we may invoke the restrictions placed on the utility function $\omega(i,y)$ and deduce that the shape of the $V(\dot{P}_0{}^e, G)$ function is as shown in fig. 7.7.

Suppose now that the expected rate of inflation fell to $\dot{P}_1{}^e$: the level of utility is higher for all G so that the $V(\dot{P}_1{}^e, G)$ curve is higher than the $V(\dot{P}_0{}^e, G)$ curve. This upward drift will continue until the curve reaches its limiting

Fig. 7.7

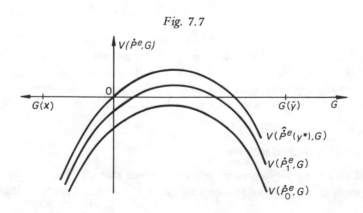

position which coincides with the curve $V(\hat{\dot{P}}^e(y^*),G)$ which, due to our felicitous choice of units, passes through the origin. The curve will cease to drift once $\dot{P}^e = \hat{\dot{P}}^e(y^*)$, since full liquidity will have been reached and no increase in utility will be achieved by a further fall in the expected rate of inflation. We are now in a position to interpret the optimality condition set out in equation (7.19) in terms of fig. 7.8. For any arbitrary point in time, the optimal value of G (and hence of y) is found by drawing a line AO through the origin in such a way that it is tangential to the $V(\dot{P}_0{}^e,G)$ function. Let A' denote the point of tangency. At A' the slope of the $V(\dot{P}_0{}^e,G)$ function, *viz.* $V_G(\dot{P}_0{}^e,G)$, is equal to the slope of the tangent, $V(\dot{P}_0{}^e,G)/G$. This optimality condition is thus satisfied at point A'. It follows that the optimal rate of decrease of the expected rate of inflation is G_0, which is found by drawing a vertical line from A' to the $G(y)$ axis. Noting that the optimal rule at time $t = 0$ requires a negative $G(y)$, we may deduce that initially a government must follow a policy of *under-utilisation* of capacity so as to drive down the expected rate of inflation.

Having located the initially optimal G, we must examine how the optimal value of G changes, if at all, with the passage of time. As we said previously, a decline in the expected rate of inflation will raise μ and shift the $V(\hat{\dot{P}}^e,G)$ curve bodily upwards. The continuing upward drift of this curve to its limiting position $V(\hat{\dot{P}}^e(y^*),G)$ implies that as time passes, the point of tangency will be drifting in a north-easterly direction and will ultimately coincide with the origin. The asymptotically optimal expected rate of inflation is $\hat{\dot{P}}^e(y^*)$, and once this expected rate of inflation is established it will remain optimal forever, since as $t \to \infty$, $G = 0$ becomes the optimal rate of change of the expected rate of inflation.

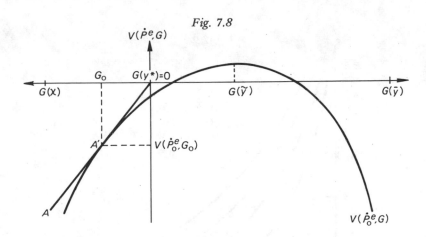

Fig. 7.8

Summary

We have seen how the optimal rule given in equation (7.19) states that, when the initial expected rate of inflation exceeds $\hat{\dot{P}}^e(y^*)$, the government should undertake a policy of under-utilisation of capacity. Following such a policy, the government would have to push the unemployment rate above its natural level, even though (as we have assumed) the statically optimal unemployment rate may be below the natural rate. This is illustrated in the more familiar Phillips curve diagram in fig. 7.9.

The natural rate of unemployment is U^* and the unemployment rate which is *statically* optimal, on the assumption that the expected rate of inflation is $\dot{P}_0{}^e$, is $\tilde{U}$. The optimal rule states that unemployment should be pushed *above* U^* in order to lower the expected rate of inflation and gradually shift the temporary trade-off relation from position I to position II. Moreover once the process of shifting the trade-off relation downwards has been set in motion, demand and employment can be steadily expanded so that in the limit, the unemployment rate will approach U^* and the expected rate of inflation will fall to $\hat{\dot{P}}{}^e(y^*)$.

It will also be noted that, starting with an excessively high expected rate of inflation, a *unique* expected rate of inflation is optimal in the limit, viz. $\hat{\dot{P}}(y^*)$. This conclusion does not square with the static approach set out in fig. 7.3 in which, depending upon the initial value of $\dot{P}^e$, a *variety* of inflation rates will yield an optimum.

When it comes to handling the situation in which the initial expected rate of inflation (e.g. $\dot{P}_1{}^e$ in fig. 7.9) falls short of the asymptotically optimal rate, new problems arise. Phelps shows that no optimal rule exists for this case unless additional assumptions are made. One assumption which sorts out this difficulty also happens to be economically very appealing and this is the assumption of positive utility discounting. It can be shown that, with positive discounting of utility, the *long-run equilibrium* expected rate of inflation, $\dot{P}_E{}^e$, always exceeds the no-discount optimum, $\hat{\dot{P}}{}^e(y^*)$, irrespective of the initial value of $\dot{P}^e$. Of

Fig. 7.9

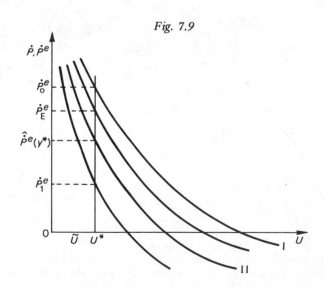

greater interest however is the nature of the optimal time path for U (or $\dot{P}^e$) when initially $\dot{P}^e = \dot{P}_1{}^e$ and when there is positive time discounting. Phelps shows that in this case the optimal policy is one of *over-utilisation* of capacity: the optimal rule requires that $\dot{P}^e$ be driven towards $\dot{P}_E{}^e$ by a policy of maintaining U below U^* (in the limit, of course, U will have to approach U^*).

Note to chapter 7

1. The existence of *involuntary* unemployment implies that the equilibrium utilisation level, y^* will not coincide with y^o. In the diagram it is assumed that $y^* < y^o$.

CHAPTER 8

Monetarists and Inflation

Up to this point we have assumed exogenous variations in the pressure of demand and in the unemployment rate without committing the analysis to any particular explanation of the forces which have operated to produce such variations. The traditional approach of macroeconomics text-books is to assume that fiscal measures are by far the most effective means of controlling the level of economic activity. Monetarists, on the other hand, reject this assertion. It is a central tenet of the modern monetarist position that, in the medium and longer runs at least, variations in nominal income are best explained, not by variations in the level of 'autonomous' expenditure which serve to shift the IS curve, but by variations in the rate of monetary expansion. The consequent displacement in the position of the LM curve will have important implications for the behaviour of other variables such as the price level and the level of real income.

In section 8.1 we shall trace the revival of the quantity theory of money which took place under the careful guidance of Milton Friedman and other economists working in the Chicago tradition. In particular we shall lay some emphasis upon the transmission mechanism whereby monetary impulses generate reaction in other sectors of the economy. Section 8.2 will be devoted to the recently formulated theory of nominal income and to an examination of the short-run dynamics of a monetarist model. The evidence indicating the relationship between money and other variables will be briefly surveyed in section 8.3. Finally in section 8.4 we shall examine some attempts to extend the scope of the monetarist model to take account of the recent upsurge in the rate of *worldwide* inflation.

8.1 The modern Quantity Theory of Money and the portfolio balance transmission mechanism

8.1.i What is a quantity theorist?

At the highest level of generality a quantity theorist is one who subscribes to both of the following propositions:

(i) that the demand for money is a stable function of a finite number of variables. The choice of arguments for the demand for money function will depend, of course, both upon personal taste and upon the level of sophistication of the analysis. What matters is that all quantity theorists have *some* stable demand function for money as the cornerstone for macro-analysis.

(ii) that the factors affecting the supply of nominal money balances can validly be separated from those which determine the demand for such balances. This amounts to saying that, although certain factors may determine the supply of money, these factors are not identical to those which determine its demand.

If the two characteristics mentioned above are held in common by *all* quantity theorists, the *majority* of them tend to proceed to make certain observations concerning the adjustment process in which the supply and demand for money are brought into equilibrium. In particular they would maintain:

(iii) that money income will be affected in both the short and the long runs by prior variations in the money supply. Now money income, Y, is the product of real income, X, and the price level, P. If a change in M produces a change in Y, how is the latter change divided between price and output variations? Most quantity theorists would subscribe to the view that the change in M will have an initial impact on X but this effect would be regarded as transitory (except in a situation of chronic under-employment equilibrium where an increase in the money stock could increase the level of output permanently). Quantity theorists have tended to assume that X (and the rate of growth of X) is determined by factors such as population growth and technical progress. In the longer period, a change in the supply of money will affect prices alone.

(iv) that the velocity of circulation of money may change either on account of short-period adjustment frictions or in response to longer-run developments in the economic system. As an example of the latter effect, Fisher (1920) long ago recognised that interest rate changes and the expectation of changing price levels would tend to produce variations in the velocity of circulation of money. The crucial point to bear in mind is that a quantity theorist, while recognising that the velocity of circulation of money may vary along with changes in economic circumstances, insists that such variations are predictable from the form of the demand for money function. More importantly he asserts that a stable velocity of circulation of money function is a useful *predictive* device, enabling the economic planner to forecast variations in important economic variables. This stands in marked contrast to the Keynesian position outlined below.

8.1.ii   Friedman on the demand for money

We have seen from chapter 2 that the Cambridge cash-balance equation for the demand for money $M=kPX$ came in for much criticism for being overly mechanistic: instead of treating k as a catch-all variable designed to pick up the effects of other, less significant variables which have been omitted from the analysis for the sake of brevity, the Cambridge k tended to be treated as a *numerical constant*. The gauntlet thrown down by Keynes in his treatment of the determinants of the demand for money was taken up by Friedman (1956) who provided the most elegant statement to date of the quantity theory approach to the demand for money which incorporates many features commonly thought of as Keynesian.

Friedman starts by asking the question: how will ultimate wealth-holders divide their asset portfolios in order to maximise utility? Since money is one of the assets that a wealth-holder may wish to include in his portfolio, an examination of the factors which determine the demand for money plants the quantity theory of money firmly in the soil of capital theory.

The demand for money will be influenced by the following variables:

(a) the volume of total wealth. A true measure of wealth would have to include a human capital component. Alternatively, since it is plausible to assume that substitution of capital between its human and non-human forms takes time, an estimate of the fraction of total wealth that is in the form of human capital would be useful. Let x denote this fraction. Moreover let Y_p, permanent income, stand as a surrogate for the total wealth variable.

(b) the expected rates of return on money and other assets. We may be more specific and restrict the range of assets to three: money, fixed-interest securities and equities. Their expected rates of return will be i_m, i_b and i_e respectively where each return variable includes the expected change in the prices of the assets.

(c) the expected rate of change of the prices of goods and services, $\dot{P}^e$.

(d) other less significant variables which are denoted by a portmanteau vector **u**.
    The resulting demand for money function is thus:

$$\frac{M_d}{P} = M(Y_p, x; i_m, i_b, i_e, \dot{P}^e; u) \tag{8.1}$$

Even in this elaborate guise, however, the quantity theory is simply a statement of the possible factors which may influence the demand for money. It cannot be regarded as a theory of prices or nominal income until a supply of money function has been specified. Once this breach has been filled the analysis is free to proceed to a detailed scrutiny of the repercussions of independent monetary disturbances using the methods of Marshallian supply and demand analysis. The simplest and most frequently invoked assumption is that the supply of money is exogenously determined by factors which fall outside the scope of the model so that $M_s = \bar{M}$ or $\dot{M}_s = \dot{\bar{M}}$ where the 'bar' symbol indicates that the determination of a variable is exogenous to the system.

8.1.iii Keynesians, Monetarists and the portfolio balance transmission mechanism

> [The] essential difference between the situation as it appears to the individual, who can determine his own cash balances but must take prices and money income as beyond his control, and the situation as it appears to all individuals together, whose total cash balances are outside their control but who can determine prices and money income, is perhaps the most important proposition in monetary theory. (Friedman, 1959)

Why do Keynesians demur at this eminently reasonable proposition? Why do they downgrade monetary policy in favour of alternative fiscal measures? In order to provide an answer to these questions, it may be useful to recapitulate the arguments against the quantity theory which were raised in chapter 2.

Under conditions of under-employment equilibrium, Keynes asserted that the velocity of circulation of money would be highly unstable and that its variation would be largely unpredictable. This is on account of the fact that if an economy is hovering just above a position of absolute liquidity preference, even large increases in the supply of money will fail to persuade wealth-holders to purchase other assets in exchange for money and hence will fail to drive down their rates of return. In other words the *LM* function will be more or less horizontal. The private sector behaves like an insatiable sponge, absorbing increasing quantities of nominal balances whenever more money is made available. This leads to the inevitable conclusion that a change in income produced, for example, by an expansive fiscal policy, will fail to alter the total holding of *real* balances. An increase in income will simply increase the transactions and precautionary demand for money at the expense of the speculative demand for money. Similarly an increase in the supply of money brought about by an expansive monetary policy will have no impact on the level of income, the effect of such a policy merely being to swell the holding of speculative balances. In both cases the model predicts supine variations in k and V.

A second line of argument dispenses with the assumption of absolute liquidity preference and allows for some degree of variation in the long-term rate of interest (i.e. the rate of interest on bonds). This variant on the Keynesian model however asserts that autonomous expenditure is highly insensitive to variations in interest rates so that even if monetary policy succeeded in affecting the rate of interest, its impact on the level of final expenditure would be minimal. The logic of this approach is to regard money and bonds as close substitutes for each other but to regard *neither* as being a substitute for real assets.

Fortunately over the past few years some measure of agreement has been struck between neo-Keynesians and monetarists on the appropriate way of tackling the detection of complex monetary influences on the real economy. Neo-Keynesians in general have abandoned the above two objections to the quantity theory in favour of a more sophisticated transmission mechanism which has come to be known as the principle of *portfolio balance*. This principle states that an increase in the supply of money will induce wealth-holders to substitute other assets for money in their wealth portfolios. Such attempted substitution will drive down the real yields on existing non-money assets by bidding up their prices. This process will work its way through a wide variety of markets for financial and real assets, leading for example to a rise in the price of equities and a fall in the yield on equities (this effect is particularly important in the work of Tobin and other neo-Keynesians of the Yale School).

According to neo-Keynesians, the all-important impact of an expansionist monetary policy occurs in the market for equities and similar securities. A rise in the market valuation of a company's stock of existing capital goods will stimulate further equity issue producing a concomitant rise in the level of real investment. 'On this reasoning,' writes Park (1972), 'the stock market plays a significant role in influencing economic activity, and indeed changes in the Dow-Jones averages give some measure of the stance of monetary policy.'

Monetarists adhere to the same simple mechanism but would insist that attention be focused not only upon equities but upon a wide variety of additional assets. Moreover the mechanism is more direct in that changes in spending are not the result of the higher level of investment influencing, via the multiplier, the level of money national income; the portfolio substitution process will directly stimulate spending upon items not normally considered to be assets at all. Friedman (1972) writes:

> The major difference between us and the Keynesians is less in the nature of the process [of portfolio substitution] than in the range of assets considered. The Keynesians tend to concentrate on a narrow range of marketable assets and recorded interest rates. We insist that a far wider range of assets and interest rates must be taken into account — such assets as durable and semi-durable consumer goods, structures and other real property. As a result, we regard the market rates stressed by the Keynesians as only a small part of the total spectrum of rates that are relevant . . .

Writing of the apparent strangeness of the monetarist approach, he continues:

> After all, it is most unusual to quote houses, automobiles, let alone furniture, household appliances, clothes and so on, in terms of the 'interest rate' implicit in their sales and rental prices. Hence the prices of these items continued to be regarded as an institutional datum, which forced the transmission process to go through an extremely narrow channel.

An additional source of contention between monetarists and neo-Keynesians has been the empirical methodology appropriate to econometric models which attempt to isolate the independent effect of monetary policy upon the level of economic activity. Monetarists tend to emphasise the extreme complexity of the interaction among monetary variables, real rates of return and aggregate expenditure. Conventional multi-equation econometric models (preferred by the

Yale School) cannot hope, they say, to capture the many and devious ways in which monetary variables affect a wide variety of other variables so that the simplest solution is to adopt a methodology which concentrates upon the relation between something large (such as money national income) and something not so large (such as the supply of money). This approach leads to a preference for reduced-form equations or very simple simultaneous systems.

This in essence is the methodology implicit in the econometric models which have proliferated in the last few years. Their object is to estimate the relative impact of changes in fiscal variables and changes in monetary variables upon the level or rate of growth of GNP (many examples of this line of inquiry can be found in the various issues of the *Federal Reserve Bank of St Louis Review*). Yale theorists, on the other hand, express grave dissatisfaction with this approach, settling instead for complex multi-equation estimation of structural relationships. Although any sort of generalisation in this area is fraught with danger, the results of the reduced-form approach have tended to attach much greater importance to monetary rather than fiscal variables while the multi-equation approach has tended to come to the opposite conclusion.

8.2 Money and prices: the theory of nominal income

The picture which was presented in the discussion of the expectations hypothesis in chapter 7 was one in which the economy is seen to be poised on a knife-edge between chronic inflation on the one side and chronic deflation on the other. Any attempt by the authorities either to over-utilise capacity (maintain $U < U^*$) or to under-utilise capacity (maintain $U > U^*$) will produce these dire consequences. The only safe road to take is the one along which capacity is being utilised at its equilibrium rate (i.e. where $U = U^*$) at each point in time after an initial period of adjustment during which, depending upon the initial value of the expected rate of inflation, a government may be forced to depress demand (when $\dot{P}_0{}^e > \hat{P}^e(y^*)$) or may be free to maintain a fairly buoyant level of activity (when $\dot{P}_0{}^e < \hat{P}^e(y^*)$). The only problem is that the government is not in a position to know what the equilibrium rate of capacity utilisation actually is. Does it correspond to an unemployment rate of 2%, 2¼% (as Professor Paish has argued) or 5%? No one, not even the most accomplished econometrician, can really know the answer.

Except, that is, for the market. It is a central premise of the modern quantity theory approach to the question of price determination that, given a stable monetary background and left to operate unimpeded by such nuisances as interventionist fiscal policies, the market will in the long run generate *automatically* the equilibrium rate of capacity utilisation. No matter what the initial position, be it one of over-utilisation or under-utilisation of capacity, an efficiently working market economy will eventually check any tendency to accelerating inflation or accelerating deflation.

The question which now must be answered is: what assumptions need to be made concerning the role of the monetary authorities if these dire prognostications of knife-edge instability are fulfilled? In particular how would the economy react to a policy in which the rate of monetary expansion were to be stabilised at some constant rate? As it stands, the quantity theory outlined in section 8.1 is ill-suited to providing answers to these questions. In section 8.2.i we shall examine a recent attempt by Friedman (1970 and 1971) to extend and transform the quantity theory from a theory of the demand for money into a fully fledged theory of prices and money income. Several untidy loose ends remain however, the most important being the age-old problem of how increases in the supply of money are divided between price and output increases. Friedman's approach to this hairy problem is discussed briefly in section 8.2.ii.

### 8.2.i	*The theory of nominal income*

The demand for nominal money balances, M_d, depends (a) upon the opportunity cost of holding money, taken to be the nominal rate of interest, i, and (b) upon the level of money income, Y. This dual dependence is expressed in the following form of the traditional Cambridge equation:

$$M_d = k(i)\, Y \tag{8.2}$$

where $k(i)$ is the desired money/money income ratio, varying inversely with the nominal interest rate.

The supply of money, M_s, is assumed to be determined exogenously by the monetary authorities. It is assumed moreover that the demand for money is continually equal to the supply of money so that M_s and M_d may be represented by the common symbol M. Bearing this in mind, equation (8.2) may be rewritten in the following manner:

$$Y = \frac{1}{k(i)} M = V(i)\, M \tag{8.3}$$

where $V(i)$ is the income velocity of circulation function. Taking proportional time derivatives of equation (8.3) produces the following equation:

$$\dot{Y} = \frac{V'(i)\, di}{V(i)\, dt} + \dot{M}. \tag{8.4}$$

The determination of di/dt is relatively straightforward. The nominal rate of interest is by definition equal to the real rate of interest, r, plus the rate of inflation, $\dot{P}$. In particular the *anticipated* money interest rate, i^*, will be equal to the anticipated real interest rate, r^*, plus the expected rate of inflation i.e. $i^* = r^* + \dot{P}^e$. To this Fisherine concept Friedman adds what he calls the 'Keynesian' assumption that the actual market interest rate will be determined by the firmly held expectations of market speculators: the rate of interest will be what it is expected to be so that $i = i^*$ at each point in time. The final assumption is that r^*, the anticipated real interest rate, is constant, presumably determined by such factors as the marginal productivity of investment. It clearly follows therefore that di/dt will be equal to $d\dot{P}^e/dt$, the rate of change of the expected rate of inflation. By invoking the adaptive expectations mechanism in which

$$\frac{d\dot{P}^e}{dt} = \beta(\dot{P} - \dot{P}^e),$$

equation (8.5) is obtained:

$$\dot{Y} = \frac{V'(i)}{V(i)} \beta(\dot{P} - \dot{P}^e) + \dot{M} \tag{8.5}$$

or

$$\left(\frac{\dot{Y}}{M}\right) = \frac{V'(i)}{V(i)} \beta(\dot{P} - \dot{P}^e). \tag{8.6}$$

Suppose the economy is initially operating at a non-equilibrium rate of capacity utilisation (i.e. $\dot{P} - \dot{P}^e \neq 0$). It is a necessary condition for convergence on a new position of monetary equilibrium that the right hand side of equation (8.6) should vanish in the limit. A necessary condition for stability is therefore that

$$\frac{V'(i)}{V(i)} \beta < 1.$$

If this condition is not met then the accelerating inflationary process will be self-financing in the sense that sufficient fuel for a higher rate of inflation will always be forthcoming, not from increases in the rate of monetary expansion, but from the continual depletion of desired real balances. (Once again the same argument applies *mutatis mutandis* to a deflationary process.)

On the plausible assumption that

$$\frac{V'(i)}{V(i)} \beta < 1,$$

therefore, a fairly clear picture of the monetarist position emerges. For a constant rate of monetary expansion, the economy will eventually converge upon a situation in which $\dot{Y}$ will equal $\dot{M}$ and in which the rate of unanticipated inflation, $\dot{P} - \dot{P}^e$, falls to zero. That is to say, the unemployment rate will converge upon the natural unemployment rate.

It will be useful for the subsequent discussion of the short-run dynamics of the monetarist model if we go into greater detail as to the long-run division of $\dot{Y}$ between inflation and real-income growth. By definition $\dot{Y} = \dot{P} + \dot{X}$. Consider a further identity: $X = (X/X^*) X^*$. The X/X^* term is a measure of the degree of capacity utilisation (similar to y in chapter 7). It compares the actual level of utilisation, X, to some hypothetical level, X^*. If we now assume that when

$X = X^*$ capacity is running at its equilibrium level, then a value of unity for (X/X^*) will indicate that the unemployment rate is at its natural level.

Returning to the identity for the rate of growth of nominal income, it follows from what has just been said that

$$\dot{Y} = \dot{P} + \left(\frac{\dot{X}}{X^*}\right) + \dot{X}^*.$$

That is, the rate of change of nominal income is equal to the sum of the rate of inflation, the rate of change of the rate of capacity utilisation and the equilibrium rate of growth of capacity. But it has already been established that the economy will eventually converge upon the equilibrium rate of capacity utilisation so that in the limit, $(\dot{X}/X^*) = 0$. The rate of growth of nominal income will be exclusively divided between the rate of inflation (which will eventually be fully anticipated) and the equilibrium rate of growth of capacity, $\dot{X}^*$.

8.2.ii *The short-run dynamics of price and output determination*

The theory of nominal income outlined above is clearly long-run in character. An increase in the rate of monetary expansion will be manifest in a higher rate of inflation and in nothing else. While insisting that variations in the rate of monetary expansion only affect nominal variables in the long run, Friedman, in common with most quantity theorists from Hume onwards, is prepared to admit that such variations will affect real variables such as the levels and rates of growth of output and employment in the short run. Apart from the rudimentary model outlined above, one of the few references to short-run dynamics in monetarist models is contained in Friedman's article (1970) in which he proposes the following equations as approximate descriptions of the short-run behaviour of prices and output in response to an exogenous change in the rate of monetary expansion:

$$\dot{P} = \dot{P}^e + \frac{\alpha}{1-\alpha}(\dot{X} - \dot{X}^*) + \frac{\delta}{1-\alpha}\log\left(\frac{X}{X^*}\right) \tag{8.7}$$

$$\dot{X} = \dot{X}^* + \frac{1-\alpha}{\alpha}(\dot{P} - \dot{P}^e) - \frac{\delta}{\alpha}\log\left(\frac{X}{X^*}\right) \tag{8.8}$$

The crucial parameter is α which indicates the proportion by which a deviation in the rate of growth of Y from its anticipated growth path will be manifested in price changes; by definition $(1 - \alpha)$ is the proportion by which such a deviation will be manifested in output changes.

Professor Tobin (1972) has pointed out that equation (8.7) may be rewritten in the following way:

$$\dot{P} - \dot{P}^e = \lambda_0 \dot{U} + \lambda_1 (U - U^*) \tag{8.9}$$

where $\dot{U}$ is the rate of change of unemployment (correlated with $(\dot{X} - \dot{X}^*)$) and $(U - U^*)$ is the deviation of the actual from the natural unemployment rate (correlated with (X/X^*)). If $\dot{U} = 0$ we are left with a modified expression for the standard trade-off relation.

Two features of the above model are worthy of note. Firstly, although an increase in the rate of monetary expansion will produce a higher rate of inflation in the long period, the process of adjustment will not be one of smooth convergence but will entail complex cyclical variations in nominal income along its new trend growth path. The virtual certainty of an oscillatory adjustment process being generated (a process which Friedman assumes to be convergent) will render the interpretation of estimated equations relating $\dot{M}$ to $\dot{Y}$ a hazardous exercise. In particular econometric equations which rely exclusively on short-period data will probably fail to pick up the full causal relationship between the rate of growth of the money stock and the rate of growth of nominal income. (For a more detailed analysis of the cyclical motion of this system, see Laidler, 1972 and Friedman, 1970.) Secondly, considering the thirty-five years which elapsed between the *General Theory* and the theory of nominal income, the mechanism whereby the system adjusts to an unanticipated change in the money stock is not too dissimilar in both models. Admittedly Keynes was less concerned with the possible cyclical properties of his model. Moreover he tended to adhere to the simplifying assumption that the full-employment level of output and capacity utilisation could not be exceeded in physical terms. Notwithstanding these and other points of difference, however, chapters 20 and 21 of the *General Theory* and the later monetarist models of disequilibrium adjustment bear a considerable resemblance to each other.

Finally a word on the empirical evidence on the division of monetary impulses between price and output variations. No firm conclusions can be drawn on this question although several commentators have, on the basis of econometric studies, hazarded inspired guesses at the relative impact of such a change over time. For the UK, A. A. Walters (1971 and 1973) has estimated that a change in the rate of monetary expansion will affect the rate of growth of real output after about a nine-month lag and upon the rate of inflation after a two-year lag. A successful anti-inflation policy which relies on a reduction in the rate of monetary expansion will therefore have little perceptible impact for about two years and even then '. . . the effects are worked out slowly over the following two or three years' (Walters, 1973). Evidence for the United States provided by the *Federal Reserve Bank of St Louis Review* indicates the presence of lags in adjustment of similar length. Recent empirical work by Friedman (1969) has tended to corroborate this time profile.

8.3 Money and inflation: some indicative evidence

The three subsections of this section will be devoted to an examination of the relation between monetary expansion and inflation in three different species of inflation. In descending order of gravity they are:

(i)   Hyper-inflation
(ii) Inflations of Latin American proportions.
(iii) Moderate inflations.

8.3.i *Hyper-inflation*

The most celebrated analysis of the dynamics of hyper-inflation is contained in
the work of P. Cagan (1956). Cagan examined the behaviour of seven European
countries which had been subject to severe hyper-inflation, and concentrated
particularly upon the monetary factors which initiated and exacerbated the
hyper-inflationary process in each country. Central to his model is an equation
linking the demand for real balances to the expected rate of inflation. Since
'... the cost of holding money ... during hyperinflation is for all practical
purposes the rate of depreciation in the real value of money or, equivalently the
rate of rise in prices ...', Cagan argues that expectations of inflation will
influence the demand for real cash balances according to the following log-linear
scheme:

$$\frac{M}{P} = e^{k(\dot{P}e) + \gamma}; \ k'(\dot{P}^e) > 0$$

or

$$\log \frac{M}{P} = k(\dot{P}^e) + \gamma. \tag{8.10}$$

Equation (8.10) states that the higher the expected rate of inflation, the
higher is the cost of holding money and the lower is the demand for real
balances. The elasticity of demand for real cash balances with respect to the
expected rate of change of prices is

$$| \ \eta_d \ | = \frac{\dot{P}^e \, d(M/P)}{(M/P) d\dot{P}^e} = k(\dot{P}^e)\dot{P}^e \tag{8.11}$$

which implies that the elasticity of demand for real cash balances is an increasing
function of the expected rate of increase in prices.

In order to generate an observable series for the expected rate of inflation,
Cagan assumed that expectations were formed according to the adaptive
expectations mechanism whereby

$$\dot{P}_t^{\,e} = (1 - \psi) \sum_{j=1}^{\infty} \psi^{j-1}\dot{P}_{t-j}. \tag{8.12}$$

Having incorporated the adaptive expectations hypothesis into equation
(8.10) Cagan ran regressions of the equation for each of the countries. In general
equation (8.10) yielded good approximations of the demand functions for real
balances. The hypothesis that $|\eta_d|$ increased as $\dot{P}^e$ rose was confirmed. It will be

recalled from equation (8.6) that price increases would be self-generating if

$$\frac{k'(i)}{k(i)} \beta > 1,$$

for in this case a rise in prices will produce a *proportionately greater* decline in real cash balances. In fact, for the seven hyper-inflation studies by Cagan, $\beta\{[k'(i)]/[k(i)]\}$ never reached this critical value so that the hyper-inflationary process was convergent and could have been halted at any time by a curtailment in the rate of expansion of the money supply. Moreover Cagan found that the weighting pattern indicated by equation (8.12) tended to become biased in favour of more recently experienced rates of inflation as prices rose at an ever increasing rate. That is, ψ becomes smaller and smaller indicating that the lag in adjustment of actual to expected inflation tends to shorten as inflation continues.

8.3.ii *Latin American inflations*

In recent times the phenomenon of rapid inflation has come to be associated principally with the economies of Latin America. Whereas the hyper-inflations which occurred in Europe were fairly shortlived (the longest being of twenty-six months' duration), Latin American experience presents a picture of prolonged and substantial increases in price in various countries at different times.

The Chilean inflation is particularly interesting on a number of counts. For a start, inflation got under way in Chile as far back as 1879 and has remained with varying degrees of intensity ever since. Moreover Chile has, by Latin American standards at least, a highly developed economy with a sophisticated network of financial institutions. It is hardly surprising that economists from more advanced economies should specifically focus upon Chile when they are examining how economies learn to live with inflation.

In an econometric study of the Chilean inflation, A. C. Harberger (1963) established a strong relationship between the rate of inflation and the rate of monetary expansion. The basic relationship which he tested was

$$\dot{P}_t = \alpha_0 + \alpha_1 \dot{M}_t + \alpha_2 \dot{M}_{t-1} + \alpha_3 A_t \tag{8.13}$$

where $\alpha_1 + \alpha_2 = 1$ and A_t is defined as $(\dot{P}_{t-1} - \dot{P}_{t-2})$; A_t is an index of the rate of change of the cost of holding cash. In general all of the parameters except for α_3 were significant and even when α_3 was significant it was small in magnitude.

An important contribution of Harberger's paper was the formulation of several empirical tests which were designed to sort out the complex inter-relationship between wage increases and expansions in the supply of money. Harberger pits the monetarist approach, which views money wage increases as the passive outcome of a general inflationary process set in motion by monetary expansion, against what he calls the 'neo-orthodox' approach which asserts that the fundamental source of inflationary pressure is to be found in an imperfectly functioning labour market. According to this position, monetary expansion merely serves to *finance* the process of wage-push inflation (see chapter 3). An example of one of Harberger's tests is as follows. Assume for the sake of argument that the neo-orthodox position is correct and let $\dot{W}_t$ (or lagged values of $\dot{W}_t$) be substituted for $\dot{M}_t$ and $\dot{M}_{t-1}$ in equation (8.13). If the resultant regression equation 'outperformed' the monetarist equation from the point of view of the accuracy of its predictions, then this would be strong evidence in favour of the neo-orthodox approach. An implication of this result is that the 'overfinancing' or 'underfinancing' of the process of cost inflation will not inhibit the ultimate rise in prices. For this to occur, of course, the velocity of circulation of money must be variable in an upward and a downward direction. If on the other hand the expansion in the money supply was more than sufficient to finance the rise in money wages and if the rise in prices was greater than would be predicted by the wage variable alone, then this would constitute strong evidence in support of the proposition that the supply of money exerts an *independent* influence upon the price level. (This sort of test is encapable of sorting out the separate influence of wage-push and monetary factors when both processes are occurring simultaneously.)

Most of the tests performed by Harberger tend to support a monetarist interpretation of the Chilean inflation. Although not all of the tests were favourable to the monetarist position, the conclusion which emerges from his study is that cost-push wage increases only occasionally had any effect upon the rate of inflation; most of the wage increases which were secured in Chile were merely defensive responses to the threat of past or future inflation. Moreover in a more extensive study of Latin American inflations, R. Vogel (1974) concludes that despite the extreme diversity in economic and social conditions, most of the inflations in Latin America could be explained by a basic monetarist model. Indeed the remarkable similarity of the structural parameters of the model between countries is regarded as being a major plus point for the monetarist model. This, of course, contrasts with the findings of Jackson, Turner and Wilkinson who tended to emphasise (with little empirical justification) the cost-push aspects of Latin American inflations (see chapter 3).

In his study of the political aspects of Chilean inflation, T. Davis (1963) supports the conclusion that the primary source of inflationary pressure was the inability or unwillingness of successive Chilean governments to control the expansion of the money supply. Political pressure groups representing business interests were unwilling to forego the *inflation subsidy* upon which many sectors of the economy had come to depend. An inflation subsidy in this context arises from the fact that nominal interest rates rarely, if ever, kept pace with the rate of price increase; the real rate of interest was actually negative for considerable periods of time. This permitted the entry of firms into an industry whose profit rates were being subsidised by government monetary policy. Any attempt to reduce the rate of inflation was resisted by business groups who feared large-scale bankruptcy resulting from the removal of the inflation subsidy.

The only way to soften the impact on the business community of the removal of the inflation subsidy appeared to be the formulation of an anti-inflation policy package which would include, *inter alia*, proposals for reducing the real wage rate. Such a measure, it was argued, would reduce the real wage bill of the public sector and permit the private sector to sever its dependence upon the inflation subsidy by maintaining real profit rates. The governments of Peru, Argentina and Chile have all attempted to implement the politically unpopular policy of real wage cuts in order to obviate the cognate evils of bankruptcy and unemployment. The outcome of these attempts has not been encouraging. Indeed the general failure to control price rises even despite draconian measures of direct control have added a greater strength to the monetarist contention that any policy to combat inflation must primarily rely upon monetary policy and to a lesser extent (if at all) on other policies.

8.3.iii   *The monetary experience of moderate inflations*

The recent revival of interest in monetary theory and policy has led, quite naturally, to a concomitant avalanche of empirical literature on the manner in which money influences and is influenced by important economic variables. In this subsection we shall concentrate upon two aspects of money which relate directly to the theory of nominal income outlined in section 8.2. The first is the evidence concerning the factors which influence the demand for money. The second aspect relates to the ongoing controversy between monetarists and neo-Keynesians on the relation between money and economic activity.

The demand for money. The impressive volume of empirical literature on the demand for money in Britain, the United States and other western countries has tended to undermine the extreme pessimism prevalent among neo-Keynesians regarding the presence of absolute liquidity preference at some finite, positive interest rate. On the other hand, the naive version of the Cambridge equation (i.e. that $M=kPX$) is also refuted by the observation that, although the demand for money function is not horizontal, neither is it vertical. The *LM* curve has a positive finite slope, indicating that monetary policy may play an important role in generating inflationary pressure by (temporarily) depressing the interest rate and stimulating investment. (This is the channel Keynesians tend to emphasise exclusively whereas monetarists view it as simply a part of a wider network.) Moreover the theoretical conjectures of Friedman's 1956 paper appear to have borne fruit in that *permanent* income (his surrogate for wealth) performs more adequately than measured income in demand-for-money equations. (For an excellent analysis of many of the theoretical and empirical studies of the demand for money, the reader is referred to Laidler, 1969.)

At full employment, the acceptance of a stable demand function for money which produces neither a vertical nor a horizontal *LM* curve constitutes strong evidence in favour of the notion that there exists a stable function for velocity of circulation of money which, once a supply of money function is supplied and the disequilibrium adjustment mechanisms are specified, can be used as a *predictive* device. We have seen that even in terms of simplified comparative statics (i.e. even in a framework where adjustment frictions and the factors influencing the supply of money are ignored) an increase in the rate of monetary expansion was regarded as being of trivial importance in Keynesian models. In order to demonstrate the efficacy of monetary policy in provoking or restraining inflationary pressure, monetarists were obliged to show how *total expenditure* was affected by monetary policy. Moreover not only did they have to show that the money supply did produce noticeable repercussions on final expenditure but they also had to show that the relationship between money and expenditure was of greater operational significance than other well-tried alternatives. This is the challenge which Friedman and Meiselman (1964) accepted.

Money and economic activity. The methodology of the Friedman/Meiselman paper is relatively straightforward. The simple Keynesian model predicts that the level of total expenditure in general, and consumer expenditure in particular, varies with the level of autonomous expenditure such as autonomous investment and government expenditure. In symbols, the Keynesian hypothesis states that:

$$C_m = C_1(E_m)$$

where the m subscripts on C and E refer to the money values of consumer expenditure and autonomous expenditure respectively. The monetarist hypothesis in contrast states that variations in consumption expenditure are more adequately explained in terms of variations in the stock of money. In symbols:

$$C_m = C_2(M).$$

Not surprisingly Friedman and Meiselman's econometric testing found that the monetarist hypothesis was better determined statistically for all periods apart from the depression years.

Ando and Modigliani (1965) on the other hand found that a theoretically more satisfactory definition of autonomous expenditure yields the contrary conclusion — that fiscal variables were more effective in explaining variations in consumption expenditure. Their principal objection to the Friedman/Meiselman approach is however of a methodological nature. They register the familiar Keynesian objection to highly simplified regression equations in which the apparently independent variables may not in fact be independent at all. They regard the application of partial equilibrium techniques to a general equilibrium problem as being less than useful.

For the UK Barrett and Walters (1966) produced inconclusive results on the basis of first-difference reduced-form equations. Monetary and fiscal variables, when considered separately, performed poorly, but when they were both included in the same equation produced superior results. A more intricate study by Artis and Nobay (1969) once again produced rather ambiguous findings. Their results indicate that, on balance, fiscal policy is more effective than monetary policy.

It should be clear by now that there is nothing approaching a consensus of professional opinion concerning the relative impact of monetary and fiscal variables in determining the level of economic activity. One tentative opinion, which will satisfy most if not all of the researchers in this area, is that both monetary variables and autonomous expenditure variables affect the level of demand and activity. It seems more likely that fiscal variables are more effective in producing *traceable* variations in activity in the *short run*. The influence of monetary factors only becomes apparent in the *longer period*.

8.4 Inflation in the world economy

In recent years a widespread dissatisfaction with the traditional income-expenditure theory of the balance of payments has emerged and a return to an older and in many ways simpler explanation of the sources of balance of payments disequilibrium has gained in popularity and influence – the so-called *monetary theory of the balance of payments*. The theoretical precursor of this approach is contained in David Hume's *On Money* (1963) but the modern proponents of this framework are, *inter alios*, H. G. Johnson, R. A. Mundell, D. E. W. Laidler and J. M. Parkin.

The cardinal premise of the monetary theory of the balance of payments is that balance of payments disequilibrium is essentially a monetary phenomenon. Such disequilibrium may be viewed as an adjustment by the wealth-holders of the country concerned of their actual real cash balances to their desired real cash balances. A balance of payments surplus is the means by which real balances are augmented and a deficit is the means by which they are depleted. Viewed in this light therefore a devaluation is the means by which the real value of nominal money holdings of a country are brought into line with the (lower) demand for such balances.

The following partial adjustment mechanism has been extensively used in the empirical literature on monetary dynamics:

$$B = B\left(\frac{M_d}{P} - \frac{M_s}{P}\right) \tag{8.14}$$

where B is the balance of payments deficit (which may, of course, be positive or negative). The restriction on equation (8.14) is that $B'(\ ) > 0$: that is, the greater the excess demand for real balances, the lower will be the balance of payments deficit.

The monetary theory of the balance of payments has been extended in a number of directions and has a direct relevance to the international propagation of inflationary pressure under a system of fixed exchange rates. In particular it has served the useful purpose of emphasising the *international* character of the inflationary process. Since money plays such an important role in a closed economy model of inflation, why should it not play a similar role for a group of trading partners linked to each other by a system of fixed or quasi-fixed exchange rates? In other words can the inflationary experience of the Western world be treated in more or less the same way as that of any other monetary union? Monetarists answer Yes to the latter question, with the proviso that sufficient allowance is made for devaluations and 'dirty' floatations of individual currencies.

The assumptions of the monetarist model. The first assumption of the monetarist model is that the western world, and the Group of Ten in particular, forms a highly integrated network of interrelated markets in which there is little or no product differentiation in the output of different countries. A second and by no means negligible assumption is that capital is highly mobile with the result that world interest rates move roughly in step. (The remarkable growth in the volume of internationally mobile capital has tended to shift emphasis away from trade flows in analyses of balance of payments accounts; for a further discussion of these and related matters see Laidler and Nobay, 1974.)

Two adjustment mechanisms. Returning to the partial adjustment mechanism of equation (8.14) the question now arises: what factors determine the adjustment of the system to disequilibrium? We saw in chapter 2 that in a closed economy the initial inequality $(M_s/P) > (M_d/P)$ where M_s is given can only be eliminated by an increase in the price level. In an open economy however an alternative equilibrating mechanism is available: wealth-holders may run a balance of payments deficit in order to eliminate their holding of excessive real balances.

Two adjustment mechanisms immediately present themselves as likely candidates for consideration, the difference between them depending upon the emphasis accorded to domestic price changes relative to the prices prevailing in the rest of the world. According to the first version (the traditional price-specie-flow mechanism), a balance of payments surplus for the ith country will imply that money balances are being acquired, not from the domestic monetary authorities, but from the rest of the world. Assuming that all countries were initially in a situation of price stability and full employment, such an inflow of money will, according to the price-specie-flow mechanism, raise prices in the ith country. This will make its products less competitive in world markets. Eventually the initial price level will be restored after some period of adjustment and balance of payments equilibrium will once again prevail (the adjustment process may, of course, be cyclical): the price-specie-flow mechanism relies mainly on *short-period* variations in P_i or $\dot{P}_i$ relative to the rest of the world.

An alternative mechanism views each country as being a price-taker in the context of the world economy so that substantial relative price changes do not occur even in the short run. Instead the money inflow occasioned by a balance of payments surplus *in itself* acts as the equilibrating mechanism. For example if $(M_s/P) < (M_d/P)$, equation (8.14) predicts that a surplus will exist, but since such a surplus represents the net accumulation of money balances, the inequality will be eliminated by direct increases in M_s: prices may in fact remain constant.

In practice these mechanisms should not be regarded as being mutually exclusive but as complementary processes which assist each other at each stage of adjustment. Moreover both mechanisms make the identical diagnosis concerning the ability of an individual national economy, operating under a regime of fixed exchange rates, to isolate itself from monetary developments taking place in the rest of the world. More precisely they both predict that, once all lags in adjustment have worked their way through the various economic systems, all countries will inflate at the same rate, that rate being determined by the rate of *world* monetary expansion.

Johnson (1972) has recently advanced a simple model of this process. He suggests that adhering too closely to a closed economy monetarist model which concentrates upon the rate of *domestic* money creation will be highly misleading for an economy such as that of the United Kingdom which depends to such a considerable extent upon international trade. This is because the money supply is defined as the sum of international reserves, R, and domestically created credit, C; i.e.:

$$M_s \equiv R + C. \tag{8.14}$$

By taking proportional time derivatives of equation (8.2) for an individual country, equation (8.15) is obtained:

$$\dot{M} = \frac{k'(i)}{k(i)} \frac{di}{dt} + \dot{P} + \dot{X}. \tag{8.15}$$

Making the simplifying assumption that competitive capital markets will keep the interest rate in line with the world rate and assuming further that this world rate is constant, equation (8.16) is obtained:

$$\dot{M} = \dot{P} + \dot{X}. \tag{8.16}$$

On the other hand, taking proportional time derivatives of equation (8.14) we obtain the following approximate result:

$$\dot{M}_s \simeq \delta \dot{R} + (1 - \delta) \dot{C} \tag{8.17}$$

where

$$\frac{R}{R + C} = \delta.$$

For overall monetary equilibrium to prevail therefore the following condition must be satisfied:

$$\dot{P} + \dot{X} = \delta \dot{R} + (1 - \delta) \dot{C} \tag{8.18}$$

or

$$\dot{P} = \delta \dot{R} + (1 - \delta) \dot{C} - \dot{X}. \tag{8.19}$$

Assuming the rate of growth of output to be exogenously determined, equation (8.19) states that the rate of inflation of an individual country will depend upon three important factors: (a) the rate of growth of domestic credit, $\dot{C}$; (b) the rate of growth of international reserves, $\dot{R}$; and (c) the ratio of international reserves to the domestic money supply, δ.

The monetarist approach to inflation would therefore assign great importance to the level and rate of expansion of international money. Viewed in this light, two recent developments in the world monetary system are seen to be important sources of inflationary pressure. The first is the continued balance of payments deficits experienced by the United States in the years down to 1972. Due to US dominance in world trade and to the fact that the dollar is the main reserve currency, the effect of such a deficit will be to pump dollars into the international monetary system. But as was shown in the previous paragraph, the expansion in the rate of accumulation of international reserves which would accompany a higher balance of payments deficit will be inflationary for the countries of the rest of the world. The second development is the rapid growth in the Eurodollar market in recent years which, fuelled by a persistent dollar outflow from the USA, led to a multiple expansion in credit within Europe. At the same time as the USA was running large external payments deficits, a European money market emerged in which unrepatriated dollar deposits in Europe were used in transactions. This is of course the Eurodollar market and its growth may be gauged by the fact that Eurodollar credits available to final borrowers rose from $9 billion in 1964 to around $85 billion in 1972.

An indication of the extent of the US balance of payments deficits is given in Table 8.1 (the minus sign denotes a deficit).

Table 8.1.   The US Balance of Payments on a Liquidity Basis ($ millions).

1965	−1,335
1966	−1,357
1967	−3,571
1968	171
1969	−7,012
1970	−4,715
1971	−22,719*
1972	−14.684*

Source: L. Sirc *Outline of International Finance* London, Weidenfeld and Nicholson (1974)
* The figures for 1971 and 1972 are calculated on a slightly different basis from those for previous years.

Some evidence on the international monetarist hypothesis. There is still considerable dissension among economists working in this area as to what constitutes a robust test of the monetarist hypothesis. Nevertheless we shall attempt to indicate at this stage the broad state of play in the literature.

Firstly, we saw earlier that Parkin, Sumner and Ward (1974) have found a significant and stable relationship between the world rate of inflation and an index of world excess demand augmented by a price expectations variable, the 'world' in this case being confined to the Group of Ten. That is, there are strong *prima facie* grounds for believing that the world is, under a system of fixed exchange rates, similar to any other monetary union: one country within the union may be undergoing an economic recession and be suffering from rising unemployment rates but, on the assumption that a sizeable proportion of its output is in the form of *tradeable* goods, the behaviour of its price level will to a large extent be determined by external economic conditions, and in particular the state of excess demand for tradeable goods in the rest of the world. Nevertheless the findings of Parkin *et al.* can do little to throw light upon the *sources* of the world excess demand: are they the monetarist variables aggregated over countries or the Keynesian expenditure variables similarly treated? We saw earlier that the period of rapid inflation in the western world coincided with the massive balance of payments deficits of the United States. In order to corroborate the monetarist hypothesis, the precise relationships linking the dollar deficits and the expansion of the Eurodollar market to the level of excess demand will have to be spelt out in greater detail.

An additional piece of evidence which tends to support the 'integrated world market' hypothesis is provided by Genberg (1973) who compared the variance of inflation rates across OECD countries with the variance of inflation rates among US cities. He found that there was no significant difference between these two variances, lending support to the view that if we are to regard the US cities as constituting a unified market network, then it is plausible to deduce that OECD countries should also be so regarded.

A more sceptical view of the monetarist interpretation of the international propagation of inflationary pressure is to be found in Hines and Nussey (1974). They question the monetarist hypothesis that individual inflation rates are converging to some common world rate and opt instead for an explanation of inflation which relies to a great extent upon 'power' variables. On a national level there is the celebrated 'trade union militancy' hypothesis which serves to explain that part of inflation which has a domestic source. On an international level there is the prevalence of demonstration effects and the increasingly intense struggle between capital and labour on the one hand and the developed and underdeveloped countries on the other to explain why world prices are rising. (These hypotheses are contrary to the findings of Ward and Zis (1974) who have shown that Hines' own 'militancy' variable, when applied on an international level, fails to perform adequately.) It should be noted however that an important objection raised by Hines and Nussey against the monetarists, namely that they fail to take account of the empirical fact that a large proportion of national wealth is non-tradeable, is specifically incorporated into an earlier paper by Parkin (1972). In this paper Parkin sets out to demonstrate that the failure of individual inflation rates to converge with anything like the expected speed can be explained by the fact that not all goods are internationally tradeable. The prices of traded goods will be dominated by the relation between supply and demand in the world economy whereas the prices of non-traded goods will depend upon market conditions in the domestic economy.

His argument runs as follows. Suppose a particular country, starting from a position of full employment and an inflation rate equal to the world rate, was suddenly to raise its rate of domestic credit expansion. This will produce an excess demand for all goods, the excess demand for traded goods leading to a balance of payments deficit. But this is not the end of the story. The same policy will also produce excess demand for non-traded goods which, on the full employment assumption, are fixed in supply in the short period. The prices of non-traded goods will be bid up relative to those of traded goods and wages in the non-traded sector will rise in line with the higher marginal value product of labour. To the extent that the wage increases in the non-traded sector are transmitted to the traded sector, the competitive position of the trading sector will deteriorate and the balance of payments deficit will worsen even more. Parkin's variant on the monetary theory of the balance of payments and inflation therefore predicts that only a part of the inflationary pressure caused by expansive monetary policies is exported: the rest remains to bid up prices in the sector for non-traded goods. Moreover a divergence between domestic inflation and world inflation will persist for as long as the monetary authorities continue to expand credit at a rate which is faster than the rate of credit expansion in other countries. The abandonment of such a policy will indeed produce a convergence in inflation rates, but this process will be much more gradual than is implied when the whole of output is regarded as tradeable on an integrated world market.

8.5   Concluding remarks

Monetarists assert that the only sure way of combating inflation is to bring the rate of monetary expansion *gradually* into line with some tolerable rate of inflation, making sufficient allowance for output growth and secular changes in the velocity of circulation of money. This will involve a reduction in the rate of monetary expansion if the initial rate of inflation is regarded as being excessively high. It is an unfortunate fact of life, say the monetarists, that the solution of monetary restraint will bring in its wake an inevitable increase in the unemployment rate above its natural level. The more obdurately individuals cling to their expectations of inflation even in the face of considerable under-utilisation of capacity (i.e. the larger is ψ), the longer will have to be the period of unemployment and the greater will be the cost of fighting inflation in terms both of lost output and the socially undesirable phenomenon of unemployment. On the other hand the more alert the population to perceived reductions in the rate of inflation (i.e. the smaller is ψ), the lower will be the cost of a restrictive monetary policy. It is with the avoidance of these unpalatable side-effects of monetary restraint in mind that monetarists have come out in favour of *indexation* as a possible way of accelerating the process of downward revision of inflationary expectations (see chapters 9 and 10). If all nominal contracts are indexed efficiently to allow for *experienced* inflation, much of the pressure upon individuals to anticipate inflation is removed.

Nevertheless many untidy ends remain in the monetarist explanation of inflation. We shall briefly touch upon two of them at this stage.

Is the natural unemployment rate the relevant concept of full employment? That is to say, is the U^* which is found by evaluating the root of the equation $f(U) = 0$ really the full-employment rate which Keynes had in mind when defining the concept? Is U^* really that unemployment rate which is consistent with the absence of involuntary unemployment? Tobin (1972) has cast doubt upon the full-employment properties of U^*.

His argument, which employs exactly the same approach of the *General Theory*, runs as follows. Assume that a given rate of inflation is fully anticipated at $\dot{P_1}^e$ and that the unemployment rate which corresponds to this fully anticipated inflation rate is U^*. Assume also a *notional* full-employment rate of unemployment U_F where $U_F < U^*$; U_F is that unemployment rate consistent with the absence of involuntary unemployment. Tobin, following Keynes, maintains that even though $\dot{P} = \dot{P}^e$, workers as a group may be prepared to accept a *general* reduction in the rate of growth of their real wage rates provided that this reduction is accomplished, not by a deceleration in the rate of growth of the *money* wage rate, but by means of a higher rate of inflation than had previously occurred. This is the inflationary counterpart of the under-employment equilibrium proposition in the *General Theory* which states that workers, although willing to accept reductions in their real wages engineered through a rise in prices, are opposed to cuts in the money wage rate. Nor is such a reaction as irrational as it at first appears. If one group accepts a cut in its money wage rate, what guarantee do they have that other groups will follow suit? None. Price increases are regarded as a neutral and equitable method of adjusting the real wage rate (and its short-term rate of growth) so as to eliminate involuntary unemployment. It is the duty of governments to accomplish this goal by means of the instruments of demand management.

Moreover once U_F has been reached through a *short-term* depression of $\dot{W}$ relative to $\dot{P}$ and the rate of growth of labour productivity, the situation may then prevail in which inflation is fully anticipated and fully allowed for in wage bargains. Real wages thenceforward will rise in line with labour productivity and all workers will begin to demand *full* compensation for price increases in their nominal wage contracts. The fact that they failed to allow fully for price increases in the process of transition from U^* to U_F is simply a reflection of the disequilibrium dynamics of the system. What appears to be irrational behaviour is simply a manifestation of the short-period dynamics of adjustment. In terms of the money illusion hypothesis, ϕ is only less than unity during the period in which U^* is falling towards U_F. Thenceforward it assumes a value of unity.

Is the supply of money exogenous? We saw earlier that a quantity theorist of necessity must subscribe to the proposition that the factors determining the demand for nominal balances are distinct from the factors which determine the supply of nominal balances. As a very rough approximation we may summarise the preceding analysis and assert that the demand for nominal balances depends upon money income and 'the' money interest rate. But suppose the supply of money also depends upon these two variables. For example if the government were to use monetary policy to control the interest rate, it would effectively lose control of the supply of money. Similarly if the monetary authorities were to validate all increases in money income produced, for example, by cost-push factors, the supply of money would then itself be a function of the level of nominal income. In both cases the supply of money would become an endogenous variable and an independent policy to control the money supply would be subordinate to other policy objectives.

In fact Friedman (1968) himself is prepared to accept a mild version of the endogeneity argument. His explanation of why governments have failed to exercise adequate control over the supply of money in the past is (a) that the printing of money is a very convenient method of imposing an inflation tax without having to go through the usual channels of raising taxation or issuing government debt: this was particularly important for the United States from the mid-1960s onwards where the expense of the Vietnam War required enormous fiscal outlays (see chapter 9); and (b) that, influenced by the writings of J. M. Keynes, governments had attached disproportionate significance to stabilising the interest rate at a low level.

The inflationary impact of this second objective, namely the goal of low interest rates, has been singled out for severe criticism by monetarists. Monetary policy, according to monetarists, cannot hope to peg interest rates for more than very limited periods. The mistaken notion that they are capable of so doing in the longer period is traceable to the Keynesian hypothesis that interest is a purely monetary phenomenon. Monetarists on the other hand propose an alternative framework in which the money interest rate is the sum of the real interest rate and the expected rate of inflation. The real interest rate will be determined at its Wicksellian natural level by the twin forces of time preference and the marginal productivity of investment. The expected rate of inflation will be determined by expansions in the money supply which had occurred in the immediate past. Should the authorities attempt to maintain a real interest rate below its natural level, the ultimate effect of this will be to *raise* the nominal interest rate on account of the inflationary pressure produced by the concomitant increase in the rate of monetary expansion. The persistent attempts of British, American and other governments to peg the rate of interest at a level inconsistent with the natural rate is to a large extent responsible for the current inflationary crisis. Only by abandoning this interest rate objective will the authorities be able to prevent the inflationary repercussions of increases in the rate of monetary expansion.

A more damaging criticism of the 'exogeneity of money' hypothesis comes both from neo-Keynesians and cost-push theorists. The monetarist contention that by manipulating the monetary base of the system the government is in a position to control the money supply *ad libitum* has been explicitly challenged by neo-Keynesian economists. Kaldor (1970) and Cramp (1970) have argued that the fact that stable velocity-of-circulation functions appear to emerge from econometric studies of the demand for money should not be allowed to obscure the fundamental causal connection between economic activity (the independent variable) and the supply of money (the dependent variable). 'In other words, in one way or another, an increase in the demand for money evoked an increase in supply. The money supply "accommodated" itself to the needs of trade: rising in response to an expansion, and *vice versa*' (Kaldor, 1970). Even though the Bank of England and the Federal Reserve Board have the monopoly of note issue, they will act in very much the same way as a constitutional monarch '. . . with very wide reserve powers on paper, the maintenance and continuance of which are greatly dependent on the degree of restraint and moderation shown in their exercise.'

As an example of what is referred to as the *supportive* function of monetary policy, Kaldor selects the relationship between consumer expenditure and the money supply in the immediate pre-Christmas period. 'Nobody would suggest (not even Professor Friedman, I believe) that the increase in note circulation in December is the cause of the Christmas buying spree.' But he poses the following question: 'Could the authorities prevent the buying spree by refusing to supply additional notes and coins in the Christmas season?' The answer is, of course, negative. 'There would be chaos for a few days, but soon all kinds of money substitutes would spring up: credit cards, promissory notes etc., issued by firms and financial institutions which would circulate in the same way as bank notes.' The fact that such near-money substitutes have not arisen for the purpose of everyday transactions is, according to this argument, an important indicator of the extreme passivity of monetary policy.

CHAPTER 9

The Effects of Inflation

Up to this point we have assumed that inflation is an unambiguously evil phenomenon and that it is one of the principal tasks of a responsible government to take the appropriate steps to reduce the rate of inflation. Nevertheless, depite the highly emotional rhetoric which issues from politicians and journalists alike, it is by no means obvious to the economist that inflation is a bad thing. It has often been argued, for example, that a price level which is changing at a constant proportional rate and which is fully anticipated and acted upon by all economic agents will have negligible effects upon economic welfare. That is, the addition of 'noughts' at the end of *nominal* quantities at regular periods may have no noticeable effect on *real* quantities.

In the first three sections of this chapter we shall attempt to gauge the effect of a *fully anticipated* rate of inflation upon three important variables:

(a) the real interest rate
(b) the level of economic welfare
(c) the balance of payments.

In the fourth and most important section of this chapter we shall attempt to indicate why the sort of inflation which is being experienced by most western economies at the present time is highly detrimental to the economic progress of these nations.

9.1   The effects of anticipated inflation on investment and real interest rates

Most of the monetarist models of inflation which we have so far encountered have depended heavily upon the Fisherine theory of nominal interest whereby the money interest rate is the sum of the real interest rate, r, (often assumed to be constant, especially in the longer run) and the expected rate of inflation, $\dot{P}^e$. That is:

$$i = r + \dot{P}^e. \tag{9.1}$$

There is not normally supposed to be a relation between the expected rate of inflation and the equilibrium real interest rate. (In the short run, of course, a failure to anticipate inflation adequately may depress the real rate of interest, but this disequilibrium will not persist into the long run.) Keynes attacked this theory in the *General Theory*, arguing that part of the impact of a higher rate of inflation would be on the marginal efficiency of capital. Even Fisher himself had doubts about the *empirical* validity of equation (9.1): '. . . When prices are rising,' he wrote 'the rate of interest tends to be high but not so high as it should be to compensate for the rise; and when prices are falling, the rate of interest tends to be low, but not so low as it should be to compensate for the fall. . . . The erratic behaviour of real interest is evidently a trick played on the money market by the "money illusion" when contracts are made in unstable money' (1930).

And there the matter rested until R. A. Mundell (1963) took up the question of the relation between the real interest rate and the expected rate of inflation.

9.1.i Mundell's model

We shall assume a closed economy with only two assets, money and equity shares. Wages and prices are perfectly flexible in both directions. Changes in prices are the result either of changes in the stock of nominal money or of saving—investment disequilibrium at full employment. A price increase, for example, may be the result either of an increase in M_s or of an inflationary gap (the excess of investment over saving at full employment). Similarly a price decline may be the result either of monetary contraction or of a *deflationary* gap (or both). Total wealth is the sum of the real value of equities, E^*, and real money balances, (M_0/P), the supply of money being fixed at M_0. There is only a transactions demand for assets which will be divided between E^* and (M_0/P), the exact division depending upon the difference between the nominal return on shares (which is the nominal interest rate, i) and the nominal return on money, σ. Real income and employment are assumed to be at their full-employment equilibrium levels and are suppressed into the functional forms of the following equations. The demand for money may therefore be written:

$$\frac{M_0}{P} = L(i - \sigma) \qquad (9.2)$$

where real income, X, is suppressed into $L(\ )$. For the moment we shall follow Mundell in assuming that the nominal return on money is zero so that $\sigma = 0$ and equation (9.2) may be rewritten:

$$\frac{M_0}{P} = L(i). \qquad (9.3)$$

Following Fisher, it is assumed that $i = r + \dot{P}^e$ where $\dot{P}^e$ is exogenously determined. If $\dot{P}^e = 0$, equation (9.3) describes the relation between (M/P) and r, which we shall label LM_1 (see fig. 9.1).

For each value of $\dot{P}^e$, a new LM relation holds. The greater the expected rate of inflation, the further to the south-west will be the relevant LM curve lie. Thus LM_2 corresponds to a positive expected rate of inflation.

Fig. 9.1

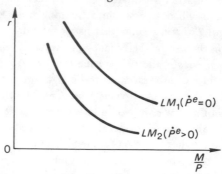

So far we have only considered the factors which determine the demand for real balances. It is now necessary to consider the factors which determine the demand for and supply of loanable funds, i.e. the factors which determine savings and investment. Investment, I, varies inversely with the real interest rate, i.e. $I = I(r)$, $I'(r) < 0$.

Saving is divided into private saving and the (positive or negative) budget surplus of the government. Private saving is a function of the real interest rate, the total volume of wealth and the level of taxation. In symbols, private saving will equal

$$S\left(r, E^* + \frac{M_0}{P}, T_0\right)$$

where T_0 is the level of taxes (assumed to be lump sum); if we assume for simplicity that government expenditure is zero, T_0 will also equal the (given) budget surplus. Total saving will then equal:

$$S = S\left(r, E^* + \frac{M_0}{P}, T_0\right) + T_0. \tag{9.4}$$

In equilibrium

$$I(r) = S(\ldots) + T_0. \tag{9.5}$$

The two variables which concern us at the moment in the equilibrium condition (9.5) are r and M_0/P. A rise in r will reduce desired investment ($I'(r) < 0$), but may in fact stimulate saving ($S_r > 0$). In all events, so long as $I'(r) < S_r$, a rise in r will have to be accompanied by a rise in M_0/P if the equilibrium condition (9.5) is to be satisfied. From the point of view of saving—investment equilibrium therefore a rise in r will be associated with a rise in M_0/P. The locus of such equilibrium combinations is the *IS* curve illustrated in fig. 9.2.

It should be continually borne in mind when reading the following three sections that we are making the assumption that the level of real income does

Fig. 9.2

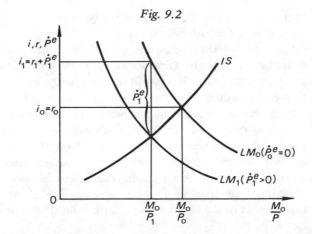

not vary as a result of various monetary and fiscal policies. The *IS* and *LM* curves which are referred to in this chapter do not therefore relate the interest rate to the level of *real income*: they relate the interest rate to the holding of *real balances*. The labels have been retained in order to emphasise the notion that an *IS* curve is a locus of points of equilibrium in the product market and the *LM* curve the locus of points of equilibrium in the money market. The choice of variables for the horizontal and vertical axes will depend upon the nature of the problem to be solved (fig. 9.2).

Full equilibrium occurs at the intersection of the *IS* curve and the relevant *LM* curve. For example, if the expected rate of inflation is zero, the equilibrium real (and nominal) rate of interest will be r_0 and the equilibrium level of real balances will be M_0/P_0. But should the expected rate of inflation rise to $\dot{P}_1^e$, full equilibrium requires that both r and M_0/P should fall to r_1 and M_0/P_1 respectively. The nominal interest·rate will rise from r_0 to $r_1 + \dot{P}_1^e$, i.e. i will indeed rise, but not by as much as the rise in $\dot{P}^e$

The mechanics of the process are as follows. A higher expected rate of inflation raises the nominal interest rate for each real interest rate; individuals attempt to run down their holdings of real balances by substituting shares for real balances in their transactions portfolio: but since it is assumed that the economy is at full employment, any increase in the demand for capital will simply bid up prices; the fall in the value of real balances which accompanies this price inflation will curtail consumption and stimulate saving at each rate of interest, which in turn will stimulate investment and drive down the real yield on shares.

9.1.ii   *The role of monetary and fiscal policy*

The two crucial assumptions underlying the above analysis are that money bears no interest ($\sigma = 0$); and that the government will allow the real interest rate to fall to r_1. That is, it is assumed that even if the government had the power to shift the *IS* curve it would refrain from doing so.

In this subsection, we shall relax the second assumption. Following the analysis of an influential paper by Professor Phelps (1965), it will be shown that a rise in the expected rate of inflation will not necessarily lead to a fall in the real interest rate. Everything depends upon the way in which inflationary expectations are generated. If inflation is generated by fiscal means (that is, by reducing T), the consequent rise in $\dot{P}^e$ (and south-westerly displacement of the *LM* curve) will accompany a north-westerly displacement of the *IS* curve which could in fact *raise* the real interest rate. If on the other hand inflationary expectations are induced by monetary means (that is, by successive open market purchases of shares), the rise in $\dot{P}^e$ will be accompanied by a *continual* downward displacement of the *IS* curve and a declining real interest rate.

The impact of fiscal policy. This is easily analysed by means of fig. 9.2. Assume that the government starts to run a budgetary deficit ($T < 0$) after a long period of budgetary balance. A government deficit will have two effects in this model. If we assume for the moment that the desired level of real balances remains constant, an increase in the size of the deficit will lead to an equal increase in the supply of money in the initial period and in all subsequent periods. The only way a deficit can be financed in this model is by increasing the trend of the money supply over time, which in turn raises the trend of prices. This effect may be called the monetary effect of a deficit. The fiscal effects are more familiar. A higher budgetary deficit raises desired consumption and reduces saving for a given level of real national income. In the short run an inflationary gap will emerge which will push up prices at a faster rate than would be produced by the *monetary* effect alone. Hence although nominal money balances are rising, real balances will fall to the point at which savings have been stimulated by an amount sufficient to restore equilibrium at a full-employment level of output. This is the celebrated *Pigou effect* which was originally invoked to demonstrate the long-run impossibility of under-employment equilibrium in an economy in which prices were downwardly flexible. The Pigou effect will therefore shift the *IS* curve to the left: a lower equilibrium level of real balances will correspond to each real interest rate. The monetary effect of a deficit induces continued expansion of the money supply and a permanently higher rate of inflation; the Pigou effect of a deficit will reinforce the inflationary impact of the monetary effect by raising prices still further by means of a temporary inflationary gap which reduces the real value of (growing) nominal balances to a point where it is consistent with full-employment equilibrium. When this new equilibrium is finally reached, inflation will still be taking place, but at a rate equal to the rate of expansion of the money supply, which in turn will equal the size of the annual budgetary deficit.

In the long run the sustained inflation produced by the monetary effect will come to be fully anticipated, the *LM* curve shifting to LM_2 at a positive expected rate of inflation of $\dot{P}_2{}^e$. What happens to the real interest rate depends upon the relative displacement of the *IS* and *LM* curves. In fig. 9.3, the real interest rate falls slightly from r_1 to r_3, but this need not necessarily occur. If the upward displacement of the *IS* function for a given *M/P* exceeds the consequent downward displacement of the *LM* function, the rate of interest will in fact rise. The essential point is that when inflationary expectations are induced by an expansionary budgetary policy, the real rate of interest will not necessarily fall, as is implied in Mundell's model where expectations are exogenously given. And even if it did fall, the decline in *r* would be very much smaller in magnitude than would be predicted by Mundell's model in which the economy moves along a *given IS* function to a new point of equilibrium at r_4.

Fig. 9.3

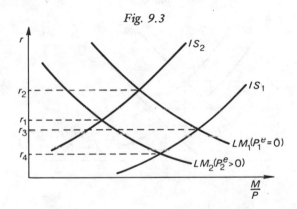

The repercussions of an expansionary monetary policy. These are less complex. In this two asset model, open market operations constitute the exchange of money for shares and *vice versa*. The purchase of shares by the monetary authorities increases the supply of money by effecting an equal fall in the supply of privately held equity shares. If equation (9.4) is to continue to hold, an increase in *M/P* is necessary to compensate for the fall in E^*; for each real interest rate the equilibrium *M/P* will have to be higher. That is, a once and for all open market purchase will shift the *IS* curve permanently to the right. Morveover, since the equilibrium *M/P* must rise, prices will have to rise by a greater proportion than the money supply is expanded. But the rise in prices is a once and for all occurrence. Sustained inflation by monetary means alone can only be induced by continual open market purchases, i.e. by a continual rightward displacement of the *IS* function. But this rightward displacement will mean that, even if the *LM* curve is slow to react to the experience of inflation, the real interest rate will still be lower, for in this case the rightward shifts in the *IS* function will be accompanied by the south-westerly displacement of the *LM*

curve, as is illustrated in fig. 9.4. If expectations are very sluggish in reacting to experienced inflation the *LM* curve will stay fixed despite the ultimate drift of the *IS* curve to IS_2. In this case r will fall to r_2 and M/P will rise to $(M/P)_2$. If on the other hand a south-westerly drift in the *LM* curve to LM_2 accompanies the shift in the *IS* curve, $r_3 (> r_2)$ and $(M/P)_3$ $(<(M/P)_2)$ will be the new real interest rate and level of real balance respectively.

Should the government wish to use monetary methods to *raise* the real interest rate, it would engage in open market sales which would shift the *IS* curve to the left. As a direct consequence of such a policy prices would tend to fall, for although the nominal money supply is being run down, a more than proportionate fall in prices is necessary if real balances are to be raised.

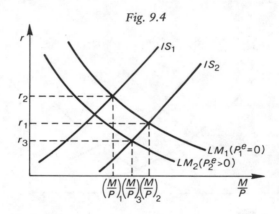

Fig. 9.4

In the light of the above analysis it follows that the government, by using the appropriate combination of monetary and fiscal instruments, is able to combine *any* real rate of interest with *any* constant rate of price inflation, positive or negative. Assume, for example, that starting from a position of price stability the government wishes to maintain a constant real rate of interest and induce a negative rate of inflation. Ignoring the consequent downward drift of the *LM* function for the moment, such objectives could be achieved simultaneously by running a budget surplus, which by itself would tend to raise r, in conjunction with an open market purchase, which by itself would tend to reduce r. If combined in the correct proportions the budget surplus could achieve the required rate of deflation and open market operations could be used to prevent r from rising. As the *LM* function drifts upwards in response to a rising expected rate of deflation, the monetary and fiscal instruments will have to be combined in different proportions. The fact remains however that when a higher or lower expected rate of inflation is induced by the active intervention of the government, the real rate of interest need not change. Higher anticipated inflation does not necessarily entail a lower real interest rate; such a fall in r will only occur if the government wishes it to occur. 'Thus the government can choose', writes Phelps (1965), 'what kind of inflation to have: an inflation with high saving and a low real rate of interest — brought about by open market purchases — or an inflation with low saving and a high real rate of interest — brought about by low taxes.'

9.2   Anticipated inflation and economic welfare

The question now arises as to the possible welfare repercussions, if any, of a fully anticipated inflation.

Retaining the assumption that money bears no interest ($\sigma = 0$), the only welfare effect of anticipated inflation will be to induce asset holders to economise on the holding of money in their transactions balances by participating in such socially wasteful activities as making more frequent trips to the bank to encash their equity shares (see appendix to chapter 8). As long as there is a difference between the nominal yield on money and other riskless and easily convertible assets, there will exist an incentive to economise on money. This incentive will be the greater the higher the nominal interest rate.

This observation led M. J. Bailey (1956) to devise a measure of the welfare cost of a higher expected rate of inflation. Starting with the Fisherine assumption that a higher expected rate of inflation produces an equal rise in the nominal rate of interest, Bailey proposed that variations in i will mainly reflect variations in $\dot{P}^e$. That is, $i = r + \dot{P}^e$ where r is constant. We shall be interested in three rates of interest: 0, i_1 and i_2. Corresponding to each interest rate will be three different rates of inflation: $\dot{P}_0{}^e = -r$, $\dot{P}_1{}^e = 0$ and $\dot{P}_2{}^e > 0$ respectively.

In fig. 9.5, the demand for real balances is measured on the vertical axis and the cost of holding money, $i - \sigma$, is measured on the horizontal axis. Since σ is assumed to be equal to zero, the cost of holding real balances will equal the nominal interest rate, i.

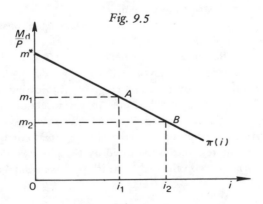

Fig. 9.5

The relation between the demand for real balances and the cost of holding money is made explicit in the $\pi(i)$ function which for expository simplicity is assumed to be linear. The cost of a positive rate of interest of i_1 is measured by the triangle m^*Am_1. Should the expected rate of inflation rise to $\dot{P}_2^e(=i_2 - i_1)$, the demand for real balances will fall to m_2 and the increased welfare cost of the positive expected rate of inflation will be measured by the area m_1ABm_2. Only a zero nominal interest rate will eliminate this welfare cost. But a zero nominal interest rate implies a *negative* expected rate of inflation equal in absolute value to the real interest rate.

Phelps' demonstration that a higher expected rate of inflation can produce a higher or lower real interest rate depending upon the means by which inflationary expectations are induced severely undermined the generality of Bailey's analysis. If for example a higher expected rate of inflation is accompanied by a fall in r (as Mundell predicted) the total change in welfare depends critically upon whether a low real interest rate is considered to be a good or bad thing. If a higher rate of investment is an important objective of economic policy, the beneficial effect of a lower r could conceivably outweigh the detrimental effect of a higher nominal rate of interest.

Phelps set out to show how an alternative analytical framework could be developed which would yield quite definite welfare conclusions. Social welfare, according to Phelps, depends upon both the nominal rate of interest and the real rate of interest. It is at a maximum when two conditions are simultaneously met: (a) when the expected rate of deflation $(-\dot{P}^e)$ equals the real interest rate: in this case, $m = m^*$ and *full liquidity* is said to prevail; (b) when the real interest rate is at a level which will produce the rate of investment required to optimise the distribution of consumption between the present and the future. Let r^* denote the optimal real interest rate. The necessary and sufficient conditions for the maximisation of social welfare are therefore that $r = r^*$ and that $\dot{P}^e = -r^*$. Let $\dot{P}^{*e}$ denote the optimal expected rate of inflation.

The reader will recall from section 9.1 that a unique LM curve will correspond to each expected rate of inflation. More particularly one and only one LM curve will correspond to an expected rate of inflation of $\dot{P}^{*e}$ viz. LM^*. This particular curve is illustrated in fig. 9.6.

But suppose the economy started out experiencing a positive (i.e. non-optimal) expected rate of inflation ($\dot{P}_1^e > 0$). The LM curve corresponding to this expected rate of inflation is labelled LM_1 in fig. 9.7. If the initial expected rate of inflation were zero, the relevant LM curve would be LM_2. In Phelps' model, LM_2 is vertical at m^* over a small range of r indicating that money and shares are close but not *perfect* substitutes in a transactions portfolio. This possibility is ignored in the succeeding discussion. We shall assume that LM_2 is asymptotically vertical as r approaches zero. The optimal combination of real balances and the real interest rate is indicated by the point $\Omega = (r^*, m^*)$ and is clearly unfeasible with the two values of $\dot{P}^e$ which we have assumed.

Fig. 9.6

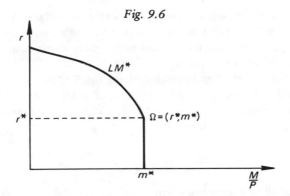

The above analysis offers the government two alternative courses of action if it is to achieve a welfare optimum. Assuming that the initial anticipated rate of inflation exceeds $\dot{P}^{*e}$, it may either engage in an active policy of deflation or it may take the advice of Professor Friedman and initiate a policy whereby interest is paid on money holdings.

As was shown in section 9.1, the first course of action would involve the appropriate combination of monetary and fiscal policy to bring about the optimal interest rate, r^*, and the optimal expected rate of inflation, $\dot{P}^{*e}$. Should the initial real interest rate fall short of r^*, the attainment of a welfare optimum will require a leftward shift in the *IS* curve. Such a shift in the *IS* curve may be accompanied by *any* rate of inflation, positive or negative; in the limit, monetary and fiscal policy will be combined in such a way as to maintain a stable *LM** curve which intersects the *IS* curve at a point $\Omega = (r^*, m^*)$.

A more painless policy for the maximisation of social welfare would be for the government to pay interest on money to the holders of money. In fact in a

Fig. 9.7

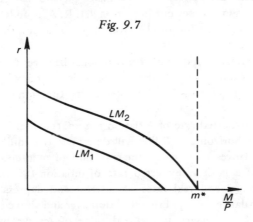

freely competitive banking system the existence of inflationary expectations would induce banks to pay interest on deposits in such a way as to maintain the difference in yields between money and other assets whose nominal yield varies with the expected rate of inflation.

Referring back to the argument underlying fig. 9.5, it was asserted that full liquidity would only prevail at m^* if the cost of holding money was zero. The cost of holding money is defined as $i - \sigma = r + \dot{P}^e - \sigma$. Full liquidity will prevail at *any* expected rate of inflation provided that the following condition is fulfilled:

$$\sigma = i = r + \dot{P}^e. \qquad (9.6)$$

Social welfare will be maximised when

$$\sigma^* = r^* + \dot{P}^e \qquad (9.7)$$

where $\dot{P}^e$ is any expected rate of inflation.

Monetary and fiscal policies will still be necessary of course, in order to achieve the optimal real interest rate r^*. But the payment of interest on money to satisfy equation (9.7) will render the anti-inflationary aspect of such policies redundant. Anticipated inflation in excess of $\dot{P}^{*e}$ will no longer have a detrimental effect on social welfare. The welfare cost of inflation will have been eliminated.

9.3   Anticipated inflation and the balance of payments

Assume that the world is divided into two areas, Europe and America, and that the exchange rate between European currency and the dollar is fixed. Assume further that the real rate of return on claims to physical assets is fixed at $\bar{r}$. (In keeping with the argument set out in section 9.1, R. A. Mundell (1971) assumes that r is an increasing function of the level of real balances; this complication is ignored in the subsequent analysis.)

In fig. 9.8, the European demand for real dollar balances ($q = R/P$, where R is the demand for nominal dollar balances and P is an index of the purchasing power of the dollar) is assumed to be a decreasing function of the nominal rate of interest.

If initially the expected rate of inflation is zero, the intersection of the $\Psi(q)$ function with the horizontal AE line will determine the equilibrium European holding of real balances at q_0 where the real and money interest rates are equal. The emergence of a positive expected rate of inflation $\dot{P}_1^e$ will drive a wedge between the nominal and real rates of interest and depress the equilibrium holdings of real balances to q_1. Price inflation over and above the expected rate of inflation will be necessary if the real value of reserve balances is to be depressed to q_1. Once European real balances have adjusted to the new

Fig. 9.8

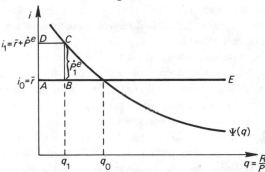

equilibrium level, Europe will be accumulating dollar holdings at a rate equal to the expected rate of inflation. That is

$$\frac{1}{R}\frac{dR}{dt} = \dot{P}_1^{\,e} \tag{9.8}$$

Equation (9.8) implies that the advent of inflationary expectations will force Europe to aim at a balance of payments surplus in order to satisfy their dollar reserve requirements. This surplus may be considered to be a form of *inflation tax* which is levied by America on Europe. The real value of the inflation tax may be expressed diagrammatically as the area ABCD in fig. 9.8 and symbolically by equation (9.9).

$$\frac{1}{P}\frac{dR}{dt} = q_1 \cdot \dot{P}_1^{\,e} \tag{9.9}$$

dR/dt and $(1/P)(dR/dt)$ are the respective nominal and real values of the European balance of payments surplus; $\dot{P}_1^{\,e}$ may be interpreted as the tax rate and q_1 as the tax base.

Under a system of fixed exchange rates therefore a positive expected rate of decrease in the value of the dollar will induce European dollar holders to reduce the real value of dollar balances to a level q_1. When European dollar balances have fallen to q_1, America will be levying an inflation tax upon Europe the real value of which will be $q_1 \cdot \dot{P}_1^{\,e}$. Balance of payments equilibrium will no longer be the object of European economic policy: in order to maintain the new (lower) desired level of real dollar balances, Europe will have to accumulate dollar reserves by running a balance of payments surplus.

Once the inflation is under way and is confidently expected to persist into the future, the abandonment of fixed exchange rates in favour of exchange rate flexibility will not free Europe from the burden of the inflation tax. The exchange rate will only vary if an imbalance between the supply of and demand for dollars threatens to emerge. But no such imbalance will emerge: America will now be 'exporting' a new commodity — real balances. By raising the expected rate of dollar inflation, an acceleration in the rate of credit expansion in America will increase the desired rate of accumulation of dollars in Europe. A higher rate of American monetary expansion will therefore induce the European monetary authorities to aim at a higher balance of payments surplus to maintain a constant (but lower) level of real dollar balances.

The analysis remains unchanged when Europe is subdivided into its individual economies. The United Kingdom, for example, will have its own demand function for real dollar balances, $\Psi_1(q)$. The European demand function is simply the horizontal sum of the demand functions for each individual European country. From the British point of view it matters little whether real balances are maintained by a budget surplus with America or a similar surplus with, say, France in a situation of anticipated dollar inflation. Since all international transactions are financed by the same international currency (the dollar) a British surplus with France is just as effective a source of dollar balances as a surplus with America. But a positive expected rate of inflation will imply that the French government, like the UK government, will aim at an overall surplus to satisfy its demand for real balances. If it runs a deficit with the UK, it must run an even greater surplus with the rest of the world (i.e. other European countries and America). Moreover if France runs an overall deficit with *all* other European countries, its necessary surplus on American transactions will be higher and the necessary surpluses of other European countries will be lower. The internal European balance of payments situation will make no difference to the total quantity of dollar reserves 'exported' by America; it will only affect the *distribution* of the American deficit between European countries.

9.4   The detrimental effects of inflation

In reading the first two sections of this chapter, the reader may be wondering precisely why inflation is regarded as the process undermining the economic stability of Western economies. If the only effects of inflation are to force economic agents to economise on their holdings of real balances by making more frequent trips to the bank and if even this inconvenience can be obviated by allowing money to bear interest, why should anyone worry about inflation at all? But then the reader will recall that the sort of inflation which was being referred to possessed two vital characteristics: (a) it was an inflation which was fully anticipated and acted upon *in the aggregate*; and (b) it was an inflation in which *all* nominal prices were expected to rise at the same proportional rate, i.e. $\dot{P}_i^e = \dot{P}^e$ where $\dot{P}_i^e$ is the expected rate of increase in prices confronting the ith economic agent. Should either or both of these conditions fail to be satisfied, then inflation will indeed have very real effects upon the economic well-being of the nation. *Unanticipated inflation* is the really disturbing phenomenon. In principle unanticipated inflation may be divided into two categories: (i) a *general* failure to anticipate the aggregate rate of inflation; and (ii) a failure to anticipate the rise in prices which affect particular economic agents. From the point of view of resource allocation, effect (ii) may be very serious indeed.

9.4.i   Unanticipated inflation

In chapter 8 the following equation was encountered which purported to describe how expected price changes would affect the current rate of inflation:

$$\dot{P} = f(U) + \phi\dot{P}^e.$$

Partial adaptation to inflationary conditions will be indicated by a fractional value of ϕ. If there is complete adaptation to anticipated inflation by all income recipients, then $\phi = 1$. The latter is the extreme monetarist position.

If ϕ is less than one there is a failure to anticipate fully the future rate of inflation. This could arise for one of two reasons: (a) the existence of money illusion in one or more income-receiving groups; (b) the existence of passive economic groups who, even though they are able to predict the future rate of inflation with a high degree of accuracy, are unable to act on the basis of such prediction. An example of such a group would be rentiers who live off assets whose rate of return had been fixed in nominal terms before the prospect of inflation had appeared. Similarly recipients of transfer payments of fixed nominal value, such as widows and old age pensioners, will suffer from inflation even though they are in a position to predict it accurately. If the disposable income of these groups were to remain constant in absolute terms, the decline in the real value of such income as a consequence of inflation will serve to redistribute income in favour of those groups who are in a position to defend their real incomes from similar erosion. Although it is doubtful whether wage-earners as a group have suffered from the recent inflation, there can be little room for doubt that the debtor-creditor relationship has shifted very much in favour of debtors in the last few years owing to the failure of the nominal interest rate to keep pace with inflation (for a detailed study of the empirical literature on the 'wage lag' and 'debtor-creditor' effects, see Foster, forthcoming).

Even if it can be assumed that each economic agent is successful in predicting the aggregate rate of inflation, it does not follow that he is in a similar position with regard to the vector prices which is most relevant to his own decision-making. For example assume that a particular employer is confident that the rate of change of money wages overall will be 20% and that his estimate, firmly held, persistently turns out to be correct. If he is an 'average' employer, this estimate of 20% will form the basis for an accurate prediction of the behaviour of money wages in his own enterprise. Most employers, on the other hand, are not 'average'. The extent to which they are able to apply their expectations concerning the performance of the whole economy to the special circumstances with which they are faced may be very limited indeed. For example what guarantee does the employer have that his employees will not put in for a wage increase well in excess of 20% which, owing to the market conditions for his product, he is unable to pass on in the form of higher prices?

It may be objected that these uncertainties arising from unanticipated changes in *relative* prices may occur even in a situation of zero inflation. This is true, although the scope for making erroneous predictions regarding the relative movement of costs and revenues will be much greater the higher the rate of unanticipated inflation. Nominal contracts are normally made at discrete intervals and the longer the time period between each bargain, the greater the uncertainty as to how the parties to the bargain are going to react to changed economic conditions. On the other hand the costs involved in making more frequent nominal contracts and in revising prices upwards more often may be quite considerable. Most of the undesirable consequences of unanticipated inflation may be avoided by the application of complete indexation to all nominal contracts.

9.4.ii Indexation

Indexation is the means by which all parties to contracts agree to terms which are fixed in *real* value. For example an indexed interest rate would be calculated to satisfy the equation $i = r_d + \dot{P}$ where r_d is some desired real return on the loan. In the past few years, of course, the *realised* real interest rate has typically been negative, reflecting a failure to anticipate inflation adequately. With indexation however, whatever the rate of inflation turns out to be, the nominal interest rate will be adjusted so as to maintain a given r_d. Similarly the rate of change of money wages will satisfy the equation $\dot{W} = \dot{P} + (\dot{X}/N)$ where $(\dot{X}/N)$ is the rate of change of labour productivity. The great advantage of this arrangement is that it removes a major part of the need to *anticipate* future price increases when making nominal contracts. Full compensation for increases in the price level will be *automatically* allowed for: the unholy scramble for wage increases which aim at compensating for *future* price increases will no longer be a dominant feature of the wage bargain.

We may express this proposition symbolically by assuming that the following vector of relative prices is optimal over a period of time:

$$P^* = \left(\frac{P_1}{P}, \frac{P_2}{P}, \ldots, \frac{P_n}{P}\right)$$

where the P_is also include factor rewards. If this vector of prices happens to prevail at a point in time and the general price level subsequently begins to rise at a faster rate, then indexation will ensure that the *ratios* of prices will remain unchanged. Since it is the ratios of prices which counts within a general equilibrium framework, such stability will prevent the misallocation of resources which would ensue from a failure to anticipate inflation.

In.terms of the analysis of chapters 7 and 8, the effect of indexation will be to accelerate the process of adjustment to a new, lower rate of inflation engineered through a reduction in the rate of monetary expansion. A completely successful indexation scheme would reduce the value of ψ in the adaptive expectations scheme to zero, implying that the expected rate of inflation in period t will simply be the experienced rate of inflation in period $t - 1$, i.e. $\dot{P}_t^e = \dot{P}_{t-1}$. Since no other terms will be involved, the adaption of the real sector of the economy to reductions in the rate of monetary expansion will be rapid. If on the other hand public confidence in the efficacy of indexation in protecting their real living standards is less than complete, indexation will merely reduce ψ. Nevertheless *any* increase in the speed of adaptation to a slower rate of inflation is to be welcomed. Indexation is therefore an integral part of a monetarist solution to the problem of inflation (see Friedman, 1974). It is designed to reduce the duration of the transition process from a high to a lower rate of inflation and to mitigate the social and economic costs of under-utilisation of capacity and resource misallocation.

CHAPTER 10

Conclusions and Policy Recommendations

In this final chapter we shall attempt to summarise the principal hypotheses which have been proposed to explain the phenomenon of inflation. The summary must of necessity be brief so that many of the wrinkles which distinguish one hypothesis from another will be glossed over.

The main line of division between economists writing on inflation is still the emphasis which is given to excess-demand factors on the one hand and to socio-political, non-market phenomena on the other. Monetarists and a large contingent of neo-Keynesians continue to adhere to more elaborate versions of the excess-demand hypothesis in which inflation is the result of past attempts to run the economy at a level of activity in excess of its full-employment level. Cost-push theories dismiss this line of reasoning, arguing instead that money wages and prices are either the outcome of some unspecified form of class struggle for shares in national income or the result of a highly rigid institutional framework within which wages and prices are set by conventional rules of thumb. Excess-demand factors may serve to exacerbate the conflict between rival groups but they do not form a necessary part of the inflationary story. Indeed, in most versions of the cost-push hypothesis, inflation may be taking place at *any* level of demand.

10.1   Theories of inflation

10.1.i   Cost-push theories

It should be clear by now that we are out of sympathy with the majority of cost-push hypotheses. The main reason for this is the failure of the adherents of such theories to provide a coherent and fairly complete model of the inflationary process. This theoretical slap-happiness is compounded by a failure to undertake empirical studies which would aim at confirming the cost-push thesis against its excess-demand rivals. It is not good enough to assert that prices are administered by non-market considerations simply by observing that the

166

relation between prices and prime costs is comparatively stable over time. Such stability is perfectly consistent with neoclassical general equilibrium theory. What needs to be demonstrated is that the mark-up which is applied to total costs is arrived at by forces which have nothing to do with prevailing market conditions. We are aware of no empirical study in which the irrelevance of market forces in wage and price setting has been demonstrated in any convincing way. On the contrary, excess-demand factors have emerged in many studies as a crucial variable in the process of price determination.

On the other hand, despite our extreme scepticism concerning the ability of the majority of cost-push hypotheses to explain the current inflation, we do not fail to recognise the important role which trade unions play in the inflationary process. Numerous empirical studies have shown that the existence of trade unions will inject a distinct inflationary bias into the system so that for a given level of excess demand the rate of inflation will tend to be higher in the presence of trade unions than in their absence. We subscribe to this point of view but we do not regard the recent acceleration in the rate of inflation as being due to an increase in the magnitude of the trade union bias. We must look elsewhere for the source of the recent upsurge in inflationary pressure.

10.1.ii Excess-demand theories

Excess-demand theories of inflation, although much criticised in the late 1960s, continue to provide, with suitable modifications, a plausible explanation of the origins of the inflationary process. The principal modifications which must be made to the excess-demand hypothesis are twofold:

(i) the cardinal role of price expectations in determining the actual rate of inflation should be explicitly acknowledged;
(ii) the international aspect of the problem whereby inflationary pressure is disseminated from one country to another should be regarded as an integral part of any complete theory of inflation.

The obvious question which must now be answered is: what was the source of the demand pressure? In this and many other issues, monetarists and many neo-Keynesians have discovered a considerable amount of common ground. Professor Kaldor (1974), for example, places the blame for the recent inflation squarely on the shoulders of successive governments who have failed to match higher public expenditure with higher taxes and/or a larger volume of domestic borrowing. 'This [failure to balance the budget] meant that the rate of growth of the money supply was stepped up from well under 10% to well over 30% a year' (Kaldor, 1974). This is exactly the same point of view adopted by Professor Friedman in a slightly different context when he refers to inflation as a very convenient and highly seductive form of taxation: 'Inflation has been irresistibly attractive to [governments] because it is a hidden tax that at first appears painless or even pleasant, and, above all, because it is a tax that can be imposed without specific legislation. It is truly taxation without representation' (1974). This reluctance of governments to impose explicit taxes to finance expenditure has led them to resort to the printing press and increase the rate of domestic credit expansion. Add to this the belief either that money does not matter or that the principal role of monetary policy is to peg the interest rate below its natural level, then an ineluctable inflationary spiral fuelled by an ever increasing rate of monetary expansion is set in motion. What appears to neo-Keynesians as sharp fiscal practice at the same time appears to monetarists as sharp monetary practice. Both explanations of inflation single out the same basic cause and prescribe the same cure, namely either to restore a balance between revenue from taxation and government expenditure or to finance the difference, not by printing money, but by borrowing domestically. In addition monetarists would advise a government to plug other sources of monetary expansion such as would arise for example from a policy of pegging interest rates.

The maintenance of fixed or quasi-fixed exchange rates between trading partners is also emphasised by monetarists as an important source of inflationary pressure. The monetary theory of the balance of payments states that the monetary links between nations will, after some lag, generalise the inflationary effects of monetary expansion in one or more of the countries involved to all of its trading partners. The balance of payments repercussions of the expansionary monetary policies of successive American administrations are still being felt throughout the rest of the world in the form of a higher rate of inflation than would otherwise have occurred. This, coupled with high rates of domestic credit expansion within the countries of the rest of the world, has led to a monetary explosion in the last few years.

If an individual country really wants to solve its inflation problem without severing its trading connections with the rest of the world, monetarists would advise its government (i) to control the rate of domestic credit expansion, and (ii) to float its currency against other currencies. The attempt to impose the latter remedy without at the same time enforcing the discipline implicit in the former is regarded as one of the principal reasons why Britain decided to abandon a 'clean' floatation of the pound sterling in favour of the present 'dirty' arrangement in which the monetary authorities continue to intervene to prevent violent fluctuations in the dollar value of sterling.

The persuasive logic of the monetarist position coupled with the ample and growing volume of evidence in support of its major predictions both for individual national economies and for the western world as a whole has led in recent years to a widespread acceptance of the monetarist explanation of inflation among academic economists and economic commentators. We regard this increased confidence in the revitalised version of the quantity theory of money as wholly justified. In the policy recommendations which follow, we shall continually refer back to the monetarist hypothesis as a frame of reference for devising an adequate anti-inflation package.

10.2 Recommendations for policy

10.2.i *Control over the rate of domestic credit expansion*

This recommendation must by definition form the core of any monetarist solution to the problem of inflation. Only by using the power at its disposal to control the supply of money arising from domestic sources will a government be able to make a start in its battle with inflation. This may not be an easy decision to make for a wide variety of political reasons. For example a government may be quite rightly deterred or at least discouraged by the prospect of the increase in unemployment which would ensue from the policy of demand restraint which is implicit in the above proposal. Moreover it may be reluctant to forego its ability to impose the inflation tax: the acceptance of the above proposal may force the government to cut back on its own expenditure and raise tax revenue in a more overt fashion.

Monetarists would also argue that the required reduction in the rate of monetary expansion should be undertaken *gradually* so as to avoid subjecting the economy to too violent a change in direction. We know too little about the precise mechanics of adjustment to be able to predict with any accuracy the reaction of the economic system to a sudden jerk occasioned by a dramatic reduction in the rate of monetary expansion. The economy should be given the opportunity to acclimatise itself to a changing monetary environment.

10.2.ii *Float the currency*

According to the monetary theory of the balance of payments, a major source of worldwide inflationary pressure was the dissemination of international liquidity through a regime of fixed exchange rates. If a country wishes to isolate itself from the inflation occurring elsewhere in the world it should float its currency and then set about controlling that part of inflation which is generated *internally* by excessive expansions in domestic credit. By conducting its affairs in this manner an open economy will be in a position to act *as if* it were a closed economy.

The reasoning behind this proposal is the notion that an important source of inflationary pressure arises from the importation of currency by means of payments surpluses. Hence the attention paid to the huge dollar deficits with the rest of the world which occurred in the late 1960s and early 1970s. Had the rest of the world floated against the dollar it would have neutralised what turned out to be a massive outflow of dollars into a world economy which was already operating near its capacity limit. (The monetary theory of the balance of payments tends to concentrate upon the monetary repercussions of changes in *trade flows*. The complications arising from large capital movements are rarely mentioned except in footnotes.)

10.2.iii   Adopt widespread indexation

In the prolonged period of transition from a high to a lower rate of monetary expansion the unemployment rate will rise and the rate of growth of output will fall. Although the monetarist proposals in sections 10.2.i and 10.2.ii get right to the heart of the inflation problem, they involve possibly quite considerable social and economic costs extending over a period of years. In order to soften the blow and shorten the period of transition we advise the widespread adoption of indexation as a means both of reducing the arbitrary inequities and misallocations produced by unanticipated inflation and of speeding up the rate of erosion of inflationary expectations. The more rapidly $\dot{P}^e$ is revised downwards, the shorter will be the period of low capacity utilisation and high unemployment. A completely successful indexation programme would reduce $\dot{P}^e$ fairly rapidly. One possible blueprint for such a policy has been amply formulated by Friedman (1974). Suffice it to say that we disagree profoundly with those who maintain that indexation is itself inflationary. Far from increasing the rate of inflation, indexation will achieve exactly the opposite effect by removing much of the incentive to *anticipate* future price increases.

10.2.iv   The implementation of a prices and incomes policy for a short period

The debate over whether or not a prices and incomes policy would be a useful anti-inflation device is fraught with difficulty. On the one hand there are the political obstacles involved when it comes to discussing whether such a policy should be statutory or voluntary in nature. On the other hand there are the traditional economic arguments which revolve around the desirability of freezing, albeit temporarily, the vector of relative prices. Those who argue against a prices and incomes policy point to the random misallocation of resources which would result from restricting the variation in relative prices. A changing economy needs a continually changing set of relative prices in order that the right signals be transmitted to the relevant economic agents who then act upon the basis of those signals to reallocate resources. The suppression of this mechanism by means of a prices and incomes policy may bring in its wake a serious misallocation of resources. Those who argue in favour of a prices and incomes policy maintain that relative prices are highly stable and that the signals, if they appear at all, are very slow to emerge. They assert that the consequent economic costs of a temporary prices and incomes policy are probably very small indeed when weighed against the costs of unanticipated inflation.

Despite the large volume of econometric evidence which tends to indicate that prices and incomes policies do not appear to work (see Parkin and Sumner, 1972), we believe that such policies can play an important role in combating inflation provided that they are part of a larger package. They can only succeed if they are part of the scheme outlined in this chapter. It would be the height of irresponsibility, for example, for a government to impose a prices and incomes policy and then to let the supply of money continue to expand at its previous rate. Nevertheless such a policy may be extremely useful in acting as a back-up to the indexation proposal so as to erode inflationary expectations more rapidly. If a prices and incomes policy can succeed in dramatically reducing the experienced rate of inflation, and if indexation is widely accepted for all nominal contracts, then a policy of reducing the rate of monetary expansion quite substantially may avoid the large-scale dislocations which would normally result from such a policy. As was pointed out earlier, the sooner the economy as a whole adjusts its expectation of inflation in a downward direction, the less will be the social and economic disruption which will accompany a restrictive monetary policy. We therefore believe that a prices and incomes policy can play an important role in accelerating the speed of adjustment of the real economy to a lower rate of monetary expansion.

Bibliography

G. Ackley (1958) 'A Third Approach to the Analysis and Control of Inflation' in *The Relationship of Prices to Economic Stability and Growth* Joint Economic Committee, Washington.

G. Ackley (1959) 'Administered prices and the inflationary process' *American Economic Review* (44).

G. Ackley (1961) *Macroeconomic Theory* London, Macmillan.

A. Ando and F. Modigliani (1965) 'The relative stability of monetary velocity and the investment multiplier' *American Economic Review*.

G. C. Archibald (1969) 'The Phillips Curve and the Distribution of Unemployment' *American Economic Review, Papers and Proceedings* (May).

M. J. Artis and A. R. Nobay (1969) 'Two aspects of the monetary debate' *National Institute Economic Review* (August).

O. C. Ashenfelter and G. E. Johnson (1969) 'Bargaining Theory, Trade Unions and Industrial Strike Activity' *American Economic Review* (LIX).

O. C. Ashenfelter, G. E. Johnson and J. H. Pencavel (1970) 'Trade Unions and the Rate of Change of Money Wages in United States Manufacturing Industry' mimeograph.

O. C. Ashenfelter and J. H. Pencavel (1974) 'A Note on Estimating the Determinants of Changes in Wages and Earnings' Working Paper 46, Industrial Relations Section, Princeton University.

M. J. Bailey (1956) 'The Welfare Cost of Inflationary Finance' *Journal of Political Economy* (April).

C. R. Barrett and A. A. Walters (1966) 'The stability of Keynesian and monetary multipliers in the United Kingdom' *Review of Economics and Statistics* (November).

R. J. Barro (1972) 'A Theory of Monopolistic Price Adjustment' *Review of Economic Studies* (January).

W. J. Baumol (1951) *Economic Dynamics* New York, Macmillan.

W. J. Baumol (1972) *Economic Theory and Operations Analysis* (3rd edn) Englewood Cliffs, Prentice-Hall.

R. J. Bhatia (1961) 'Unemployment and the Rate of Change in Money Earnings in the United States, 1900–58' *Economica* (XXVIII).

R. G. Bodkin (1966) *The Wage-Price-Productivity Nexus* Pennsylvania University Press.

W. G. Bowen (1960) *The Wage-Price Issue: A Theoretical Analysis* Princeton University Press.

W. G. Bowen and R. A. Berry (1963) 'Unemployment Conditions and Movements of the Money Wage level' *Review of Economics and Statistics* (XLV, 2).

J. K. Bowers et al. (1970) 'The Change in the Relationship between Unemployment and Earnings Increase: A Review of Some Possible Explanations' *National Institute Economic Review* (54, November).

J. K. Bowers, P. C. Cheshire, A. E. Webb and R. Weedon (1972) 'Some Aspects of Unemployment and the Labour Market 1966–71' *National Institute Economic Review* (62, November).

F. P. R. Brechling (1968) 'The Trade-off between Inflation and Unemployment' *Journal of Political Economy* (July/August).

F. P. R. Brechling (1972) 'Wage Inflation and the Structure of Regional Unemployment' University of Essex Discussion Paper no. 40, mimeographed. Reprinted in Laidler and Purdy (1974).

M. Bronfenbrenner and F. D. Holzman (1963) 'A survey of inflation theory' *American Economic Review* (September).

172

P. Burrows and T. Hitiris (1970) 'Incomes Policy: A Comment', mimeographed.

J. Burton (1972) *Wage Inflation* London, Macmillan.

P. Cagan (1956) 'The monetary dynamics of hyperinflation' in Friedman (1956a).

P. Cagan (1969) 'Theories of mild, continuing inflation: a critique and extension' in S. W. Rousseas (ed.) *Inflation: Its Causes, Consequences and Control* Wilton Conn., The Calvin K. Kazanjian Economics Foundation Inc.

J. A. Carlson (1972) 'Elusive Passage to the Non-Walrasian Continent' University of Manchester, mimeograph.

J. A. Carlson and J. M. Parkin (1973) 'Inflation expectations' University of Manchester Inflation Workshop Discussion Paper 7305.

A. B. Cramp (1970) 'Does money matter?' *Lloyds Bank Review* (October).

D. E. Cullen (1956) 'The Inter-Industry Wage Structure, 1899–1950' *American Economic Review* (June).

T. Davis (1963) 'Eight decades of inflation in Chile: a political interpretation' *Journal of Political Economy* (August).

G. de Menil (1971) *Bargaining: Monopoly Power Versus Union Power* Cambridge Mass., MIT Press.

L. A. Dicks-Mireaux (1961) 'The Interrelationship Between Cost and Price Changes, 1948–59. A Study of Inflation in Post-War Britain' *Oxford Economic Papers* (Vol. 13).

L. A. Dicks-Mireaux and J. C. R. Dow (1959) 'The Determinants of Wage Inflation: United Kingdom, 1946–1956' *Journal of the Royal Statistical Society* (CXXII, 2).

L. A. Dicks-Mireaux and J. R. Shepherd (1962) 'The Wages Structure and Some Implications for Incomes Policy' *National Institute Economic Review* (November).

P. H. Douglas (1930) *Real Wages in the United States, 1890–1926* Boston, Houghton Mifflin.

J. C. R. Dow (1956) 'Analysis of the Generation of Price Inflation, A Study of Cost and Price Changes in the United Kingdom, 1946–1954' *Oxford Economic Papers* (October).

N. W. Duck, J. M. Parkin, D. Rose and G. Zis (1975) 'The Determination of the Rate of Change of Wages and Prices in the Fixed Exchange Rate World Economy: 1956–70' in J. M. Parkin and G. Zis (eds.) (1975) *Inflation in the World Economy* Manchester University Press.

J. T. Dunlop (1950) *Wage Determination Under Trade Unions* New York, Kelley.

J. Duesenberry (1950) 'The mechanics of inflation' *Review of Economics and Statistics* (Vol. 32).

O. Eckstein and T. A. Wilson (1962) 'The Determination of Money Wages in American Industry' *Quarterly Journal of Economics* (Vol. 76).

I. Fisher (1920) *The Purchasing Power of Money: Its Determination and Relation to Credit, Interest and Crises* New York, Macmillan.

I. Fisher (1930) *The Theory of Interest* New York, Macmillan.

J. I. Foster (forthcoming) 'The redistributive effects of inflation: questions and answers' University of Manchester Inflation Workshop.

M. Friedman (1951) 'Some Comments on the Significance of Labor Unions for Economic Policy' in D. McC. Wright (ed.) (1951) *The Impact of the Union* New York, Harcourt and Brace.

M. Friedman (ed.) (1956a) *Studies in the Quantity Theory of Money* Chicago University Press.

M. Friedman (1956b) 'The quantity theory of money: a restatement' in Friedman (1956a).

M. Friedman (1959) 'Statement on monetary policy' in *Employment, Growth and Price Levels* US Government Printing Office.

M. Friedman (1968) 'The role of monetary policy' *American Economic Review* (April).

M. Friedman (1969) *The Optimum Quantity of Money* London, Macmillan.

M. Friedman (1970) 'A theoretical framework for monetary analysis' *Journal of Political Economy* (March/April).

M. Friedman (1971) 'A theory of nominal income' *Journal of Political Economy* (March/April).

M. Friedman (1972) 'Comment on the critics' *Journal of Political Economy* (September/October).

M. Friedman (1974) *Monetary Correction* Institute of Economic Affairs.

M. Friedman and D. Meiselman (1964) 'The relative stability of monetary velocity and the investment multiplier in the United States, 1897—1958' in *Stabilization Policies: A Series of Research Studies Prepared for the Commission on Money and Credit* Englewood Cliffs, Prentice-Hall.

J. W. Garbarino (1950) 'A Theory of Interindustry Wage Structure Variation' *Quarterly Journal of Economics* (May).

H. A. Genberg (1973) 'Aspects of the monetary approach to balance of payments theory: an empipirical study of Sweden' unpublished manuscript (August).

L. G. Godfrey (1971) 'The Phillips Curve: Incomes Policy and Trade Union Effects' in Johnson and Nobay (1971).

W. Godley and W. D. Nordhaus (1972) 'Pricing in the Trade Cycle' *Economic Journal* (September).

B. Hansen (1951) *A Study in the Theory of Inflation* London, Allen & Unwin

B. Hansen (1970) 'Excess Demand, Unemployment, Vacancies, and Wages' *Quarterly Journal of Economics* (Vol. 84, February).

A. C. Harberger (1963) 'The dynamics of inflation in Chile' in Christ *et al. Measurement in Economics: Studies in Mathematical Economics and Econometrics in Memory of Yehuda Grunfeld* Stanford, California.

J. R. Hicks (1935) 'A suggestion for simplifying the theory of money' *Economica* (February).

A. G. Hines (1964) 'Trade Unions and Wage Inflation in the United Kingdom: 1893—1961' *Review of Economic Studies* (Vol. 31, October).

A. G. Hines (1969) 'Wage Inflation in the United Kingdom 1948—62. A Disaggregated Study' *Economic Journal* (LXXIX, March).

A. G. Hines (1971) 'The Determinants of the Rate of Change of Money Wage Rates and the Effectiveness of Incomes Policy' in Johnson and Nobay (1971).

A. G. Hines and C. Nussey (1974) 'The international monetarist theory of inflation: the story of a mare's nest' Birkbeck College, London, Discussion Paper in Economics No. 23.

C. C. Holt (1971a) 'Job Search, Phillips' Wage Relation, and Union Influence: Theory and Evidence' in Phelps (1971a).

C. C. Holt (1971b) 'How Can the Phillips Curve be Moved to Reduce Both Inflation and Unemployment?' in Phelps (1971a).

F. D. Holzman (1950) 'Income determination in open inflation' *Review of Economics and Statistics* (Vol. 32).

David Hume (1963) 'On Money' in *Essays Moral, Political and Literary* Oxford University Press.

L. C. Hunter (1974) 'The Economic Determination of Strike Activity' Glasgow University Discussion Paper in Economics No. 1 (mimeo).

D. Jackson, H. A. Turner, F. Wilkinson (1972) *Do Trade Unions Cause Inflation?* University of Cambridge Department of Applied Economics Occasional Paper 36, Cambridge University Press.

H. G. Johnson (1972) *Inflation and the Monetarist Controversy* Amsterdam, North-Holland Publishing Company.

H. G. Johnson and A. R. Nobay (eds.) (1971) *The Current Inflation* London, Macmillan.

J. Johnston (1974) 'A Model of Wage Determination Under Bilateral Monopoly' in Laidler and Purdy (1974).

N. Kaldor (1959) 'Economic Growth and the Problem of Inflation' *Economica* (November).

N. Kaldor (1970) 'The new monetarism' *Lloyds Bank Review* (July).

N. Kaldor (1974) Letter to *The Times* (12 February).

M. Kalecki (1954) *Theory of Economic Dynamics* London, Allen and Unwin.

J. M. Keynes (1936) *The General Theory of Employment, Interest and Money* London, Macmillan.

J. M. Keynes (1940) *How to Pay for the War* London, Macmillan.

L. R. Klein and R. J. Ball (1959) 'Some Econometrics of Absolute Prices and Wages' *Economic Journal* (September).

E. Kuh (1967) 'A Productivity Theory of Wage Levels — An Alternative to the Phillips Curve' *Review of Economic Studies* (Vol. 34).

D. E. W. Laidler (1969) *The Demand for Money: Theories and Evidence* Scranton, Pa., International Textbook Co.

D. E. W. Laidler (1971) 'The Phillips Curve, Expectations and Incomes Policy', in Johnson and Nobay (1971).

D. E. W. Laidler (1972) 'A monetarist model of simultaneous fluctuations in prices and output' University of Manchester Inflation Workshop Discussion Paper 7207.

D. E. W. Laidler (1973) 'The Influence of Money on Real Income and Inflation: A Simple Econometric Model' *The Manchester School* (December).

D. E. W. Laidler and D. L. Purdy (eds.) (1974) *Inflation and Labour Markets* Manchester University Press.

D. E. W. Laidler and A. R. Nobay (1974) 'Some current issues concerning the international aspects of inflation' University of Manchester Inflation Workshop Discussion Paper 7405.

A. Leijonhufvud (1968a) *On Keynesian Economics and the Economics of Keynes* Oxford University Press.

A. Leijonhufvud (1968b) 'Is There a Meaningful Trade-Off Between Inflation and Unemployment?' *Journal of Political Economy* (Vol. 76).

H. M. Levinson (1951) 'Unionism, Wage Trends and Income Distribution' *Michigan Business Studies* Ann Arbor, University of Michigan.

H. M. Levinson (1960) 'Pattern Bargaining: a case study of the automobile workers' *Quarterly Journal of Economics* (May).

H. M. Levinson (1966) *Determining Forces in Collective Wage Bargaining* New York, Wiley.

H. G. Lewis (1963) *Unionism and Relative Wages in the United States* Chicago, Chicago University Press.

R. G. Lipsey (1960) 'The Relation Between Unemployment and the Rate of Change of Money Wage Rates in the United Kingdom, 1862—1957: A Further Analysis' *Economica* (February).

R. G. Lipsey (1965) 'Structural and demand deficient unemployment reconsidered' in A. M. Ross (ed.) (1965) *Employment Policy and the Labour Market* Berkeley, University of California Press.

R. G. Lipsey and M. D. Steuer (1961) 'The Relation Between Profits and Wage Rates' *Economica* (May).

K. M. McCaffree (1963) 'A Further Consideration of Wages, Unemployment, and Prices in the United States, 1948—1958' *Industrial and Labour Relations Review* (XVI).

D. I. McKay and R. A. Hart (1974) 'Wage Inflation and Regional Wage Structure' in J. M. Parkin and A. R. Nobay (eds.) (1974) *Contemporary Issues in Economics* Manchester University Press.

J. E. Maher (1965) *Labour and the Economy* Boston, Allyn and Bacon.

S. Maital (1972) 'Inflation, taxation and equity: *How to Pay for the War* revisited' *Economic Journal* (March).

F. Machlup (1960) 'Another View of Cost-Push and Demand-Pull Inflation' *Review of Economics and Statistics* (Vol. 42).

D. Mortensen (1971) 'A Theory of Wage and Employment Dynamics' in Phelps (1971a).

C. Mulvey (1968) 'Unemployment and the Incidence of Strikes in the Republic of Ireland' *Journal of Economic Studies* (July).

C. Mulvey and J. A. Trevithick (1974) 'Some Evidence on the Wage Leadership Hypothesis' *Scottish Journal of Political Economy* (February).

R. A. Mundell (1963) 'Inflation and Real Interest' *Journal of Political Economy* (June).

R. A. Mundell (1971) *Monetary Theory: Inflation, Interest and Growth in the World Economy* Goodyear Publishing Co. Inc.

R. R. Nield (1963) *Pricing and Employment in the Trade Cycle* Cambridge University Press.

OECD (1970) *Inflation: The Present Problem* Paris.

OEEC (1961) *The Problem of Rising Prices* Paris.

F. W. Paish (1968) 'The Limits of Incomes Policies' in F. W. Paish and J. Hennessy *Policy for Incomes* Hobart Paper 29, Institute of Economic Affairs.

Y. C. Park (1972) 'Some current issues on the transmission process of monetary policy' *International Monetary Fund Staff Papers* (March).

J. M. Parkin (1972) 'Inflation, the balance of payments, domestic credit expansion and exchange rate adjustments' University of Manchester Inflation Workshop Discussion Paper 7211.

J. M. Parkin (1974) 'The Causes of Inflation: Recent Contributions and Current Controversies' University of Manchester Inflation Workshop Discussion Paper 7405.

J. M. Parkin and M. T. Sumner (eds.) (1972) *Incomes Policy and Inflation* Manchester University Press.

J. M. Parkin, M. T. Sumner and R. Ward (1973) 'Wage Behaviour in an Open Economy, Excess Demand, Generalised Expectations and Incomes Policies in the UK' in K. Brunner and A. H. Meltzer (eds.) *Proceedings of the Conference on Wage-Price Controls at Rochester University*.

J. M. Parkin, M. T. Sumner and R. Ward (1974) 'The effects of excess demand, generalised expectations and wage-price controls on wage inflation in the UK' University of Machester Inflation Workshop Discussion Paper 7402.

J. H. Pencavel (1970) 'An Investigation into Industrial Strike Activity in Britain' *Economica* (XXXCLL).

G. L. Perry (1966) *Unemployment, Money Wage Rates, and Inflation* Cambridge Mass, MIT Press.

G. L. Perry (1971) 'Changing Labor Markets and Inflation' *Papers of the Brookings Institute*.

M. H. Peston (1971) 'The Micro-Economics of the Phillips Curve' in Johnson and Nobay (1971).

E. S. Phelps (1965) 'Anticipated Inflation and Economic Welfare' *Journal of Political Economy* (February).

E. S. Phelps (1967) 'Phillips curves, expectations of inflation and optimal unemployment over time' *Economica* (August).

E. S. Phelps (1968) 'Money-wage dynamics and labour-market equilibrium' *Journal of Political Economy* (July/August).

E. S. Phelps (ed.) (1971a) *Microeconomic Foundations of Employment and Inflation Theory* London, Macmillan.

E. S. Phelps (1971b) 'Introduction: The New Microeconomics in Employment and Inflation Theory' in Phelps (1971a).

E. S. Phelps (1971c) 'Money Wage Dynamics and Labour Market Equilibrium' in Phelps (1971a).

E. S. Phelps and S. Winter (1971) 'Optimal Price Policy Under Atomistic Competition' in Phelps (1971a).

E. H. Phelps Brown (1971) 'The Analysis of Wage Movements Under Full Employment' *Scottish Journal of Political Economy* (November).

A. W. Phillips (1958) 'The Relation between Unemployment and the Rate of Change of Money Wage Rates in the United Kingdom, 1861—1957' *Economica* (November).

G. Pierson (1968) 'The Effect of Union Strength on the US Phillips Curve' *American Economic Review* (LVIII).

M. V. Posner (1973) Letter to *The Times* (4th September).

D. L. Purdy and G. Zis (1973) 'Trade Unions and Wage Inflation in the UK. A Reappraisal' in J. M. Parkin and A. R. Nobay (eds.) (1973) *Essays in Modern Economics* London, Longmans.

D. L. Purdy and G. Zis (1974) 'On the Concept and Measurement of Union Militancy' in Laidler and Purdy (1974).

D. Rose (1972) 'A general error-learning model of expectations formation' University of Manchester Inflation Workshop Discussion Paper 7210.

A. M. Ross (1948) *Trade Union Wage Policy* Berkeley, California University Press.

A. M. Ross and W. Goldner (1950) 'Forces Affecting the Inter-industry Wage Structure' *Quarterly Journal of Economics* (May).

P. A. Samuelson (1968) 'What classical and neo-classical monetary theory really was' *Canadian Journal of Economics*.

P. A. Samuelson and R. M. Solow (1960) 'Analytical aspects of anti-inflation policy' *American Economic Review* (Vol. 50, May).

J. D. Sargan (1971) 'A Study of Wages and Prices in the UK 1949—1968' in Johnson and Nobay (1971).

P. G. Saunders and A. R. Nobay (1972) 'Price expectations, the Phillips curve and incomes policy' in Parkin and Sumner (1972).

M. Segal (1964) 'Union Wage Impact and Market Structure' *Quarterly Journal of Economics* (February).

G. Seltzer (1951) 'Pattern Bargaining and the United Steelworkers' *Journal of Political Economy* (August).

N. J. Simler and A. Tella (1968) 'Labour Reserves and the Phillips Curve' *Review of Economics and Statistics* (Vol. 49).

S. H. Slichter (1952) 'Wage Policies since World War II' *The Commercial and Financial Chronicle* (4th December).

A. Smithies (1942) 'The behavior of money national income under inflationary conditions' *Quarterly Journal of Economics* (November).

R. M. Solow (1969) *Price Expectations and the Behaviour of the Price Level* Manchester University Press.

J. Taylor (1970) 'Hidden Unemployment. Hoarded Labor and the Phillips Curve' *Southern Economic Journal* (July).

J. Taylor (1972) 'Incomes Policy, the Structure of Unemployment and the Phillips Curve: the United Kingdom experience: 1953–70' in Parkin and Sumner (1972).

R. L. Thomas (1974) 'Wage Inflation in the UK: a multi-market approach' in Laidler and Purdy (1974).

R. L. Thomas and P. J. M. Stoney (1970) 'A Note on the Dynamic Properties of the Hines Inflation Model' *Review of Economic Studies* (XXXVII).

R. L. Thomas and P. J. M. Stoney (1972) 'Unemployment Dispersion as a Determinant of Wage Inflation in the United Kingdom, 1925–1966' in Parkin and Sumner (1972).

J. Tobin (1968) 'Unemployment and inflation; the cruel dilemma' in Almarin Phillips and Oliver E. Williamson (eds.) *Prices: Issues in Theory and Public Policy* University of Pennsylvania Press.

J. Tobin (1972) 'Inflation and unemployment' *American Economic Review* (March).

J. A. Trevithick (1975) 'Keynes, inflation and money illusion' *Economic Journal* (March).

S. J. Turnovsky (1972) 'The expectations hypothesis and the aggregate wage equation: some empirical evidence for Canada' *Economica* (February).

S. J. Turnovsky and W. L. Wachter (1972) 'A test of the "expectations hypothesis" using directly observed wage and price expectations' *Review of Economics and Statistics*.

J. Vanderkamp (1966) 'Wage and Price Level Determination: An Empirical Model for Canada' *Economica* (XXXIII).

R. C. Vogel (1974) 'The dynamics of inflation in Latin America, 1950–1969' *American Economic Review* (March).

A. A. Walters (1971) 'Inflation and real output growth' in *Money in Boom and Slump* Institute of Economic Affairs (3rd edition).

A. A. Walters (1973) Letter to *The Times* (26 November).

R. Ward and G. Zis (1974) 'Trade Union Militancy as an Explanation of Inflation: An International Comparison' *Manchester School* (March).

P. Wiles (1973) 'Cost inflation and the state of economic theory' *Economic Journal* (June).

J. Williamson (1967) 'The Price-Price Spiral' *Yorkshire Bulletin of Economic and Social Research* (May).

Author Index

178

Subject Index